# A History of
# the Baltic States

Andres Kasekamp

palgrave
macmillan

First published 2010 by
PALGRAVE MACMILLAN

Palgrave Macmillan in the UK is an imprint of Macmillan Publishers Limited, registered in England, company number 785998, of Houndmills, Basingstoke, Hampshire RG21 6XS.

Palgrave Macmillan in the US is a division of St Martin's Press LLC, 175 Fifth Avenue, New York, NY 10010.

Palgrave Macmillan is the global academic imprint of the above companies and has companies and representatives throughout the world.

Palgrave® and Macmillan® are registered trademarks in the United States, the United Kingdom, Europe and other countries.

ISBN-13: 978–0–230–01940–9 hardback
ISBN-13: 978–0–230–01941–6 paperback

This book is printed on paper suitable for recycling and made from fully managed and sustained forest sources. Logging, pulping and manufacturing processes are expected to conform to the environmental regulations of the country of origin.

A catalogue record for this book is available from the British Library.

A catalog record for this book is available from the Library of Congress.

10   9   8   7   6   5   4   3   2   1
19   18   17   16   15   14   13   12   11   10

Printed in China

# Contents

# List of Maps and Tables

MAPS

TABLES

# Preface

This book provides a concise survey of developments on the territory comprising the present-day countries of Estonia, Latvia and Lithuania from the end of the last ice age to the present; it is not just the histories of the three independent republics in the narrow sense (1918–40; 1991–) as might be inferred from the title, nor is it only that of the ethnic Estonians, Latvians and Lithuanians. As will become apparent, it was not preordained that these three countries together would today be commonly known as the Baltic states. They are not the Baltic States with a capital 'S', as in the United States, nor the lazy shorthand 'Baltics', patterned after the 'Balkans'.

Although often referred to as tiny, the territory of the smallest Baltic state, Estonia, is 45,227 sq. km., slightly larger than many of the old European states such as Denmark, Switzerland and the Netherlands. Compared to these countries, however, the Baltic states are sparsely populated. Estonia is the smallest continental European country to maintain a national system of higher education and state administration in its own indigenous language.

'Baltic' is not a term originally used by the peoples living along the coast of what is now known as the Baltic Sea, even though an etymological connection is often claimed with the Latvian and Lithuanian stem *balt*, denoting 'white' or 'swamp'.[1] In the eleventh century, the German chronicler Adam of Bremen first described the sea as *Mare Balticum*, deriving the name from the Latin word for 'belt' (*balteus*), since in the local imagination the sea extended eastwards like a belt.[2] This appears to have been his own invention since seafarers referred to the sea as the East Sea in the Germanic languages (*Ostsee* in German; *Östersjön* in Swedish; *Østersøen* in Danish) and even in Finnish (*Itämeri*), which borrowed the name from Swedish. The Estonians logically called it the West Sea (*Läänemeri*). Latvian fishermen called it the Big Sea (*Lielā jūra*), in contrast to the Little Sea – the Gulf of Riga.[3]

The term 'Baltic languages' – named after the Baltic Sea – was coined by German linguist G. H. F. Nesselmann when researching the extinct Prussian language at the University of Königsberg in 1845.[4] The Baltic languages, like the Slavic, Germanic and Romance languages, are a branch of the family of Indo-European languages. Latvians and Lithuanians speak related Baltic languages, whereas Estonian is a Finno-Ugric language which is most closely related to Finnish. Linguistically, therefore, Latvian and Lithuanian are closer to most European languages (such as English or French) than they are to neighbouring Estonian. However, when cultural patterns are examined, a different picture emerges: as a result of long centuries of common institutions under the German ruling elite, the Latvians and the Estonians are the most similar. Prior to the twentieth century, the Lithuanians had more in common with the Poles than with the Latvians.

The meaning of the term 'Baltic' has transformed over time. In the early twentieth century, a 'Balt' did not refer to an ethnic Estonian, Latvian or Lithuanian. The name was consciously brought into use in the mid-nineteenth century as a term of self-identification by the German ruling elite of the three Russian provinces of Estland, Livland and Courland, collectively known as the *Ostseeprovinzen* of the Russian Empire. In 1918 the Baltic Germans almost succeeded in uniting the three provinces into a Baltic duchy under the German Kaiser. Only after World War I did the term 'Baltic states' come into use. Even then, it was a fluid term, at times encompassing other states which had emerged from the collapse of tsarist Russia. Finland was frequently included among the Baltic states, but Finland and the Baltic states diverged as a consequence of World War II and she subsequently managed to rebrand herself as a 'Nordic' country. As republics of the USSR, Estonia, Latvia and Lithuania were referred to in Russian as a common region known as *Pribaltika*. Their shared experience within the Soviet system, and their close cooperation in achieving their independence from it, solidified their common Baltic identity. After the end of the Cold War, a wider Baltic Sea regional identity, including all the Baltic littoral countries (heralded by the establishment of the Council of Baltic Sea States in 1992), began to evolve. This tendency was greatly strengthened by the enlargement of the European Union in 2004, after which all of the states around the Baltic Sea, with the exception of Russia, belonged to the EU.

The focus of this book is on political history and particularly on the modern era. I have endeavoured to restrain my natural tendency to view events from an Estonian perspective and have tried to devote an equal amount of space to all three countries. The greatest challenge has been to write an integrated, comparative history, rather than the parallel histories of three separate countries. Although the titular nations are the main protagonists in these pages, I have tried to devote attention to the achievements of all of the peoples who have lived in this territory. Surprisingly few works have taken such an approach. 'Baltic' history initially was synonymous with the history of the Baltic Germans as the ruling elite in the Baltic provinces. These studies focused narrowly on *das Baltikum*, the area of German settlement. The pioneer of comparative Baltic history, Georg von Rauch, felt it necessary to justify to his German readers as late as 1970 why he had included Lithuania among the 'Baltic states'.[5]

While there have been several excellent individual country studies of Estonia, Latvia and Lithuania, thus far there have been only two general histories of the three Baltic states in English.[6] The first was a translated secondary-school textbook, written by a team of Estonian, Latvian and Lithuanian historians;[7] the second was a more readable survey by a young American specialist on Russian history, Kevin O'Connor.[8] However, these publications have not managed to supersede the earlier work of von Rauch, whose book remains the standard study of the first independence era, and that of Romuald Misiunas and Rein Taagepera, whose pioneering work on the Soviet period remains unsurpassed.[9] In the 1990s David Kirby broadened our perspective by writing about a wider 'Baltic world', including all the peoples living on the rim of the Baltic Sea.[10] German historians have recently begun referring to 'North-eastern Europe' (*Nordosteuropa*) as a distinct historical region.[11]

Writing about three separate countries, which have been ruled by several neighbouring powers through the centuries, creates a challenge in maintaining consistency and clarity for the reader, while adhering to names and terms which are historically accurate. For place names, I have mostly used the version in official usage at the time. One exception is Vilnius where I have used the Lithuanian rather than the Russian or Polish forms throughout. To aid the reader, a table with historical and alternative place names in the relevant languages is included at the end of the book. A particular challenge is the usage of the names of the three Baltic provinces under tsarist rule. In order to avoid confusion in relation to different administrative units with the same name during prior or subsequent historical periods, I have preferred the German terms used by the ruling elite at the time – Estland and Livland – rather than the English or Latin – Estonia and Livonia – but have retained the anglicised Courland. Well-known place names outside the Baltic region, such as Moscow and Warsaw, are referred to in their generally recognised English form. Proper names are mostly written in their original language. The names of Christian rulers are mainly given in the anglicised form (for example, Charles XII, not Karl XII, and Nicholas II, not Nikolai II). I beg the reader to forgive any inconsistencies which remain.

I am indebted to Karsten Brüggemann, Matthew Kott, Saulius Sužiedėlis, Rein Taagepera and Bradley Woodworth for having read through the draft manuscript and pointed out errors, inconsistencies and questionable interpretations and for having offered highly useful suggestions based on their extensive knowledge. My gratitude is also extended to Juhan Kreem and Olaf Mertelsmann for their insights and to the two anonymous reviewers of the manuscript who provided extremely constructive and helpful criticism. Nevertheless, I alone am responsible for any shortcomings or errors in the text. Finally, I am most grateful to my parents, Ilmar and Siina, for their constant encouragement, to my wife Johanna for her patience, to our children, Kaisa and Joona, for showing me what is truly important in life, and to my grandparents – those whom I knew and those whom I never had a chance to meet – their life stories sparked my passion for exploring the past of their, and my, homeland.

**Andres Kasekamp**

# 1

# Europe's Last Pagans

After the retreat of the Scandinavian ice sheet, the eastern Baltic littoral was able to support human habitation, with the first settlers arriving around 11,000 BC. For several millennia, these people were hunter-gatherers, a gradual transition to farming was not completed until the Bronze Age. People speaking Finno-Ugric languages moved into the northern part of the region and were followed by Indo-European Balts who settled in the southern part of the Baltic littoral during the Neolithic era. By the Late Iron Age, these tribes were loosely politically organised and interacted with Scandinavia and the neighbouring lands of Rus' for purposes of trade, as well as hostile raids. German and Danish crusaders subjugated the proto-Latvian and Estonian tribes and converted them to Christianity with fire and sword during the thirteenth century. The Lithuanian tribes united under a single ruler and successfully resisted the encroachments of the Teutonic Knights.

## EARLY INHABITANTS

Geography has been an influential factor in shaping the lives of the inhabitants of the Baltic region throughout history. The Baltic region lies on a latitude between 54° and 60° north and a longitude of 21° to 28° east. Compared to other regions at an equally northerly latitude, the eastern Baltic littoral has a milder climate as a result of the moderating effects of the Atlantic Gulf Stream. The territory of the present-day Baltic states is quite flat: the highest peak is only 318 m above sea level. The landscape's characteristic features are the numerous forests and swamps, and the sandy Baltic coastline. In the north, Estonia's western coastline is dotted with over 1500 islands and some, such as Saaremaa, are fairly large

($2673$ km$^2$). There are abundant bodies of water, the largest being Lake Peipus, the fifth largest lake in Europe. There are also numerous rivers, the longest being the Daugava (Zapadnaya Dvina), which flows for 1020 kilometres, emptying into the Baltic Sea near Rīga.

The territory of the present-day Baltic states can be divided into three geographical zones: the western coastal areas, the central zone with fertile soils, most suitable for agriculture, and the eastern region which contains the most lakes, swamps and forests. There are significant differences in climate from west to east and south to north. As the Baltic states lie in a transitional zone from maritime to continental climate, there are substantial variations in precipitation and temperature from the mild climate of the western coastal areas to the more extreme temperatures (warmer summers and colder winters) further inland to the east. Lithuania enjoys a growing period which is three weeks longer than that of Estonia because of the longer summers in the south.[1]

The landmass of the present-day Baltic states gradually began to emerge around 14000 BC at the end of the last ice age as the Scandinavian ice sheet retreated. The receding ice sheet shaped the landscape, creating numerous lakes. In the wake of the melting ice sheet, the Baltic Ice Lake, predecessor of the Baltic Sea, was formed. Northern Estonia did not emerge from under the ice sheet until 11000 BC, with the western coastal area of Estonia rising gradually above sea level during the following millennia. As the glacial climate warmed and vegetation began to grow, animals roamed into the area. The first humans ventured into the tundra landscape of Lithuania in pursuit of reindeer around 11000 BC near the end of the Paleolithic era (Early Stone Age). These were small bands of nomadic hunters who set up temporary camps at rivers and lakes. Those who came from the south were bearers of the Swidrian Culture and those from the west of the Magdalen-Ahrensburgian Culture. The essential difference between these two archaeological cultures is in how they chipped the flint from which they made their tools and weapons.[2]

The transition from the Paleolithic to the Mesolithic era witnessed further dramatic geological and climatic changes. The Baltic Ice Lake flowed out into the ocean across present-day Sweden and drained to sea level (dropping 25 metres), forming the short-lived brackish Yoldia Sea. The rising Scandinavian land mass soon cut off the Yoldia Sea from the ocean and around 9000 BC it became the freshwater Ancylus Lake. When ocean levels rose, however, saline water poured through the Great

Belt (Denmark) to reconnect with the ocean, creating the Littorina Sea and finally evolving to a shape similar to the Baltic Sea today. These changes were accompanied by a warming of the climate from Preboreal to Atlantic. By the end of the Mesolithic era around 5000 BC, the climate had warmed to the extent where broad-leafed vegetation dominated, as opposed to the coniferous trees of preceding periods. This was the warmest period in the history of the region (a couple of degrees warmer than at present). The warmer climate attracted new species such as elk and wild boar, while the reindeer departed. The region, with its abundant game and its bodies of water teeming with fish, was now able to support a growing human population, whose temporary camps had gradually became permanent settlements. These first settlements were situated along the rivers and lakes of the interior and later also by the sea coast where seal-hunting provided sustenance.[3]

At the start of the Mesolithic (Middle Stone Age) period (9000–5000 BC) the first indigenous culture evolved from the Swidrian Culture. This was known as the Kunda Culture after the site on the northern Estonian coast which was the first to be studied in depth. The Kunda Culture stretched from northern Lithuania to southern Finland and embraced part of north-western Russia as well. These people were hunter-gatherers: there was as yet no agriculture and they occupied themselves with hunting, fishing and seal-hunting in the coastal areas. In the seventh millennium BC another closely related local culture, the Nemunas Culture, began to form in southern and central Lithuania.[4] Flint deposits were abundant in this area hence the Nemunas Culture produced more flint tools and weapons than the bearers of the Kunda Culture and its successor, the Narva Culture, both of which relied more on bone and antlers.

The beginning of the Neolithic era (New Stone Age) in the Baltic region (5000–1800 BC) is marked by the beginning of the production of ceramic vessels. The Neolithic period is also characterised by the rudiments of agriculture – the cultivation of wheat and barley, utilising a two-field system, with one lying fallow for a year, and the domestication of livestock – cows, goats, sheep and pigs. During the Neolithic era two distinct new cultures emerged: the first, Comb Ware Culture (4000–1800 BC), characterised by pottery decorated with imprints made with comb-like objects, and the second, Corded Ware Culture (3000–1800 BC), characterised by pottery decorated with cord imprints. The latter is also identified by its boat-shaped axe head. The Comb Ware Culture is commonly associated with the arrival of Finnic-speaking peoples and the Corded Ware Culture with the influx of Indo-Europeans, the Balts. Recent research has questioned whether the advent of these two new archaeological cultures can indeed be ascribed to a new wave of settlers displacing the former inhabitants and has suggested instead a more gradual and complex process which involved an intermingling of cultures and language exchange.[5] There is considerable evidence of intermingling and assimilation, particularly in the area of present-day Latvia.

By the end of the Neolithic period the linguistic map of the Baltic region was relatively clear, with speakers of Finnic languages situated north of the Daugava river and speakers of Baltic languages south of it. Finnic Livs inhabited the northern part of the Courland peninsula. From the advent of the Corded Ware Culture until the end of the Iron Age, the Daugava river also marked the cultural border between the northern and southern Baltic regions.[6] This can be seen in the development of burial customs: the finds at grave sites provide archaeologists with the major source of information on Baltic societies.

The ethnogenesis of the people inhabiting the Baltic region is, nevertheless, an open question. Linguists, archaeologists and geneticists employ different tools and methods, but evidence from all these fields is necessary to piece together a plausible interpretation of the ethnic and linguistic development of the area. A number of different interpretations have been offered. The conventional theory holds that the Finno-Ugrians arrived from the east, having originated from the Urals, and that the Balts arrived later from the south-west. Some recent research has challenged these assumptions and suggested that the ancestors of the Finno-Ugrians had arrived several millennia earlier, and not from the Urals but from the south and west. This theory, however, has not found wide acceptance.[7] Indeed, the earlier assumptions which posited a clear connection between archaeological cultures and ethnicity are now considered overly simplistic. Ethnogenesis was a multilayered process involving language exchange among natives and newcomers, rather than migration. Genetically, it is clear that Estonians, Latvians and Lithuanians are almost identical, having the same genetic forefathers (DNA lines).[8]

The end of the Stone Age and the beginning of the age of metals in the eastern Baltic is generally dated as 1800 BC when the first bronze items appeared in the region. During the Bronze Age (1800–500 BC), stone and flint tools and weapons were gradually superseded by weapons made of bronze, initially imported from Scandinavia and Central Europe. This period saw the advent of small hillfort settlements, which were the centres of bronze-casting. Fortified settlements were also associated with the spread of livestock-breeding (since valuable animals had to be protected from potential raiders). Along with the importation of bronze from Central Europe, the custom of cremation gradually gained popularity.

The next transition – from bronze to iron tools – proceeded more rapidly, taking only three centuries. Iron was simpler to make and the necessary ore could be obtained locally from bogs. Bronze-casting had required larger fortified settlements and the maintenance of a trade network but these were largely abandoned because iron could be forged almost anywhere.[9] Slash-and-burn farming methods necessitated the cultivating of new plots and also contributed to the dispersal of the larger communities of the Bronze Age. There was a move inland from the shores of larger bodies of water to areas more suitable for agriculture. The use of iron farming implements, such as ploughshares, hoes, sickles and scythes, increased agricultural yields and enabled the spread of land cultivation to new forested areas which would have been too difficult to till with more primitive tools. By the Early Iron Age (500 BC–AD 450), the gradual transition from the hunting-fishing-gathering subsistence lifestyle to a pattern of settlement based on a single-farm system was completed.[10] The expansion of farming contributed to population growth, and the Early Iron Age appears to have been a peaceful time for the region.[11]

PREHISTORIC SOCIETIES

By the beginning of the Iron Age, social stratification had developed, evidenced by distinct differences in burial customs. The upper stratum lived on the dominant farm within a settlement or in hillforts. They were buried in stone graves and were accompanied by important artefacts. Ordinary farmers were buried with only modest grave goods. The remains of the poorest people, those who were probably dependent on the larger farms, were placed in earthen graves or simply laid on the ground at designated areas.[12]

During the Roman Iron Age (AD 50–450), the dead were buried in above-ground graves: *tarand* graves[13] in Estonia and northern Latvia; stone barrows in Lithuania and southern Latvia. By the eighth century new burial customs had spread across all of Lithuania and soon began to spread northwards: first inhumations and then, by the ninth century, cremations.[14] There were notable differences in the burial customs in the region, which allow archaeologists to delineate the settlement areas of the various Baltic tribes. For instance, during the Late Iron Age (800–1200), the Lettigallians buried the men with their heads facing to the east and the women with their heads facing to the west. Men were usually buried together with an axe and two spears. A custom practised only by the Lithuanians was the ritual burial of horses after the death of their owner.[15]

Written sources about the peoples of the eastern Baltic before the second millennium are sparse. The Roman historian Tacitus in his *Germania*, written in AD 98, was the first to describe Baltic tribes, most likely the Prussians, whom he referred to as the Aestii. He describes them as worshipping a Mother of the Gods and gathering amber from the sea.[16] In Roman times, amber was the commodity of the region which was most highly valued by traders. The Vistula river provided the trade route by which the amber reached the outposts of the Roman Empire.

During that time, the Baltic tribes inhabited a much wider area than at present: from the Vistula to beyond the Dnieper river in central Russia. After the collapse of the Roman Empire, the great migrations in the fifth and sixth centuries, particularly of the Slavs, pushed the Balts into a more compact area and also further northwards into the territory inhabited by Finnic-speaking peoples, particularly the Livs.

The Lithuanians consisted of two large groups: the Žemaitians or Samogitians ('Lowlanders') who lived around the mouth of the Nemunas river, which emptied into the Baltic Sea, and the Aukštaitians ('Highlanders') who lived further upriver to the east. Both of these groups themselves consisted of several tribal territories, or lands. Other Baltic tribes closely related to the Lithuanians, living to their west and southwest, were the Scalvians, Yotvingians and Prussians, inhabiting the territory of what is today north-eastern Poland and the Kaliningrad oblast of the Russian Federation.

The largest Baltic tribe inhabiting the territory of today's Latvia, and from whom the name Latvians or Letts later derived, were the Lettigallians. They were the last tribe to arrive, having been pushed out of present-day Belarus by Slavic migration into the eastern part of Latvia north of the Daugava river. The other proto-Latvian tribes were the Selonians south of the Daugava river. The lands of the Semigallians were also south of the Daugava but immediately to the west of those of the Selonians. The lands of the Curonians were along the western coast of present-day Latvia and Lithuania. The coast around the Gulf of Riga was inhabited by the Livs, close linguistic relatives of the Estonians. Although the proto-Estonians were not split into ethnically distinct tribes, there were notable cultural differences among those Estonians inhabiting the south and the north of the country, as well as those who lived in the western coastal areas and the islands and who were most directly exposed to Scandinavian influence. In the north-eastern corner of Estonia lived another Finnic tribe, the Votes (Votians), whose territory of inhabitation extended to the area of present-day St Petersburg.

Throughout the Iron Age, agriculture developed, evolving from the slash-and-burn system to a two-field rotational system, and eventually to a more efficient three-field system. By the end of the first millennium a strip-field system had emerged, which facilitated the formation of villages.[17] Villages banded together to form political communities ruled by elders. These districts were typically centred on a hillfort. Later, with Christianisation, these hillfort districts usually formed the basis of parishes which became the primary administrative units until the twentieth century. Larger territorial units were formed in the early second millennium when several of these districts united together to form a land or chiefdom.[18] For instance, the area inhabited by the Livs consisted of four lands; that inhabited by the Semigallians consisted of seven distinct lands. These were sovereign units which themselves determined their relationship with neighbouring lands. While a common language formed a strong bond, these territories made their own decisions about going to war, in a similar fashion to the raising of war-bands by chieftains among Celtic, Germanic and Slavic tribes.

The development of hillforts and open settlements demonstrates the evolution of social and political structures – that is to say the ambitions of the elite – in the Baltic region. Hillforts were erected first in Lithuania in the early Roman Iron Age, in Latvia at the end of the Roman Iron Age and finally in Estonia during the sixth century. The differences in the level of social and political development during the late Iron Age are illustrated by the number of hillforts: there were approximately 700 hillforts in use in Lithuania, almost 200 in Latvia and fewer than 100 in Estonia.[19] These figures also suggest that society in the Lithuanian areas was more hierarchical and placed greater emphasis on martial virtues, whereas further north, especially in the Estonian areas, communities remained more egalitarian, and feminine values were still important. By the twelfth century some hillforts, such as Jersika (Gerzika) on the Daugava, had evolved into sites of permanent inhabitation, with military chieftains and their escorts residing there. Kernavė in Lithuania was the largest and most important hillfort settlement and was thought to have had 3000 inhabitants in the thirteenth century. The population density in the Baltic at the end of the Iron Age has been estimated to have been roughly three people per square kilometre.[20]

Compared to Central Europe, Baltic society was noticeably less stratified and egalitarian.[21] Apart from slaves, mostly women and children, obtained from raids into neighbouring lands, the majority of people were free peasants. One can differentiate between the social structure which had developed by the end of the Iron Age in the coastal and western areas and that in the south-eastern area of Estonia, eastern Latvia and central and eastern Lithuania. In the former, social stratification began earlier, with the emergence of a numerically significant tier of superiors (though with few possessions and weak powers), while in the latter areas, stratification began later and was more intense: the number of superiors remained small, but the size of their territory and scope of their authority was significantly greater.[22] In the former areas, Scandinavian influences were pronounced; in the latter, East Slavic Rus'ian influences had more impact.

It is not possible to say with certainty anything about the pre-Christian religion. Stone Age religious practice was typified by ancestor and fertility cults. The belief system of the natives can be described as animistic: a belief that everything in the natural world had a spirit. By the beginning of the Iron Age, people had begun to worship personified and anthropomorphic heavenly gods as well.[23] Later written sources mention most prominently the deities Perkūnas (Baltic) and Taara (Estonian), both gods of thunder, akin to the Scandinavian Thor. The religious structure was not elaborate: shamans guided the spiritual life of communities and worship was conducted in sacred groves, particularly oak tree groves; there were no pagan temples or hierarchical priesthood.

Although Baltic history before the arrival of the crusaders at the end of the twelfth century is considered prehistory because of the lack of written sources, there are multiple references to the Baltic and Finnic tribes in Scandinavian sagas and Rus'ian chronicles. Lithuania is first mentioned in a German chronicle written in 1009 which records the martyrdom of a Christian missionary named Bruno. During the Viking Age (800–1050), Scandinavian warriors regularly raided the eastern shores of the Baltic Sea. Archbishop Rimbert of Bremen's *Life of Saint Ansgar* records the crushing defeat of a Danish maritime expedition against the Curonians and a subsequent victorious Swedish campaign against the Curonians in the 850s.[24] A testament to the intensity of interaction across the Baltic Sea are surviving eleventh-century runestones in Sweden recording warriors who fell in battle on the eastern shore of the Baltic. With the exception of a Swedish colony on the south-western coast of Latvia at Grobiņa during the eighth century, local resistance prevented Scandinavians from establishing a presence in the Baltic lands.[25] In any case, the Vikings were more tempted by the riches to be obtained further east and south. Two major trade routes to the east used by the Vikings traversed Baltic lands: the first, through the Gulf of Finland along the Estonian coast, up the Neva river to Lake Ladoga and down to Novgorod or east to the Volga to reach the Caspian Sea; the second, along the Daugava to the Dnieper river, south to Kiev and across the Black Sea to Constantinople. A lesser route went via the Nemunas river through Lithuanian territory to reach the Dnieper further downstream. Evidence of the indirect contacts with the Near East established through these trade routes to Byzantium are hoards of Arabic silver coins (dirham) from the ninth century, which have been uncovered in the Baltic region. One colourful saga which recorded interaction in the Baltic Sea region is that of Norwegian King Olaf Tryggvason who as a child was taken captive en route to Novgorod by Estonian pirates and sold into slavery.[26] Viking (Varangian) princely dynasties played a major role in the formation of the earliest Russian state, Kievan Rus', during the ninth century.

The Rus'ian principalities were active in expanding westwards and northwards in the tenth and eleventh centuries. Rus'ian chronicles record that in 1030 the Estonian hillfort settlement of Tartu was captured by the Grand Duke of Kievan Rus', Yaroslav the Wise, who also moved against the Lithuanians a decade later (1040). In the twelfth century, Rus'ians penetrated further west, into Black Rus', establishing a fort at Novogorodok (Navahrudak).[27] However, the initiative passed to the Lithuanians by the end of the century as the Kievan Rus' state fragmented; in the thirteenth century Novogorodok was used as a Lithuanian ducal residence. The proto-Latvian tribes were most closely tied with the Rus'ians. The Lettigallians paid tribute to the neighbouring Rus'ian principalities of Pskov and Polotsk, and the Lettigallian land of Jersika, in the middle reaches of the Daugava, was ruled by a vassal of Polotsk. Some Lettigallian chieftains converted to Orthodox Christianity. The Selonians and Livs who lived along the banks of the Daugava also paid occasional tribute to Polotsk.[28]

Until the beginning of the eleventh century and the Christianisation of Scandinavia, Viking raiding activity had been mainly in one direction – Scandinavian Vikings raiding eastern Baltic shores. The Scandinavian Viking era was succeeded by a Baltic Viking era, with seaborne raids

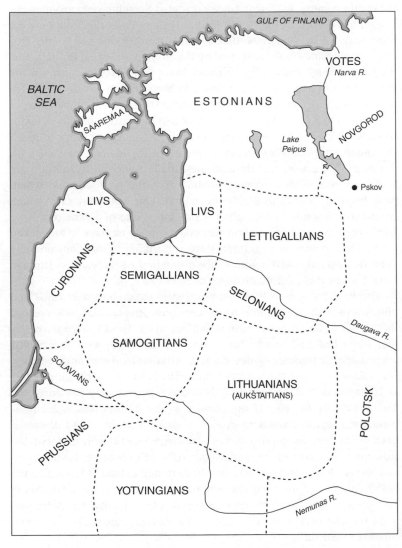

**Map 1** The Baltic region at the end of the Iron Age (*c*. 1150)

mounted by Curonians and Estonians from the isle of Saaremaa (Ösel).[29] Prayers read in Danish churches for protection against the Curonians attest to the ferocity of these raids.[30] In 1187 Estonians from Saaremaa even ransacked Sweden's principal city, Sigtuna, prompting the Swedes later to build a new capital at Stockholm.[31] Christian Swedish and Danish kings launched retaliatory expeditions against the Curonians and Estonians, but prior to the thirteenth century these raids primarily sought to neutralise the threat of eastern Baltic piracy, not to conquer territory or to convert the natives to Christianity.

## THE NORTHERN CRUSADES

By the end of the twelfth century the peoples living on the eastern shores of the Baltic were the last remaining pagans in Europe; neighbouring peoples – Scandinavians, Rus'ians, Poles – had accepted Christianity two centuries earlier. A new, fateful presence on the Baltic Sea was that of the Germans. The first crusade against pagans living on the Baltic littoral was launched against the Slavic Wends in 1147. In its wake, Henry the Lion, the Duke of Saxony, established Lübeck as the first German town on the Baltic coast in 1159. From Lübeck, German merchants expanded their activities to the north-east, establishing their most important trading centre at Visby in the 1160s on the Baltic Sea island of Gotland. From there, they were able to develop and expand their contacts on the eastern coast of the Baltic and rapidly came to dominate the old Scandinavian trade routes in the Baltic Sea region.

Along with the traders came the missionaries. Missionary work among the peoples of the eastern Baltic had been conducted earlier by Scandinavians without any great determination or success. A few churches were temporarily erected along Baltic trade routes by Christian merchants in the eleventh and twelfth centuries. In the 1150s, the Swedes began their gradual Christianisation and incorporation of Finland, which they completed at the end of the thirteenth century. The first mission approved by the papacy was initiated by Eskil, the Archbishop of Lund (then part of Denmark), who consecrated the French monk Fulco as Bishop of Estonia in 1167. Although Pope Alexander III called on Scandinavian Christians to support Fulco's mission with money and arms, Fulco's mission was an utter failure. The Estonians were not receptive and the Danish Crown was much more interested in territories along the southern shore of the Baltic Sea.[32]

One of the motives of the papacy to support crusades in northern Europe was to prevent the area from coming under the influence of the rival Orthodox Church. Indeed, the Baltic peoples encountered Christianity first from the east in its Orthodox form, as demonstrated by a number of basic religious terms in the Estonian, Latvian and Lithuanian languages which are derived from East Slavic. By the end of the twelfth century, Orthodox churches existed in Koknese and Jersika on the Daugava. However, unlike the Germanic crusaders, Rus'ian rulers and the Orthodox Church demonstrated little interest in converting neighbouring pagan peoples.

German merchants based at Visby began to trade along the Daugava river. They were accompanied by Meinhard, an Augustinian canon from Holstein, who remained as a missionary with the Livs living around the mouth of the Daugava in 1180. In 1186 the archbishop of Hamburg-Bremen named him Bishop of Üxküll, after the fort that he had constructed on the Daugava river – the first stone building in the region, built by stonemasons from Gotland – to protect the Liv converts from Lithuanian raids. Meinhard's relations with his converts soured when the Livs refused to pay taxes for this protection. The second bishop, Berthold, the Cistercian abbot of Loccum (consecrated in 1197), decided that a more forceful approach was necessary and secured a Bull for a crusade against the Livs from Pope Innocent III (1198–1216) in 1198. Berthold raised a force of Saxon knights who had no difficulty in defeating the overawed Livs, but Berthold himself was killed in the encounter. As soon as the crusaders departed, the Livs washed off their baptism.

The third bishop, Albert von Buxhoevden, the nephew of the Archbishop of Hamburg-Bremen (consecrated in 1199), was a shrewd diplomat, ambitious politician, and highly capable strategist who learned from the travails of his predecessors. He prepared the ground well, securing support from both the Pope and the Holy Roman Emperor, Philip of Swabia. In 1199 Pope Innocent III proclaimed a crusade to defend the converts in Livonia. The pilgrims who took up arms to fight the heathens would be granted indulgences equal to a pilgrimage to holy sites in Rome and, for those who fell in battle, the complete remission of their sins. Albert led a convoy of 23 ships carrying 500 crusaders from Lübeck to the mouth of the Daugava river in 1200. One of his first decisions was to move his headquarters downriver to a more defensible location where he founded Riga in 1201.

Albert returned frequently to Germany to preach the crusade and recruit new 'pilgrims', primarily from Saxony and Westphalia, for the annual summer campaigning season. Among these was Henricus, who would become a priest among the Lettigallians. His *Chronicle of Livonia*, written during the mid-1220s, is a vivid first-hand account of the crusade and one of the most remarkable chronicles of its era in Europe.[33] It marks the beginning of recorded history for Latvia and Estonia, whose peoples had only been mentioned fleetingly in earlier Scandinavian and Rus'ian chronicles.

To protect and expand the mission after the crusaders had returned home, Albert needed a permanent military force. In 1202, with the Pope's blessing, Albert created the *Fratres militiæ Christi Livoniae* (Brethren of the Militia of Christ of Livonia), who were called the Swordbrothers after the emblem of a red cross and sword on their white mantles. Since Livonia did not offer any attractions or treasure even remotely comparable to those of the Holy Land, Albert attempted to increase its allure by naming it Mary's Land (*Terra Mariana*), after Christian Europe's most venerated saint.[34] The Swordbrothers were patterned after the Knights Templar, the order of monk-warriors, who took a vow of poverty and chastity. To provide the Swordbrothers with income, Albert permitted them to retain one-third of the conquered territories. In the course of their new conquests, their portion actually grew considerably larger. This arrangement fuelled their lust for further conquest and led to future conflicts about the division of territorial spoils.

The mission in Livonia was transformed into a permanent crusade in 1204 when Pope Innocent III approved the automatic renewal of the proclamation of a crusade. Nevertheless, the Pope was not the initiator of an aggressive expansion of Christendom – he was responding to the appeals of the missionary bishops in northern Europe. The Danish and Swedish kings were also eager to obtain the Pope's support in this regard. The Danes mounted a major expedition against Saaremaa (Ösel) in 1206, which followed previous raids and counter-raids by the Danes and the Saaremaa Estonians and Curonians, but now the Danish campaign had an ideological justification. Under Innocent's successor, Pope Honorius III (1216–27), the complete crusade indulgence was extended to the eastern Baltic littoral in 1217–18, elevating the struggle against the pagans in northern Europe to an equal footing with the earlier and ongoing crusading efforts in Spain and the Holy Land.[35]

The first tribe subjugated by the crusaders was the Livs, whose resistance was broken in 1206. One of their elders, Caupo, had been given an audience with the Pope and was awed by the splendour of Rome. After their baptism, the Livs became the Swordbrothers' first allies. As the first tribe encountered by the missionaries, their name – Livonia (Livland) – was extended to cover the entire region later conquered by the crusaders. Next were the Selonians, further inland along the Daugava trade route, who were easily subjugated in 1208. East of the Livs were the Lettigallians, whose elders decided not to resist the Swordbrothers. In voluntarily submitting in 1208, they gained a strong ally against their more powerful neighbours: the Rus'ians, to whom they had had to pay tribute, and the Lithuanians and Estonians, from whose incursions they had repeatedly suffered. The invaders astutely exploited rivalries between the indigenous peoples, who had frequently engaged in raids on their neighbours for booty and slaves.

The Swordbrothers and their new allies, the Lettigallians and Livs, moved northwards against the Estonians in 1208. The Estonians were not politically united, and the southern lands of Ugandi (Ugaunia) and Sakala (Saccalia) initially fought the invaders alone. In 1217 a united Estonian army suffered a major defeat by the crusaders and their Liv and Lettigallian auxiliaries in one of the rare battles in the open field. The leading Estonian elder, Lembitu, was killed, as was Caupo. As a result, southern and central Estonia came under the control of the Swordbrothers. In campaigns against the remaining free Estonian lands, the crusaders also employed newly baptised Estonians.

In addition to Albert and the Swordbrothers, the Kingdom of Denmark – the strongest power in northern Europe at the time – was a major protagonist in the northern crusades. After his two previous military expeditions in 1206 and 1208 failed to establish a foothold in Estonian territory, the Danish king, Valdemar II, personally led a large force to northern Estonia in 1219. The Estonians almost overwhelmed the Danish encampment, but, according to legend, the king was inspired to victory by a red banner with a white cross falling from the sky: this became the *Dannebrog*, the oldest existing state flag in the world today.[36] Valdemar built a castle (Reval) near the site of the vanquished Estonian fort at what later came to be known as Tallinn.[37] The Swedish king, John I, also sought a piece of the action. In 1220, he landed in western Estonia, but the garrison he left behind at Lihula was annihilated by the Saaremaa Estonians. After this blow to their ambitions, the Swedes turned their attention northwards and renewed their efforts to conquer the rest of Finland. Valdemar also landed on Saaremaa in 1222 where he had temporary success.

Prior to the arrival of the crusaders from the west, the Rus'ian Duke of Polotsk, Vladimir, had been the major external actor in the Baltic region, receiving tributes from the Livs and Lettigallians. When he finally realised the magnitude of the newcomers' ambitions, the duke unsuccessfully besieged the crusaders' fort at Holm (Mārtiņsala) together with the rebellious Livs in 1206. After the loss of influence over the Livs and Lettigallians, the neighbouring Rus'ian principalities of Novgorod and Pskov continued to be actively involved in the region.[38] During the crusade on Estonia, the Rus'ians, rather opportunistically, alternately raided and pillaged Estonians lands or assisted the Estonians when the latter almost succeeded in driving the Swordbrothers out of their homeland in 1223–4. However, by 1227, the final Estonian resistance on Saaremaa was broken. This is where Henricus' *Chronicle of Livonia* ends, conventionally marking the successful conclusion of the crusade against the Estonians, although the people of Saaremaa repeatedly rose up against the foreigners during the following decades.

The Danes, Albert and the Swordbrothers quarrelled among themselves over how to divide the territorial spoils. Their disputes were also related to the pervasive power struggle in Europe between the papacy and the Holy Roman Emperor. After the conquest of the Estonians, the rivalry between the Swordbrothers, the Danes and the Archbishop of Riga broke out into open conflict. The Swordbrothers seized Reval and the Danish Duchy of Estonia for themselves in 1227. Attempts by papal envoys to resolve the dispute failed because the Swordbrothers had no alternative source of income – they had to support themselves by taxation or by the conquest of new territories.

The core of the crusaders were the monk-warriors of the Swordbrothers quartered in the forts spread across the newly conquered territory. The Swordbrothers never numbered more than a few hundred, but they were reinforced every spring by new crusaders recruited from northern Germany who generally sailed home in the autumn. The Swordbrothers soon learned to adapt their military campaigning methods to the local conditions. After 1211, campaigning was conducted primarily in the winter months, when frozen rivers functioned as highways for the knights and the natives could not hide in ambush in (nor flee to) the forests and swamps. The fierce Estonian mariners of the island of Saaremaa were only conquered when the Swordbrothers' army crossed the sea ice in 1227. The crusaders' decisive advantage over the natives was the professionalism of their warrior class and their superior military technology: the crossbow, catapults and siege-engines; the armoured knight on horseback was the equivalent of the tank in modern times.[39] The Swordbrothers subsequently built a network of new stone castles on the sites of the native wooden hillforts, which enabled them to maintain control over the freshly conquered territory. They capitalised on the political disunity of the natives and exploited their rivalries, using the subjugated tribes to help conquer their neighbours. Native allies and auxiliaries always formed the majority of the manpower in the crusaders' force. Similarities can be noted with the contemporaneous subjugation of the Welsh by the English or even the conquest of the Americas a few centuries later.

After defeating the Estonians, the Swordbrothers thrust southwards against the Curonians, achieving early successes. However, they soon ran up against the most feared warriors in the region: the Samogitians and Lithuanians, whose incursions the Swordbrothers had already experienced during their crusade against the Livs and Estonians. To appease the thirst for action by fresh crusaders, who had arrived from Holstein in the late spring of 1236 and wanted to return home before the sea froze, the Swordbrothers carelessly undertook a risky summer expedition, and were ambushed and annihilated by the Samogitians and Semigallians at the battle of Saulė. The surviving Swordbrothers merged with the Teutonic Order in 1237, becoming its Livonian branch. The Teutonic Knights had originally been established in 1190 in Acre as the Order of the Hospital of St Mary of the Germans in Jerusalem, but soon became a military order and took up the invitation of Conrad, the Polish Duke of Mazovia in 1226 to help fight the pagan Prussians. After the Teutonic Knights conquered the Prussians during the 1230s, Samogitia and Lithuania became their next targets.

The Teutonic Knights sought to heal the Swordbrothers' rift with the papacy by returning Estonia to Denmark in 1238. Their primary concern remained the crusade in the Holy Land, and it was not until the end of the thirteenth century that the Teutonic Order finally gave up its main goal of reconquering Jerusalem. Subsequently, the Grand Master of the Teutonic Order established his headquarters at the mighty fortress of Marienburg (Malbork) in Prussia.[40]

The order fought not only pagans but also, on occasion, neighbouring Christian powers. Papal legate William of Modena sought to unite the rival crusader factions by engaging them in a joint campaign of eastward expansion.[41] Novgorod, the only Rus'ian principality which had escaped devastation by the Mongol Tatars during 1237–40, appeared to be an easy target. The order, Danish vassals and their Estonian levies moved eastwards across the Narva river against the pagan neighbours of the Estonians, the Finnic Votes, who were tributaries of

Novgorod, and occupied Pskov in 1240, with the collusion of some leading Pskovians who sought independence from Novgorod. Novgorodian Prince Alexander Nevsky ousted the order from Pskov and defeated the Livonian knights in the famous Battle on the Ice at Lake Peipus in 1242. The significance and scale of this battle has since been embellished to such an extent that it has achieved epic proportions and it has been misleadingly portrayed as part of a highly coordinated papal strategy to bring the Russian Orthodox Church under its control.[42] The mythification of the battle was emphasized later, in the sixteenth century, when Alexander Nevsky was made an Orthodox saint. Later propagandists have often claimed that this engagement set the limit of the *Drang nach Osten* (German colonisation eastwards) and marked the borderline between Western and Eastern, Catholic and Orthodox civilisations.[43]

The Livonian brethren subsequently turned their attention southwards, seeking to connect their territory with that of the Teutonic Order in Prussia. The Curonians were subjugated in the 1240s and a network of castles was established, with Goldingen (Kuldīga) being the most imposing and strongly garrisoned. Of key strategic importance in establishing a short-lived land bridge between Livonia and Prussia along the sea coast, was the Memel fortress built in 1252, which later evolved into the city of Memel (Klaipėda). The order's relentless advance brought it into direct conflict with the Samogitians and Lithuanians, who would prove to be its most formidable opponents.

By this time, the Lithuanian tribes had been united under one ruler, Mindaugas, whose own patrimonial lands lay between the Neris, Nemunas and Merkys rivers in the territory known as *Lietuva* (Lithuania). This area formed the cradle of the future state and contained all its early administrative centres: Kernavė, Trakai and Vilnius. In addition to Lithuania proper, other ethnically Lithuanian lands were Nalšia to its east, Deltuva and Upytė to its north, and Neris to its west. Together, the peoples of these lands were known as Aukštaitians (Highlanders) as opposed to the Žemaitians (Lowlanders) who lived downriver to their west in Samogitia (Žemaitija).[44] By the thirteenth century, these lands had formed a loose confederation, often participating in common military expeditions. The unification of these lands was accomplished by Mindaugas, the most skilled and cunning Lithuanian duke, who rose to be supreme ruler through successful military campaigns as well as by exiling and murdering potential rivals. The destruction of Kievan Rus' by the Mongols presented Mindaugas with a golden opportunity to spread his authority southwards and eastwards. By the mid-1240s, Mindaugas managed to assert his supremacy over an area stretching from Samogitia in the west to Minsk in the east to Black Rus' in the south.

Mindaugas' ruthless consolidation of his power, however, resulted in internecine war. His uncle and nephews, whom he had dispossessed and expelled, forged an alliance with neighbouring powers, the Archbishop of Riga and the Galician Rus'ians. To undermine the coalition attacking him, Mindaugas entered into an alliance with the Livonian branch of the Teutonic Order. In return for accepting baptism from the order in 1251, the Pope approved the crowning of Mindaugas as King of Lithuania in 1253. Peace was concluded with the order, but Mindaugas had to cede Samogitia to the order as the price for the crown. Mindaugas also erected the first Christian cathedral in Vilnius. His choice was political: with external aid, he defeated his internal enemies, he secured peace in the west to concentrate on expansion in the east and he achieved international recognition of his realm. Mindaugas did not lose much by ceding Samogitia because it had been only nominally under his rule and the Samogitians had no intention of bowing to the order (or to Mindaugas, for that matter).[45]

The Samogitians adopted an offensive strategy and dealt a crushing defeat to the order at the Battle of Durbe (Durben) in 1260. This proved the catalyst for recently subjugated native tribes, starting with the Prussians, to rise up against the crusaders. The order faced a desperate situation on both fronts simultaneously, as, in Livonia, the Curonians and Saaremaa Estonians rebelled and the Semigallians broke their uneasy alliance with the order. These events persuaded Mindaugas to reassess his strategy and to support the Samogitians against the order. He expelled the Christian clergy from Lithuania. However, his reign was terminated in 1263, when he was assassinated by a rival from within his own clan. Six years of internecine warfare followed, during which Mindaugas' three immediate successors were all killed. Hardly any traces of Christianity survived Mindaugas; Lithuanian society had clearly not been prepared for the acceptance of Christianity. Indeed, Mindaugas' baptism did not mean his rejection of his former pagan deities nor the conversion to Christianity of others beyond his immediate retinue. Although fratricidal rivalries threatened to break up the newly created realm, Mindaugas' greatest accomplishment, the unification of the state, endured.

By the time internal stability was restored with the emergence of Traidenis as supreme ruler in 1269, the Lithuanians had lost the opportunity to unite the Baltic tribes and to deliver a concerted blow to the highly vulnerable Teutonic Order. Although the Lithuanians were able to conduct successful raids deep into Livonia (as in the case of the auda-cious expedition over the frozen sea to pillage Saaremaa in 1270), the order recovered the initiative. By the time of Traidenis' death in 1282, most of the Baltic tribes neighbouring the Lithuanians had been subju-gated by the crusaders. The Curonians capitulated in 1267, the Prussian uprising was finally suppressed by reinforcements from Germany in 1274, and, to the southwest, the Yotvingian lands were divided among the Teutonic Order, the Poles and the Rus'ians by 1283. The final Baltic tribe to be conquered was the Semigallians, whose last redoubt surrendered to the Livonian knights in 1290. Thousands of irreconcilable Semigallians moved south into Samogitia. Thus the conquest of the proto-Latvian tribes was completed and the borders of medieval Livonia (roughly cor-responding to present-day Estonia and Latvia), which would endure for almost three centuries, were fixed. Although the order would occasionally gain temporary control over further territory in the south, the subjugation of the Semigallians was their last permanent territorial conquest.[46] This military frontline between pagans and Christians of 1290 would roughly correspond to the present Latvian and Lithuanian border. The Lithuanians and Samogitians, however, remained unbowed and the most resolute ene-mies of the crusaders. Samogitia would continue to be the main theatre of war for more than a century. The major threat from the Teutonic Order now came from the west along the Nemunas river after the Prussians had finally been subdued. The unrelenting aggression of the order pushed the Samogitians into closer union with the Lithuanians.

# 2

# Lithuania's Expansion and Medieval Livonia (1290–1560)

Lithuania remained Europe's last pagan state and greatly expanded its territory in the east while under continuous attack from crusaders in the west. Lithuania formed a dynastic union with Poland in 1386 and converted to Christianity in order to neutralise the threat from the Teutonic Order. The Lithuanian nobility was able to strengthen its leading position in the Grand Duchy and increase its authority over the peasantry by securing additional privileges from successive rulers eager for their support.

Feudal relations were introduced in the lands of the Estonian and Latvian tribes under German and Danish colonial rule during the Middle Ages. The conquerors established a network of castles and towns across Livonia. The towns enjoyed flourishing international trade and prosperity during the heyday of the Hanseatic League in the fourteenth and fifteenth centuries. Although the Livonian towns and bishoprics were often in conflict with the order, a Livonian Confederation was formed in the fifteenth century. The Protestant Reformation in the 1520s undermined the old order in Livonia and it collapsed under the pressure of Muscovite invasion in 1558.

## LITHUANIA ASCENDING

The most important development which caused the future paths of the history of the Baltic peoples to diverge was the fact that the Lithuanians alone managed to resist the onslaught of the Teutonic Order in the thirteenth century and establish their own state under a single ruler. This was the result of Mindaugas' ruthless ambition and the fact that the Lithuanians and Samogitians were the most ferocious warriors in the region, but was also the consequence of a more fortunate geographical location than those of the other Baltic tribes who had encountered the Germanic crusaders earlier. The Lithuanian lands were shielded from the Teutonic invaders by a barely penetrable wilderness of thick forest and swamps and they were not on the major river trade routes. Thus the Lithuanians had additional crucial decades of time to prepare for the conflict with the new advancing enemy.

The fratricidal competition in the ruling clan after Mindaugas' assassination did not tear the state asunder. Traidenis' successor Pukuveras (ruled until 1295) initiated the Gediminian dynasty which in the following century would make Lithuania one of the major powers in Eastern Europe. For a century, the Gediminian rulers all faced similar challenges: warfare with the order in the north and west, with the Rus' in the east and with the Poles in the south. They were unable permanently to resolve the dilemma of simultaneously combating threats on different fronts and they seldom had the luxury of focusing solely on one enemy.

Pukuveras' son, Grand Duke Vytenis, was primarily concerned with repelling the attacks of the order. After his death in 1316, Vytenis was succeeded by his younger brother, Gediminas, after whom the dynasty was named. Grand Duke Gediminas (ruled 1316–41) was the most significant ruler of pagan Lithuania and was credited with consolidating and expanding the state. Gediminas built his citadel at Vilnius in 1323 and fostered economic development. Realising that an economy based on slave-raiding was not sustainable, he invited Hanseatic merchants and tradesmen to Lithuania.[1] Among those he welcomed were Jews. Gediminas allowed Catholic priests into the country in order to minister to foreign merchants, but not to proselytise. Under Gediminas, Lithuania expanded further into the lands of Rus', annexing most of the territory of present-day Belarus. Expansion also served the needs of the dynasty by providing territories for Gediminas' plentiful kinsmen to rule over. They did not establish their own hereditary rule in the Rus'ian principalities, but were appointed and shifted around by the grand duke.[2]

Lithuania was unusual in that it was a pagan realm which ruled over a majority Christian population. One Orthodox and two Catholic churches, for eastern and western merchants respectively, existed in Vilnius alongside the pagan temple erected by Gediminas on the ruins of Mindaugas' cathedral.[3] The temple housed the idol of Perkūnas, the sky god, chief of the Lithuanian deities. The pagan temple, however, was a late development, mimicking Christianity, since Baltic pagan worship was conducted outdoors in sacred groves or at sacrificial stones. There was no hierarchical pagan priesthood: the grand duke himself was the supreme religious authority and officiated at the most important rituals. The chancellery of the grand duke retained Franciscan scribes who corresponded in Latin with western powers, and Ruthenian scribes who communicated in chancery Slavonic with eastern subjects and allies. At that time, Lithuanian had not yet developed into a written language. More than twice as many Orthodox Christian Eastern Slavs (Ruthenians) lived in the Grand Duchy than did Lithuanians. The former owed their religious allegiance to the Metropolitan of Kiev, who had moved his residency to Muscovy in 1325. In a rivalry with Muscovy, the Gediminians sought the creation of an Orthodox metropolitanate of Lithuania as a means of enhancing their control over the lands of Rus'.

During the thirteenth and fourteenth centuries, the Lithuanian pagan state was locked in a fierce struggle with the Teutonic Order along the northern and western border territories. Periods of peace alternated with warfare. Negotiations to convert to Catholicism were used on several occasions by Lithuanian grand dukes as an instrument to buy temporary peace and to forestall aggression, or to forge a temporary alliance with the order (since Christian powers were forbidden to sign peace treaties with pagans). This was clearly a negotiating ploy: actual conversion to Catholicism would have faced strong resistance from Lithuanian society, particularly in Samogitia which adhered most stubbornly to the old ways, as well as from the Orthodox territories of the state. Lithuanians even formed alliances within the Livonian confederation, on occasion allying themselves with the Archbishop of Riga against the order in internal Livonian struggles, as during the years 1298–1313 when a pagan Lithuanian garrison was stationed in Riga to protect the city against encroachment by the order.[4] Although this was denounced as duplicity by the order, the merchants of Riga valued their trade with the Lithuanians. Gediminas and his successors were astute diplomats who shrewdly managed to make use of rivalries and conflicts between neighbouring Christian powers, most often in alliance with Riga or Poland against the order.

While the recruits for the Teutonic Order came primarily from northern Germany, the crusades against Lithuania were multinational expeditions, with knights from all over Europe participating. The campaign of the winter of 1336–7 was led by Duke Henry of Bavaria and included Charles of Moravia (the future Holy Roman Emperor) and knights from

22

Burgundy, France, Spain and the Low Countries. In the fourteenth century, participation in the nearly annual campaign against the Lithuanian heathens became almost a common rite of passage for European knights, such as the future King of England, Henry IV, who campaigned with the Teutonic Knights in 1390. Campaigning against the pagan Lithuanians provided an enticing opportunity to redeem one's sins, and, at the same time, embark upon action and adventure, perhaps even enrich oneself and return home with tales of courage and achieve local fame. King John of Bohemia brought poets along with him for the 1328–9 campaign in order to publicise his exploits throughout Europe.[5]

While defending itself against the Teutonic Order in the west, Lithuania was simultaneously expanding its territory in the east. In the wake of the Mongol Tatars' destruction of Kievan Rus' in 1240 and subjugation of most of the Rus'ian principalities, several western Rus'ian principalities had sought Lithuanian protection. Although a pagan power, Lithuania respected the established traditions in the Rus'ian principalities. Most of the Lithuanian dukes and plenipotentiaries sent to rule over Rus'ian lands converted to Orthodoxy. As the Mongol grip weakened in the latter part of the fourteenth century, Lithuania expanded its influence further. Resistance to the Mongol hegemony was led by Moscow, which also aggressively sought to 'gather the lands of Rus" under its own domination. Hence Lithuania and Muscovy became competitors for the patrimony of Kievan Rus'. In the south, Lithuania was also in competition with, and occasionally at war with, Polish rulers over control of the Rus'ian principalities of Galich-Volynia and Podolia from 1340 to 1392.

Gediminas' son Algirdas ascended to the throne in 1345 and more than doubled Lithuania's territory during his lengthy rule as the grand duke. Algirdas entrusted his brother Kęstutis with defending the realm in the west against the order, while he concentrated on expanding the boundaries of the state in the east. Algirdas succeeded in annexing more new territory than any other Lithuanian grand duke. In 1368 and 1372 Algirdas even led military campaigns right up to the walls of the Moscow Kremlin. Algirdas' conquests in the east resulted in most of present-day Ukraine, including Kiev, coming under the control of the Grand Duchy. The Gediminians also extended their influence in the lands of Rus' through the utilisation of strategic dynastic marriages. On the western front, however, Lithuania faced mounting pressure from the order, whose military expeditions, launched from Prussia and Livonia, became more frequent and penetrated deeper into the heart of the state during the 1370s.

As Europe's last remaining pagan state surrounded by Christian powers, Lithuania was isolated and without reliable allies and its existence was continually under threat. Algirdas and Kęstutis successfully defended and expanded their realm, but they were constantly in the saddle leading military expeditions on several fronts. As a consequence of this incessant warfare and continued adherence to paganism, the modernisation or 'Europeanisation' of the state and society was delayed.[6]

## JOGAILA AND VYTAUTAS

The uncommonly harmonious partnership did not survive Algirdas' death in 1377. His son Jogaila was eager to take over the reins of power from Kęstutis and disagreed sharply with his uncle on the main orientation of the state's external policy: specifically, whether to focus on war in the east or in the west. Jogaila made an alliance with the Golden Horde against Muscovy, but did not arrive in time (possibly to await the outcome) for the battle of Kulikovo in 1380, where Muscovy for the first time defeated the Mongols. Open conflict erupted between Kęstutis and Jogaila when the former learned that the latter had secretly signed a treaty with the order. Jogaila reasserted his authority by incarcerating Kęstutis and his son Vytautas at the castle of Kréva in 1382. Kęstutis was murdered there, but Vytautas escaped and found refugee with the order. Vytautas roused opposition to Jogaila in Samogitia, where Kęstutis had been duke. After two years of costly strife, Jogaila offered to restore Vytautas' ancestral lands. As a sign of their reconciliation, Vytautas burned down several of the order's forts from where he had previously attacked Jogaila. The tumultuous relationship between these two cousins is one of the most intriguing and significant in Lithuanian history.

Both Jogaila and Vytautas realised that the only viable long-term solution for the security of Europe's last remaining pagan state was voluntary Christianisation. Three options existed: accepting Christianity from the order, from Muscovy or from Poland.[7] Jogaila flirted with all three. In 1382 he negotiated an alliance with the order under which he promised to become baptised, but subsequently backed out of the deal. Two years later, he rejected his mother's plan for him to marry the daughter of Dmitry Donskoi, the Grand Duke of Muscovy. A Polish alliance seemed to be the best of the three options since it would stem the growing threat from the Teutonic Order whose attacks in recent years had penetrated deeper into Lithuania's heartland. A golden opportunity presented itself when Polish lords sought to prevent the marriage of Jadwiga, the heiress to the Polish throne, to her betrothed Austrian Habsburg prince. In 1385 Jogaila concluded the Act of Krėva (Krewo) by which he contracted to marry Jadwiga and convert Lithuania to Roman Catholicism. As a result, in 1386 he was crowned Polish King Władysław II Jagiełło, establishing the Jagiellonian dynasty which would rule over much of East Central Europe for the next two centuries. The following year, he began the Christianisation of Lithuania. The significance of the Act of Krėva has remained a matter of controversy between Polish and Lithuanian historians: the former often assert that it marked a significant step towards the union of the two states: the latter sometimes interpret it as little more than a marriage contract.

Jogaila (Jagiełło) took up residence in the Polish royal city of Cracow (Kraków), and appointed his brother Skirgaila as viceroy in Lithuania. His cousin Vytautas revolted against this arrangement and again formed an alliance with the Teutonic Order. Civil war was ended by Jogaila's offer of the viceroyship to Vytautas in 1392. Skirgaila was dispatched to rule over Kiev. Nine years later Jogaila clarified the relationship between Poland and Lithuania by naming Vytautas Grand Duke of Lithuania, while maintaining the title of supreme duke for himself. In effect, this granted Vytautas autonomous power in Lithuania. Vytautas immediately began to centralise power in the Grand Duchy by expelling Gediminian regional dukes and replacing them with loyal deputies. He also encouraged the strengthening of the Lithuanian nobility. Vytautas promoted trade by inviting the Jews who were escaping the persecutions which followed the Black Plague in Central Europe to settle in Lithuania. In 1388–9 he granted them charters (privileges), allowing religious and economic freedom and placing them under ducal protection. Injuring a Jew was subject to the same sanctions as injuring a nobleman.[8]

Vytautas' ambitions matched those of Jogaila: it was under his rule that the Grand Duchy stretched from the Baltic to the Black Sea and was the largest state in Europe. Vytautas led an ambitious expedition including the Poles and the order against the Mongol-Tatar Golden Horde in 1399, although he had to yield sovereignty over Samogitia to the order to gain its participation in the venture. For the Catholic world, he framed the campaign as a crusade, demonstrating the genuineness of the former pagan ruler's conversion. However, this unique opportunity to gain European Christendom's support for Lithuania's easterly expansion suffered a crushing defeat at the hands of the Horde at the Battle of Vorskla in 1399.

Vytautas' alliance with the Teutonic Order did not survive much longer. Vytautas supported the Samogitian rebellion against the order in 1409 and, together with Jogaila, entered a final showdown with the order. The order managed to attract knights from western Europe to its banner by claiming that the conversion of the heathen Lithuanians was not genuine. The Teutonic Knights, however, went into battle without the support of their Livonian branch, who honoured their earlier truce with Lithuania. In 1410, in one of the greatest battles of medieval Europe, a joint Polish–Lithuanian force, led by Jogaila and Vytautas, defeated the Teutonic Knights at the Battle of Tannenberg (Pol: Grunwald; Lith: Žalgiris).[9] The elite of the Knights, including Grand Master Ulrich von Jungingen, fell in battle. Vytautas and Jogaila followed up their great victory by besieging the imposing headquarters of the order at Marienburg. However, they had no siege engines and their noble levy returned home to their estates, enabling the order to recover from the brink of total defeat. Lasting peace between Lithuania and the Teutonic Order was finally concluded at Melno in 1422. The order gave up its claim to Samogitia, although it retained Memel. Lithuania's western border with Prussia was demarcated with Lithuanian territory along the Baltic Sea coast separating Livonia from Prussia, an arrangement which held until the nineteenth century. The boundary in the north between Livonia and Lithuania, agreed upon a few years earlier, corresponded approximately to the present-day Lithuanian–Latvian border.

While the struggle with the order continued, Vytautas and Jogaila made a show of unity with the Acts of Horodło in 1413, which stipulated that after the former's death the election of the new Lithuanian grand duke would have to be approved by the Polish king. Catholic Lithuanian noble families were granted the use of the Polish noble coats of arms. Although this was a significant first step on the road to the polonisation of the Lithuanian nobility, the privileged position of Lithuanians within the Grand Duchy was institutionalised since Orthodox Ruthenian nobles were not included in this arrangement. Furthermore, the Grand Duchy brought its territorial administration into line with Polish practice by reorganising its territory into palatinates (voivodships).

Nevertheless, Vytautas not only continued to assert the independence of Lithuania and his supremacy in the Grand Duchy but also managed to gain Holy Roman Emperor Sigismund's consent to have himself crowned as King of Lithuania in 1429. Vytautas' planned coronation, however, was thwarted by Polish lords who intercepted the crown sent by Sigismund. After this setback, Vytautas met with Jogaila, who apparently

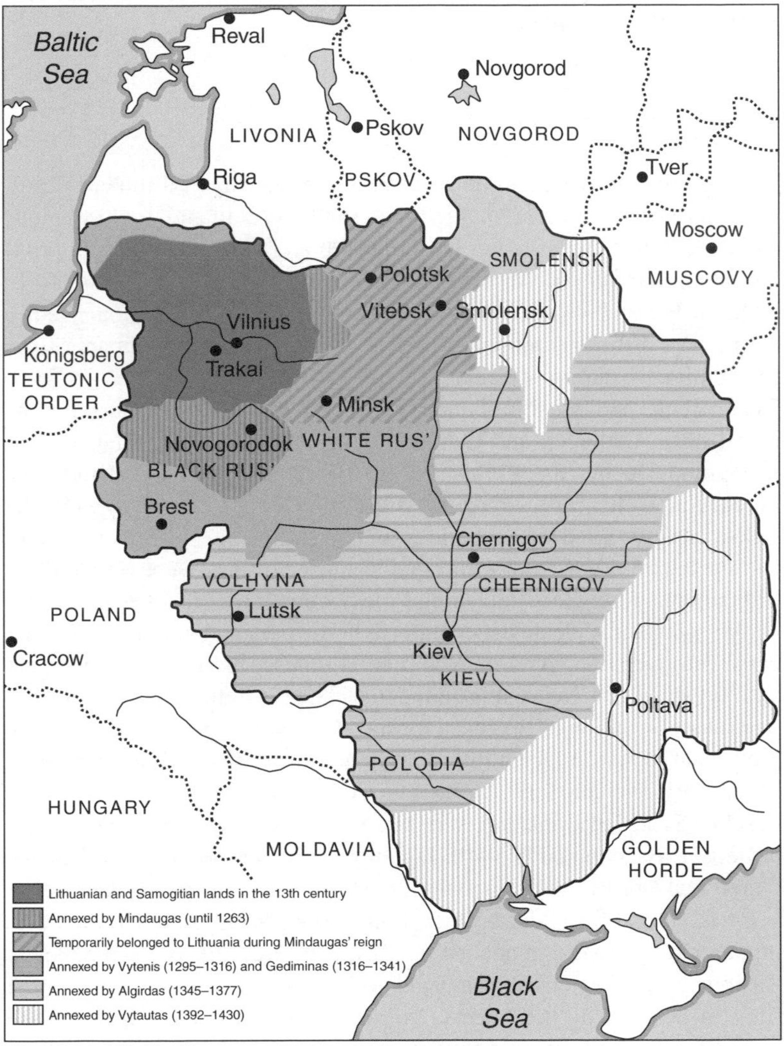
Baltic Sea
Reval
Novgorod
LIVONIA
Pskov
NOVGOROD
Riga
PSKOV
Tver
Moscow
SMOLENSK
MUSCOVY
Polotsk
Vitebsk
Smolensk
Vilnius
Königsberg
Trakai
TEUTONIC ORDER
Minsk
Novogorodok
WHITE RUS'
BLACK RUS'
Brest
Chernigov
VOLHYNA
CHERNIGOV
POLAND
Lutsk
Cracow
Kiev
KIEV
Poltava
PODOLIA
HUNGARY
MOLDAVIA
GOLDEN HORDE
Black Sea
Lithuanian and Samogitian lands in the 13th century
Annexed by Mindaugas (until 1263)
Temporarily belonged to Lithuania during Mindaugas' reign
Annexed by Vytenis (1295–1316) and Gediminas (1316–1341)
Annexed by Algirdas (1345–1377)
Annexed by Vytautas (1392–1430)

**Map 2** The Grand Duchy of Lithuania (*c.* 1430)

approved of a new coronation since Vytautas was heirless and one of his two sons would presumably have inherited Vytautas' throne. However, this did not happen because, before he could be crowned, Vytautas died in 1430 at the ripe old age of 80.[10]

## THE JAGIELLONIANS

Through conquest and immigration, the Grand Duchy of Lithuania developed into a remarkable multiethnic, multicultural and multireligious state. Gediminas first invited Jews to settle and gave them trading privileges, and these privileges were extended and expanded by Vytautas. In addition to the Jews, two small ethnic groups, which have managed to maintain a distinct community to this day, migrated to Lithuania from the south-east during Vytautas' reign: the Karaim, a Turkic people of Judaic faith, and Muslim Tatars. They both provided warriors for the grand duke. Orthodox and Catholic clergy both had important roles in the Grand Duchy: the Ruthenian, or Slavic, clergy manned the state bureaucracy (chancery Slavonic was the official state language) while the Polish clergy steered the Catholic church in Lithuania. Nevertheless, non-Lithuanians did not enjoy full equality: state offices were reserved for Lithuanians; foreigners (including Poles) were barred from owning land.

After Vytautas' death the endurance of the personal union with Poland came into question. As Vytautas died childless, his brother Sigismund and Jogaila's son Švitrigaila plunged Lithuania into a decade of civil war over possession of the ducal throne. Švitrigaila enlisted the Livonian brethren, Rus'ian principalities and Tatars to his side, while Sigismund relied on Polish support. At the decisive battle of Pabaiskas (Swienta) in 1435 Švitrigaila was defeated, but Sigismund's rule was short-lived, as he was assassinated in 1440. Jagiełło's youngest son Casimir became Grand Duke of Lithuania in 1440 and was elected King of Poland seven years later, after his elder brother, Polish King Władysław III, died during a reckless campaign against the Turks. In order to secure the crown, Casimir granted extensive privileges to Lithuanian nobles, including the right to be tried by their peers, exclusive rights to state offices in the Grand Duchy, and full title to their lands and authority over their peasants. Peasants living on the gentry's land were exempted from state taxes, but became subject to increasing demands for labour duties by their lords.[11] Casimir also upheld the territorial integrity of the Grand Duchy and its independence from Poland. Thus in 1447 a personal dynastic union was created whereby the Grand Duke of Lithuania was elected King of Poland. Henceforth, the sovereign resided mainly in Cracow and the Grand Duchy of Lithuania was ruled in practice by a council of Catholic Lithuanian magnates.

By this time, the structure of the leadership of the Grand Duchy had become well established: the highest official was the Grand Marshal who supervised the court and proclaimed ducal decisions. He was followed by the Chancellor who ran the state administration, the Treasurer, and the Grand Hetman who commanded the noble military levy in war.[12] These offices were monopolised by a group of about twenty noble families, the magnates, who owned the largest landed estates and formed the ruling elite. The grand duke appointed palatines for life to govern the twelve palatinates forming the territory of the Grand Duchy. Among these, the Palatine of Vilnius was the senior figure and was customarily appointed to the post of Chancellor. In addition to the palatinates, Samogitia retained its traditional autonomous status and was the staunchest bastion of maintaining old customs, finally converting to Christianity only in 1417. These high officials formed the core of the Council of Lords, which became an increasingly powerful state institution. The Council's powers were greatly extended in 1492, so that in practice the Council ruled the Grand Duchy, while the grand dukes merely implemented the policies crafted by the Council.[13] The institution of a Lithuanian *Sejm* (diet) evolved gradually and from 1507 began to meet annually. It discussed mostly military and financial matters (war and taxes), and it served mainly as an extension of the Council's influence over the grand duke. Unlike the Council, which was mostly Lithuanian, the members of the *Sejm* came from all parts of the Grand Duchy. Thus, the *Sejm* signified the consolidation of the gentry of the Grand Duchy as a political estate.[14] The differences between the rights and privileges of Catholic Lithuanian and Orthodox Ruthenian nobles faded over time, and in 1505 the latter achieved legal equality in the Grand Duchy.[15]

Casimir, ruling as King Casimir IV, increased the international influence of the Jagiellonian dynasty by marrying Elizabeth of Habsburg, daughter of the Holy Roman Emperor. Their eldest son Władysław became King of both Bohemia and Hungary. Their second son, the devout Casimir, died in 1484 at the age of 25 and was later canonised as the patron saint of Lithuania and Poland. Their next son, John Albert, became King of Poland, while their fourth son, Alexander, was elected Grand Duke of Lithuania in 1492. After John Albert's death in 1501, Alexander succeeded to the Polish throne. From that date onwards, the Polish king and Lithuanian grand duke were always one and the same person. Alexander attempted to consolidate the interests of the Jagiellonian dynasty even further through the Melnik Act of 1501, which united the Lithuanian and Polish states and dropped the separate election of the Lithuanian grand duke.[16] However, this act was quashed by the Lithuanian diet. Alexander died childless in 1506 and is the only Polish king buried in Vilnius.

He was succeeded by his brother Sigismund (the Old). A very significant development during his rule was the adoption, in 1529, of the first state legal code, the Statute of Lithuania, written in chancery Slavonic. Sigismund married the Italian princess Bona Sforza who promoted Renaissance influences in Lithuania and also encouraged the ambitions of the Jagiellonian dynasty against the Habsburgs in Central Europe. To this end, Sigismund took the unprecedented step of proclaiming their nine-year-old son Sigismund II Augustus as Grand Duke of Lithuania in 1529 and King of Poland a year later. Sigismund Augustus began to rule in Lithuania in 1544 and mounted the Polish throne upon his father's death in 1548.

Sigismund Augustus implemented radical agricultural reform in Lithuania in 1557, by promulgating a law which entailed land being surveyed and divided into 'hides' (Lith: *valakas*; Pol: *volok*).[17] The aim was to improve efficiency and increase revenue from Crown estates. Seeing the successful results of the reform, noble landlords soon followed the Crown's example. The reform transformed the appearance of the Lithuanian countryside, creating clustered villages with manors at their heart. The three-field system became the general rule on the estate lands. This led to a dramatic expansion of *corvée* (labour rent) and a corresponding decline of money rent paid by 'free wages', which resulted in an increased enserfment of the peasantry. Samogitia remained a partial exception because the gentry there consisted mainly of petty landlords who could not develop large-scale *corvée*-based farming.[18] The serfdom of the peasants was codified by the third Lithuanian Statute of 1588.

Lithuania's eastward expansion was halted, and gradually reversed, by the growing power of Muscovy. After the fall of Constantinople to the Ottoman Turks in 1453, Muscovy had begun to develop the powerful ideological message of its succession to Constantinople as the capital of Orthodox Christianity, with a mission to unite all the Rus'ian Orthodox lands under its dominion. Under Grand Prince Ivan III (ruled 1462–1505) the 'gathering of the lands of Rus'' by Muscovy accelerated as it claimed the patrimony to the entire territory of the ancient Kievan Rus' state.

Lithuania was hard-pressed to counter Muscovy's advance and failed to provide effective aid to prevent its ally Novgorod from being subjugated by Muscovy in 1478. King Casimir was more interested in the Jagiellonian dynasty's fortunes in Central Europe than in pursuing an active policy in the east. Muscovy's prestige and influence grew substantially when Ivan III managed to throw off the last vestiges of Mongol-Tatar overlordship in 1480. In 1494 Lithuania suffered its first territorial losses to Muscovy and grudgingly recognised Muscovy's claim to be 'Lord of All Rus".[19] Muscovy gained further territory at Lithuania's expense in 1503.[20] During Sigismund the Old's rule, war with Muscovy lasted intermittently for thirty years: 1507–8, 1512–22, 1534–7. However, the only notable result of this series of conflicts was Muscovy's capture of the strategically key fortress city of Smolensk in 1514.

## FEUDAL LIVONIA

The lands of the Liv, Lettigallian, Selonian, Estonian, Curonian and Semigallians tribes conquered by the German crusaders during the thirteenth century were carved into four bishoprics: Riga, Dorpat, Ösel-Wiek, and Courland. Riga was elevated to an archbishopric in 1255. These ecclesiastical territories were interspersed with the possessions of the Livonian branch of the Teutonic Order, the largest landholder. Together with the newly founded towns, this conglomerate of territories, covering the approximate territory of present-day Latvia and the southern half of Estonia, was known as Livonia. Its nominal head was the archbishop of Riga, who received his authority from the Pope in Rome and enjoyed the status of a prince of the Holy Roman Empire of the German Nation as of 1207. The next to be enfeoffed by the emperor was the Bishop of Dorpat, Albert's brother, Hermann von Buxhoevden, in 1225, followed a few years later by the Bishops of Ösel-Wiek and Courland. Nevertheless, their connection with the Holy Roman Empire remained tenuous. In the north, the territory conquered by Denmark became the Duchy of Estonia.

The crusaders formed the new ruling classes. Feudal relations were established, with the new rulers granting land to foreign nobles who, in return, pledged to provide military service whenever required by the bishops and the order. Initially, some native elders were also co-opted as vassals, but within a couple of generations they had completely assimilated into the colonisers. Outside of the towns and the network of castles, the presence of the colonists was very thin on the ground. Unlike in Prussia, the colonisers never embarked on a programme of the settlement of German peasants and the assimilation of the natives. The conquerors did not intend a class of free peasantry to be a major component of the social structure. Furthermore, the harsh climate and the fact that Livonia could only be reached by sea militated against peasant colonisation. An exception was the Bishop of Ösel-Wiek who, in the latter part of the thirteenth century, began to attract Swedish settlers to his thinly inhabited territory along the north-western coast and islands of Estonia.

Christianisation involved cultural transfer and new technologies.[21] Immediately after the conquest, parishes, based mostly on boundaries of earlier pagan hillfort districts, were created, each having a church (mostly with thick stone walls and narrow window slits to serve also as defensive fortifications if necessary) as its centre. Compared to western Europe, the Livonian parishes were widely dispersed and weakly developed. Baptism during the crusade had been simply a mere formality. Because the distance between one church and another in the countryside was often great and because the office of priest in a Livonian parish attracted few candidates, the most important role in introducing the Christian faith to the people was played by mendicant friars who served as roaming preachers and administers of sacraments. The first monastic order established in Livonia was the Cistercians who founded the first monastery at Dünamünde (Daugavgrīva) in 1207. The Dominicans, however, soon became the dominant monastic order. The Franciscans also established themselves in Livonia in the fifteenth century. By the start of the Reformation there were about thirty monasteries in Livonia.

The order was the strongest military force and greatest landholder in Livonia, with its headquarters originally in Riga but later in Wenden (Cēsis) near the centre of Livonia. During the course of the fifteenth century the Livonian brethren gradually managed to emancipate themselves from the Teutonic Order in Prussia. In contrast to the ecclesiastical lands, the order had its own permanent military force and network of castles, and thus had less reason to invite knights–vassals to settle on its territories. Although the knights–brothers of the order numbered only a couple of hundred, manpower for their force was provided by native levies and supplemented by the vassals of the bishops. During the thirteenth and fourteenth centuries, more than a hundred and fifty stone castles were erected in Livonia, a much larger number than in Lithuania where their number by the end of the sixteenth century was just twenty.[22] This network of castles in Livonia served not only to provide a defensive line

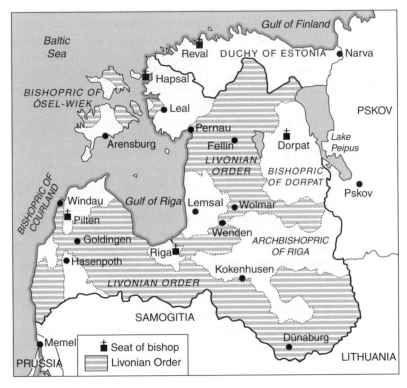

**Map 3** Medieval Livonia (*c.* 1340)

against external invaders but also to maintain control over the subjugated countryside. The order's own officials administered its territory. In their daily lives the brothers of the order were engaged in religious services and in directing the economic activities on their lands.

Donation of land to vassals was most intense in Estonia because the Danish Crown was unable to exercise effective control over its overseas possessions. The Danish Crown donated three-quarters of its Estonian lands as fiefs, mainly to German knights.[23] The weakness of the Danish Crown also tempted the order increasingly to encroach on its territory. The more numerous vassals in Danish Estonia meant that feudal relations developed more swiftly and the establishment of manors spread more rapidly than in Livonia. This development hastened the process of reducing the rights of the natives and increasing the burdens imposed upon them, provoking the massive and bloody St George's Night uprising in 1343 when Estonian insurgents slaughtered all the Germans and Danes they could lay their hands on. The Danes and their vassals had no option other than to turn to the order for protection. The order routed the rebels outside the walls of Reval while the latter were awaiting assistance from Swedish forces in Finland. The order, nevertheless, found itself hard-pressed, since the uprising spread across Estonian inhabited lands and coincided with Lithuanian and Pskovian raids into Livonia. As in previous struggles, the last Estonians to be subdued were those on the island of Ösel (Saaremaa) in 1345. The following year, the Danish Crown, burdened with debts, sold Estonia to the order for 19,000 silver marks (four tons of silver).

After Denmark sold its territory, the composition of Livonia was as follows: the largest territory belonged to the order (67,000 km²); this was followed by the Archbishopric of Riga (18,000 km²), and then the bishoprics of Dorpat (9600 km²), Ösel-Wiek (7600 km²) and Courland (4500 km²). The area of the bishop's spiritual authority (diocese) was larger than the territory where the bishop was the temporal ruler. An anomalous position was held by the Bishop of Reval, who formally remained the suffragan of the Archbishop of Lund after the Danes sold Estonia, but his *de facto* overlord was the order.[24]

The colonisers were frequently in conflict with one another, especially the bishops and the cities with the order. In these civil wars, the city of Riga even occasionally recruited the pagan Lithuanians as allies against the order. The Livonian bishops and the order often made representations at the papal court in Rome, each complaining about the other having exceeded its authority. This local conflict between the bishops and the order was frequently influenced by or mirrored the larger, complex power struggles between pope and emperor in medieval Europe, with the Livonian bishops relying on the support of the papal curia, while the order could usually count on the backing of the emperor.

The order's position in Livonia was greatly strengthened by its purchase of Estonia. The order refused to give up properties it had occupied in the Riga archbishopric, leading Pope Innocent VI in 1354 to declare an interdict against the order which lasted for 30 years.[25] However, even such a strong ecclesiastical sanction could not stem the order's growing self-confidence. In 1366 the Archbishop of Riga lost his nominal suzerainty over the order's Livonian possessions. The order steadfastly pursued a policy of bringing the Livonian bishoprics under its control, by ensuring that the canons of the cathedral chapters were members of the order. In the internal Livonian power struggle, the order scored a great victory in 1397 when Pope Boniface IX supported its position that even the Archbishop of the Riga must be a member of the order. The order's triumph, however, was short-lived as the Archbishop of Riga persuaded Pope Martin V to rescind the Bull in 1426. Nevertheless, the order persisted and convinced Pope Nicholas V to reissue the Bull in 1452. Although formally the order triumphed in the end, the power struggle (which even involved armed conflict) continued, since the cathedral chapter rejected the order's attempt to impose its authority over it, and the city of Riga continued to resist the order's designs for hegemony in Livonia.

To resolve the disputes among the composite territories of Livonia and prevent the order from accomplishing complete dominance, the Archbishop of Riga convened a Livonian diet (*Landtag*) in 1422 at Walk (Valga, Valka). Consisting of four estates, the bishops and clergy, the order, the knights–vassals, and representatives of the towns, the diet met irregularly, mostly in Walk or Wolmar (Valmiera), both near the centre of Livonia. As the diet mainly discussed matters of external relations and defence, the master of the order was its dominant figure. Closer political cooperation, in the form of a Livonian Confederation, was finally made possible in 1435 by the order's momentary weakness after it suffered a crushing defeat in the Lithuanian civil war.[26] The Livonian branch of the order had been torn between two factions since the defeat of the Teutonic Knights at Tannenberg: brothers originating from Westphalia who sought greater independence from the Prussian branch of the order, and those from the Rhineland who desired greater integration. Significantly, the master of the order in Livonia and most of his senior officers who perished at the Battle of Pabaiskas were from the Rhineland faction. Despite this strengthening of their cooperation, internal frictions between the bishops, the order and the cities hobbled the Livonian entity to the end.

## TOWNS, TRADE AND THE PEASANTRY

No towns existed in the Baltic area before the arrival of the crusaders. By the end of the Middle Ages, there were 15 towns in Livonia. Only a few of them had any continuity with the pre-Christian hillfort settlements or trading centres.[27] Riga, the first town to be founded, has to this day remained the largest centre. Already in the 1220s Riga enjoyed the same rights as Visby, but adopted the Hamburg city charter in 1290. The other Livonian towns copied Riga. Reval received the rights of Lübeck in 1248, followed by the other Estonian towns. Lithuanian towns received their own charters only after Lithuania's conversion, more than a century later. Vilnius was the first, receiving the charter of Magdeburg in 1387. Thus, the Baltic towns shared a common legal and cultural space with the northern German cities.

The Livonian towns were organised in a corporate structure based on guilds of merchants and craftsmen developed during the fourteenth century. In the largest cities, Riga and Reval, there was the Great Guild for merchants, the Guild of the Black Heads (named after patron Saint Mauritius) for unmarried merchant-journeymen, and dozens of other guilds for the various artisans and craftsmen.[28] Only guild members could legally practise these specific professions. The road from being an apprentice and journeyman to finally becoming a master of a trade was a long and demanding one. The citizens (burghers) of the towns were mainly German colonists, but the natives – referred to dismissively as the non-Germans (*Undeutsche*) – formed a substantial proportion of the urban population and provided most of the menial and manual labour. The German colonists excluded the natives from trading activities (becoming merchants) and membership in most of the guilds. Towns and cities were ruled by an oligarchic town council (*Rat*), whose members were co-opted for lifetime tenure from an exclusive group of the city's wealthy, established merchant families.[29]

As the Livonian towns grew in size and gained wealth, they increasingly sought and obtained greater independence from their feudal lords. They were part of an extended community of towns along the shores of the Baltic Sea and northern Europe which shared the same values and legal systems enshrined in their charters and used the same language,

Low German. There was considerable interaction and mobility among the merchants and artisans of these towns.

The establishment of trading centres in Livonia was initially led by the German merchants from Visby, but they were soon overtaken by Lübeck, the leading Hanseatic city. The Hanseatic League at its zenith in the fifteenth century consisted of 200 towns, mostly in northern Germany, but stretching from Livonia in the east to the Low Countries in the west. It almost monopolised trade in the Baltic Sea during the fourteenth and fifteenth centuries and had offices from London in the west to Novgorod in the east. Its fiercest rival was the kingdom of Denmark, which sought to control shipping through the Sound, the narrow entrance from the North Sea into the Baltic. Riga became the first Hanseatic city in Livonia in 1282. It was followed by seven other towns in present-day Latvia: Wenden, Wolmar, Goldingen (Kuldīga), Kokenhusen (Koknese), Lemsal (Limbaži), Roop (Straupe) and Windau (Ventspils), and four in present-day Estonia: Reval, Dorpat (Tartu), Pernau (Pärnu) and Fellin (Viljandi). Of these, Riga, Reval and Dorpat were the most active in the affairs of the Hanseatic League. No Lithuanian towns were ever members of the Hanse. Lithuanian trade flowed out to the Baltic Sea primarily via Riga and Königsberg.

By far the most important import trade article reaching the eastern Baltic littoral was salt (for the preservation of food), initially from Lüneburg, but then supplanted by cheaper and more abundant salt from the Bay of Biscay. Other significant imports were herring, spices, wine, cloth and luxury goods. However, the volume of exports exceeded that of imports. Exports consisted mainly of Russian timber, flax, grain, furs, beeswax and naval stores. After Muscovy annexed Novgorod in 1478, the Hanse office there was closed down. The Livonian ports thus became the last outposts for western trade with Russia. The important trading towns of Livonia flourished in the late Middle Ages, the largest towns being Riga, whose population rose to almost 15,000 by the sixteenth century, Reval with a population of 7000 and Dorpat with 5000.[30] The total population of Livonia reached 650,000 by the mid-sixteenth century. A sign of this affluence was the slender spire of St Olaf's Church in Reval, an important landmark for navigators, which at 159 metres was the tallest building in the world from 1549 until struck by lightning in 1625.

The Hanseatic League declined in the sixteenth century as the role of Dutch trading companies steadily increased in the Baltic trade. Nevertheless, Riga, Reval and Narva prospered as the growing demand for grain in the Low Countries made Dutch companies circumvent Lübeck and the northern German cities to trade directly with the towns of eastern Baltic littoral. There was also growing demand for timber and other products used for shipbuilding such as tar, pitch and hemp. Protecting access to the Baltic ports where they obtained supplies for naval stores became a strategic priority for the Dutch and the English.

A sharp increase in the demand for Baltic grain (by the burgeoning population of western Europe, especially the Low Countries) led land-owners to impose ever greater demands on the peasants.[31] Gradually during the sixteenth century, Baltic peasants lost their rights and generally became enserfed. Manorial estates had already begun to be established in Livonia in the thirteenth century, but their number grew exponentially during the late fifteenth and early sixteenth centuries. Initially peasants were required to work for the estate for only a few days a year and were then supplied with food and drink, but by the mid-sixteenth century they were generally providing labour several days a week in the summer – from St George's Day (23 April) to Michaelmas (29 September) – without any provisions being supplied by the manor. The general tax had been increased from one-tenth to one-quarter of the peasant's produce in the fifteenth century. Increasingly, peasants fell into debt and therefore landlords sought to restrict their movement. Debt did not belong to the individual peasant, but to his farm/household and thus the burden was transferred to the following generations. The Walk *Landtag* of 1424 introduced the principle that peasants fleeing debt had to be returned.[32] As the towns and manors competed for labour, escaping peasants often managed to build a new life for themselves in the towns. As a rule, manorial lords could not demand the return of an escaped peasant who had managed to reside in a town for a period of at least a year. A well-known saying of the period stated that the city air made one free.

The deterioration of the peasants' situation was related not only to economic developments but also to the transformation of European warfare as a consequence of the introduction of gunpowder. Until the fifteenth century, the peasants still had an important military role to fulfil, but by the close of the century the requirement for peasants to do military service for the order had been abolished, and freemen lost the right to bear arms in 1507. After the defeat at Tannenberg and the end of the crusade against Lithuania, the order had difficulty attracting good recruits from German lands. It came to rely increasingly on hiring mercenaries, and therefore needed to increase its income to pay for their services.[33] The easiest way to boost its revenues was to expand grain exports, an increase that could be obtained only by forcing the peasants to labour more intensively on the order's estates. Nevertheless, the Baltic peasantry should not be viewed as an undifferentiated mass – there were significant variations in their status and obligations under various lords. Among the natives a small number of freeholders, who held their fiefs on the same legal basis as German vassals, existed until the eighteenth century.[34] Swedish peasants and fisherman in the north-western coastal areas were untouched by the gradual process of enserfment and managed to retain ownership of their land and personal freedom.

## THE REFORMATION AND THE DISINTEGRATION OF LIVONIA

The Protestant Reformation against the practices of the papacy was launched by Martin Luther in Saxony in 1517 and spread quickly to the Livonian cities and provoked a wave of iconoclasm. The German burghers of Riga, Reval and other Livonian cities shared the same cultural space with the northern German cities which championed Luther's reforms. By 1524, the Reformation had triumphed in the major Livonian cities, although the Catholic Church hierarchy remained in place, and in the countryside the nobility remained wary of social upheaval. The Reformation also had political and material ramifications: the citizens of Riga seized the opportunity to rid themselves of their feudal overlords, the order and the archbishop of Riga (and expropriate their property). The monasteries were dissolved.

Protestantism took longer to gain adherents in Lithuania. The key centre for the spread of its ideas to Lithuania was Königsberg University in neighbouring Prussia, founded in 1544.[35] Previously, Lithuanian students had studied mainly at the Jagiellonian University in Cracow. By the 1550s the Reformation had made a breakthrough in Lithuania. Protestantism in its Calvinist form was championed by the pre-eminent Lithuanian noble magnate family Radvila (Radziwiłł) and was particularly popular among the magnates, wealthier nobles and urban population. The Protestants were under the protection of Mikolaj Radziwiłł (Mikalojus Radvila) 'The Black', the holder of the highest public offices in the Grand Duchy: Grand Hetman, Chancellor and Palatinate of Vilnius. Radziwiłł sponsored the first Polish translation of the complete Bible, published in Brest in 1563. Although the predominant strand of Protestantism in Lithuania was Calvinism, Lutheran and Arianist congregations were also founded. Unlike elsewhere in Europe, Protestants of different denominations cooperated among themselves and sectarian strife was avoided in Lithuania.

The rulers during this time, Sigismund the Old and Sigismund Augustus, both remained Catholic, but demonstrated tolerance.

The success of the Protestant Reformation was greatly facilitated by the invention of the printing press and the spread of the written word. A fundamental tenet of Protestantism was that people should be able to read the word of God themselves, a notion that resulted in the first publications in the vernacular. The earliest books printed in the region were *The Acts of the Apostles* translated into Ruthenian by the Belarusian humanist Francysk Skaryna in Vilnius in 1522 and Andreas Knopken's Low German Lutheran hymn book in Riga in 1530.[36] The first Estonian-language Lutheran catechism was published in 1535 in Wittenberg, and the first Lithuanian-language book, also a Lutheran catechism, was printed in Königsberg in 1547. The earliest surviving Latvian-language work is a Catholic catechism published in Vilnius in 1585. It is highly probable that there were even earlier religious texts in the native languages from the 1520s, but none of these have survived.[37] These, and later religious publications, had a fundamental role in the development of the Estonian, Latvian and Lithuanian written languages and the spread of literacy. The use of the vernacular helped to spread the faith to the native population for whom Christianisation had been superficial. The peasants could mimic the rituals, but the spiritual message remained an alien creed. Illustrative is the fact that the first Lithuanian catechism devoted as much space to admonishing the people not to worship the old pagan deities as to the teachings of Luther.[38]

The Protestant Reformation fatally weakened the ideological underpinnings holding the ecclesiastic territories of Livonia together. It also severed the link between the Livonian and Prussian branches of the Teutonic Order. After the Protestant Reformation, Wolter von Plettenberg, master of the order in Livonia, could have followed the example of Albert von Hohenzollern, the last grand master of the Teutonic Order who, in 1525, secularised the order's land in Prussia and became the first Duke of Prussia, a vassal of the King of Poland. Plettenberg, however, was a conservative believer in the universal Catholic Church. He chose to acquire the rank of imperial prince in 1526 and thus the lands of the order in Livonia formally became part of the Holy Roman Empire.[39] However, this connection to the distant empire proved to be too tenuous to counteract Livonia's internal weaknesses, and the rise of powerful and assertive neighbouring powers. By the sixteenth century, monk-warriors of the order had become an anachronism; the Livonian towns relied mainly on hired mercenaries for their defence. Medieval Livonia had from the beginning been riven by internal contradictions and domestic strife, and, in the end, the Reformation undermined the ideological foundations which held it together. Livonia's political fragmentation became a fatal liability at a time when neighbouring states were consolidating power in the hands of the monarch. The decline of the order during the sixteenth century coincided with the rise of the Kingdom of Sweden in the west, Muscovy in the east and Poland–Lithuania in the south. The order-dominated feudal Livonian Confederation was undermined by its own internal divisions, the Lutheran reformation and the transformation of the methods of European warfare, finally collapsing under the pressure of Muscovite expansion.

Muscovy became a direct neighbour of Livonia after her conquest of Novgorod in 1478. Despite occasional conflicts, the Livonian border with the Rus'ian lands had been stable for more than two centuries, with mutual trading interests dominating the Livonian relationship with Novgorod and Pskov.[40] After the first Muscovite incursion into Livonia in 1481, Grand Prince Ivan III prepared the ground for future conflict by erecting the strategic Ivangorod fortress directly across the river from the order's fortress at Narva in 1492. The first serious Muscovite invasion came in 1501 in response to a Livonian attack in alliance with Lithuania. After Plettenberg's inconclusive victory at the battle of Smolino in 1502, Livonia concluded a truce with Muscovy, which enabled Livonia to exist peacefully for another half-century. However, this was only a temporary respite. Livonia's eastern neighbour, Pskov, one of the last independent Rus'ian principalities, was annexed by Muscovy in 1510. The end for feudal Livonia came with Muscovy's first full-scale effort to conquer Livonia in 1558. The order's troops were badly outnumbered by the Muscovites and the once-proud Livonian knights were decimated at the Battle of Ermes (Ērģeme) in 1560.

The invasion by Tsar Ivan IV (the Terrible) drew neighbouring powers into the competition for Livonian territory. The Livonian bishops and cities desperately scrambled for protection from the Muscovite onslaught. The Bishop of Ösel-Wieck sold western Estonia to Danish King Frederick II in 1559, who installed his younger brother Duke Magnus of Holstein as ruler. Magnus purchased the Bishopric of Courland in 1560 and had greater ambitions. In 1561 the city of Reval and the knights of northern Estonia placed themselves under the protection of Swedish King Eric XIV. Thus began the meteoric rise of the Swedish Empire, which would become the dominant power in northern Europe in the seventeenth century.

The master of the order in Livonia, Gotthard Kettler, negotiated a *Pacta Subjectionis* with Polish King and Lithuanian Grand Duke Sigismund Augustus, and on 28 November 1561 Kettler swore allegiance to Sigismund. All of Livonia north of the Daugava river not under Swedish or Muscovite control initially came under direct Lithuanian rule, and as of 1569 under joint Polish–Lithuanian administration as the Duchy of Livonia (Inflanty). The final curtain for the *Ordenstaat* came on 5 March 1562 when Kettler, following the example of Albert von Hohenzollern's Teutonic Knights in Prussia, secularised the order and became the first Duke of Courland and Semigallia, a hereditary fief under Polish suzerainty, consisting of the territory of Livonia south and west of the Daugava. The only part of medieval Livonia which initially managed to maintain its independence was the city of Riga, which eventually in 1581 also submitted to the Polish–Lithuanian Crown. Almost all of present-day Latvia and the southern half of Estonia, therefore, came under Polish–Lithuanian sovereignty for almost seventy years (1561–1629). However, this quadripartite division of Livonia contained the seeds of further conflict. This was just the beginning of a series of 'northern wars' which would ultimately determine the shape of the region until the twentieth century.

# 3

# The Polish–Lithuanian Commonwealth and the Rise of Sweden and Russia (1561–1795)

The period from 1558 to 1721 was one of almost continuous warfare in north-eastern Europe, with a respite only in the latter part of the seventeenth century. Muscovy, Sweden and Poland–Lithuania contended for domination of the Baltic region in a series of major conflicts: the First Northern War (the Livonian War) 1558–83, the Second Northern War, 1655–60, and the Great Northern War, 1700–21. In between these wars, there were several bilateral conflicts among these same powers. The era began with the collapse of Livonia under the pressure of Muscovite invasion, and the union between Poland and Lithuania: events which led to Polish–Lithuanian and Swedish ascendancy in the region. It ended with the defeat of Sweden and the advent of the Russian Empire in Europe. War was accompanied by devastating famine and plague, but subsequent years of peace in the eighteenth century enabled demographic recovery. The internal weaknesses of the Polish–Lithuanian Commonwealth left it exposed to manipulation by expansionist neighbours, Russia, Prussia and Austria, who gradually partitioned it until the state disappeared from the map of Europe altogether in 1795.

## THE POLISH–LITHUANIAN UNION AND THE STRUGGLE FOR HEGEMONY IN LIVONIA

Ever since the sealing of the dynastic union between Lithuania and Poland in 1386, Polish nobles had wanted to integrate the Grand Duchy into Poland, but Lithuanian magnates had fiercely clung to their independence and parried Polish advances. However, the relentless expansion of Muscovy and the imminent extinction of the Jagiellonian dynasty forced Lithuanian magnates to reconsider their options. In 1558 Ivan the Terrible had invaded Livonia, precipitating its collapse and partition by four neighbouring powers. However, the Tsar was not content with this outcome, and sought the Polish–Lithuanian share of Livonia for himself. Ivan opened a new front against Lithuania in 1562 and conquered the key fortress town of Polotsk in 1563. Although Lithuania gained a temporary respite with a successful counter-offensive which helped trigger Ivan's bout of insanity in 1565 when Muscovy descended into seven years of internal bloodletting of the *Oprichnina*, it became increasing clear that the Lithuanians needed Polish military assistance against the growing threat from the east.[1] Negotiations between Lithuanian and Polish representatives at Lublin were deadlocked until King Sigismund Augustus pressed the reluctant Lithuanian nobles into finally accepting the Polish terms for a union in 1569 by transferring the Grand Duchy's Ukrainian possessions to Poland.[2] In one stroke, the Grand Duchy's size was halved. Its territory now amounted to just under 300,000 km$^2$.

The Union of Lublin in 1569 created one of the largest states in Europe, the Republic (*Rzeczpospolita*) of Two Nations, usually referred to as the Commonwealth. Under the terms of the Union, the Commonwealth would be ruled by a single elected sovereign crowned in Cracow, still titled King of Poland and the Grand Duke of Lithuania (though there would no longer be a separate election of the grand duke), and a joint parliament (*Sejm*) which would meet biannually in Warsaw (closer to Lithuania than Cracow). Reflecting Poland's larger population, Polish representatives outnumbered the Lithuanians in the *Sejm* by three to one. Poland–Lithuania would henceforth conduct a common foreign policy, they would have common coinage, and Polish and Lithuanian nobles would be permitted to obtain property in the other part of the Commonwealth. The Two Nations retained separate governments, armies, treasuries and legal codes. Polish historians have mostly celebrated the Union as a milestone for the flowering of the Polish state, while Lithuanian historians have usually bemoaned the Union as heralding the eclipse of Lithuania.[3]

The Union proved to be a strong impetus for the cultural polonisation of the Lithuanian elite; the Polish language and customs were attractive for Lithuanian nobles who regarded them as more refined than those of Lithuania. The Lithuanian clergy had already been polonised since Christianisation. Polish officially replaced chancellery Slavonic as the state language of the Grand Duchy in 1697. The Kingdom of Poland increasingly became the dominant partner in the Union, as is witnessed by the fact that the Commonwealth is often referred to in the literature simply as Poland. This terminological shorthand is understandable since western Europeans were in much closer contact with the Poles. Nevertheless, the Lithuanian nobility still retained a strong sense of distinct identity and struggled tenaciously to maintain the Grand Duchy's formally equal status within the Commonwealth. A clear example of their determination was the third and final Lithuanian Statute (law code) promulgated in 1588, which hardly refers to the Commonwealth and clearly states the primacy of Lithuanian law. To raise the status of Lithuanian nobles to equal that of the Polish and other European noble nations, a myth claiming that the Lithuanians' ancestors were descendants of the Romans was constructed and popularised during the sixteenth century.[4]

After the death of the heirless Sigismund Augustus in 1572 brought the Jagiellonian dynasty to an end, royal power began to erode as the nobles were able to impose restrictions on royal prerogatives and obtain greater privileges for themselves. Henry Valois, the brother of French King Charles IX, was elected in 1573 and assumed the Polish–Lithuanian throne after acquiescing to conditions set by the electors which defined and restricted his powers. Among the Henrican Articles, the new king had to promise to respect religious freedom and to convene the *Sejm* at least every two years. The right to declare war and levy new taxes belonged to the *Sejm*, not the monarch. Furthermore, the king acknowledged the right of the nobility to disobey him if he acted illegally.[5] This set a precedent for all subsequent Polish–Lithuanian sovereigns, who in addition to adherence to the Henrican Articles had to negotiate an individual *Pacta Conventa* stipulating additional specific conditions before being crowned. Henry's rule, however, lasted only a few months until he returned hastily to France to claim the French throne after his brother's death.

The Polish–Lithuanian throne was hotly contested, with neighbouring European powers, such as the Austrian Habsburgs, putting forward their candidates. The next Polish king and Lithuanian grand duke, the Hungarian Stefan Batory, Prince of Transylvania, husband of Sigismund Augustus's sister, possessed a martial spirit which was the opposite of that of the effeminate Henry. He modernised the army and embarked on a campaign to recover territory lost to Muscovy. In the meantime, Ivan had returned to the offensive and in 1570 promoted Danish Duke Magnus as a self-styled King of Livonia to rule over Muscovy's expected conquest. Although the Muscovites were able to control eastern Livonia, the high-water mark of their campaign was the unsuccessful siege of Reval in 1577, which was followed later that year by their defeat at the hands of a joint Swedish and Commonwealth force at the Battle of Wenden. With this loss, momentum passed to Muscovy's rivals. The energetic Batory besieged Pskov in 1581, forcing Ivan to sue for peace in 1582 and relinquish his Livonian conquests to the Commonwealth. Simultaneously, the Swedes pressed eastwards in Estonia, capturing Narva. Ivan finally abandoned his hopes for expansion into the Baltic littoral by concluding peace with Sweden in 1583, thus ending the twenty-five-year series of conflicts known as the Livonian war (or first Northern War).

The border between Swedish and Polish–Lithuanian control over the territory of medieval Livonia set the boundary line between Estland (Estonia) and Livland (Livonia) until the twentieth century. Sweden consolidated its newly acquired four territories of Harrien (Harjumaa), Wierland (Virumaa), Wiek (Läänemaa) and Jerwen (Järvamaa) in the northern part of Livonia into the province of Estland, with the seat of its governor in Reval in 1584. Livonia (Inflanty) now connoted the Polish–Lithuanian ruled area between Swedish Estland and the Duchy of Courland. In 1582 Batory introduced Polish administrative institutions in Livonia, but maintained toleration of Lutheranism. During the years of warfare, many devastated manors were abandoned and they became Polish Crown estates which were mainly granted to Polish and Lithuanian nobles. Jesuits were dispatched to Livonia to promote the Catholic Counter-Reformation. Although the Jesuits established colleges in Riga (1566) and Dorpat (1583), they were unable to dislodge the dominant position of the Lutheran Church in Livonia. A more lasting achievement on the part of Batory was the establishment in 1579 of the University of Vilnius, on the basis of the Jesuit college founded in 1570, the most easterly university in Europe. This university served as a bridgehead for the advancement of the Counter-Reformation. The most renowned Vilnius university faculty members were Mathias Casimirus Sarbievius, the foremost Latin poet of seventeenth-century Europe, and the theologian/philosopher Martinus Smiglecius, whose book *Logica* (1618) was widely used in European academies.

After Batory's death in 1586, Sigismund III Vasa was elected Grand Duke of Lithuania and King of Poland in 1587. Sigismund, the son of Swedish King John III and Catherine, the sister of Sigismund Augustus, was raised as a Catholic. Under the Vasa dynasty from 1587 to 1668 the Commonwealth reached its zenith, but also began its long decline. The Vasa kings often brought the Commonwealth into conflict with Sweden where Polish Vasa kings laid claim to the Swedish throne. This inter-dynastic rivalry was complicated by the religious dimension since the Swedish Vasas were Lutherans, while the Polish Vasas were Catholic. When John III died in 1592, his son, Polish King Sigismund, succeeded him as King of Sweden. He resided in Poland and left the governing of Sweden to his uncle, Duke Charles. In 1598 Charles challenged Sigismund's power, defeated his troops in Sweden and deposed Sigismund as King of Sweden in 1599. The following year Estland submitted to Charles, who then moved southwards against the Polish–Lithuanian Commonwealth in 1600, triggering a series of three wars, fought mainly in Livonia. In the early phases of the war, the Lithuanians were triumphant. Lithuanian Grand Hetman Jan Karol Chodkiewicz's hussars slaughtered Charles's numerically superior force at Kirchholm (Salaspils) in 1605. However, Chodkiewicz was unable to follow up on his brilliant victory because the *Sejm* refused to approve funds for his army.[6]

The Poles were more eager to take advantage of the succession conflict in Muscovy, known in Russian history as 'the Time of Troubles'. Sigismund's forces occupied Moscow in 1610 and his son Władyłsaw was named Tsar. Although the Poles were driven out of Moscow two years later, the Commonwealth was able to maintain control of some of the reconquered territory, including Smolensk. During this period of multiple conflicts, the interests of Poland and Lithuania often diverged. The Lithuanians were not enthusiastic about Sigismund's adventure against Muscovy, being more concerned with Swedish advances in Livonia.[7]

The situation in Livonia turned in Sweden's favour with the landing of King Gustav II Adolf in Livonia in 1621, whose reforms had transformed the Swedish army into the most effective fighting force in Europe. The nobles and burghers of Livonia were favourably inclined towards Sweden since it had maintained the privileges of their brethren in neighbouring Estland, while the Commonwealth had promoted religious Counter-Reformation and integrative administrative policies in Livonia. The military struggle for the control of Livonia ended with the victory of Sweden, confirmed with the Peace of Altmark in 1629. Riga became the largest city in the entire Swedish realm, and the seat of the governor of the Swedish province of Livland. Swedish domination of Livonia was completed when the island of Ösel (Saaremaa) was gained from the Danes in 1645. For the first time, all of ethnic Estonian territory came under one central authority.

Three territories of medieval Livonia remained part the Commonwealth: its south-eastern section, Inflanty (Latgale, also known as Polish

Livonia), the Duchy of Courland and the Bishopric of Courland. As a consequence of Polish rule, Inflanty would develop an identity distinct from the other parts of ethnic Latvian lands where the lords were Lutheran Germans. Inflanty became a mainly Catholic province with a mixture of Polish, Lithuanian, German and Ruthenian land-owners. Unlike Inflanty, which was administratively integrated into the Commonwealth, the Duchy of Courland and Semigallia remained an intriguing anomaly under Polish suzerainty. Polish King Sigismund Augustus had guaranteed the right of the Lutheran faith and the use of the German language and law in 1561. Gotthard Kettler (1517–87), the last master of the order in Livonia, had become the Duke of Courland and the Livonian knights had transformed themselves into the land-owning nobility, with Kettler reserving one-third of the order's possessions as ducal domains.[8]

Kettler and his successors were constantly at odds with the nobility, who were able to strengthen their position at the expense of the duke. In 1617, Duke Friedrich (reigned 1587–1642) was forced to agree to a constitution and law code which increased the nobility's role in governance and expanded the generous privileges already granted by Kettler in 1570, conceding to the nobility almost absolute rights over their property, including their peasants. Serfdom became the norm on the landed estates; peasants were treated somewhat better on ducal domains, but these shrunk over time.[9] In 1620, the Courland nobility organised themselves into an exclusive corporation consisting of 121 families, without whose assent the dukes found it almost impossible to impose their will. Kettler's most talented descendant was Duke Jacob (ruled 1642–82), who energetically pursued mercantilist policies and built up an impressive navy, merchant fleet and manufacturing facilities. He brought shipbuilders from the Netherlands to Windau (Ventspils), and even briefly established colonies in West Africa (Gambia) and the Caribbean (Tobago).[10] On the north-western tip of the Courland peninsula was the former Bishopric of Courland, centred on the small town of Pilten (Piltene), which had been sold by Denmark to the King of Poland in 1585. Although the Dukes of Courland briefly succeeded in extending their control over it (from 1685 to 1717) the Lutheran nobility of Pilten zealously maintained their rights of self-government until 1795.[11]

Lithuanian and Polish rule over Slavic lands in the east had a decisive influence on the development of distinct nationalities among the Ruthenians – the Ukrainians and Belarusians. Tsar Feodor (reigned 1584–98) raised the Moscow Metropolitanate to the status of patriarchate in 1589, claiming its authority over all Orthodox Eastern Slavs.

Orthodox bishops of the Commonwealth who rejected this presumptuous claim convened the Synod of Brest in 1596 which established the Uniate Church. The Uniates (often referred to as 'Greek Catholics') accepted the authority of the Pope in Rome, but maintained their eastern Christian rites. The Catholic Church promoted the creation of the Uniate Church in order to counter the attraction of Protestantism among the Grand Duchy's Orthodox nobility, many of whom had opportunistically converted to Protestantism, following the example of the Lithuanian magnates holding the chief offices of the Grand Duchy.[12] Since many Orthodox bishops rejected the Uniate Church, a confessional divide arose among the Orthodox believers in the Ruthenian lands of the Grand Duchy.

The ascendancy of the Commonwealth in eastern Europe suffered a serious reversal after the Cossack uprising against Polish lords in Ukraine in 1648 (during which tens of thousands of Jews were slaughtered by the Cossacks). With the treaty of Pereyaslav in 1654, the rebellious Cossacks placed themselves under the protection of Muscovy (temporarily in the view of the former, permanently in the eyes of the latter). Subsequently, Muscovy resumed its westerly expansion at the expense of Poland–Lithuania. Vilnius fell for the first time when Tsar Alexis (reigned 1645–76) sacked it in 1655. Swedish King Charles X (reigned 1654–60) took advantage of the Commonwealth's difficulties in the east by successfully invading Poland. By October 1655 both Warsaw and Cracow were in Swedish hands. This stunningly rapid military collapse of Europe's second largest state and its occupation by two neighbouring powers became aptly known as the 'deluge' in Polish historiography.

The Swedish invasion also spelled the end for Courland's remarkable commercial achievements. Although Duke Jacob adhered to a policy of neutrality, the Swedes imprisoned him in 1658. He was restored to the throne two years later and ruled for another twenty years, but Courland never again attained its former level of dynamic prosperity. Jacob's heirs would never aspire to the same level of ambition.

With Muscovy occupying the eastern part of the Grand Duchy and the Poles having capitulated to the Swedes, Lithuanian leaders sought terms for Swedish protection against further Muscovite advances. Calvinist Lithuanian Grand Hetman and Palatinate of Vilnius Janusz Radziwiłł (1612–55) hoped to replace the union with Poland with an equal union with Protestant Sweden. He led 1172 mainly Protestant Lithuanian nobles in signing the Act of Kėdainiai on 20 October 1655, which severed the union with Poland and acclaimed Charles X Grand Duke of Lithuania.[13] The majority of Lithuanian magnates adhered to Protestantism of the

Calvinist variety, which also served as an expression of Lithuania's independent identity vis-à-vis Poland. The Protestants were under the protection of the Radziwiłł magnate family, the holders of the highest public offices in the Grand Duchy. Although the Third Lithuanian Statute of 1588 enshrined religious toleration, the position of the Lithuanian Protestants was gradually eroded by the Jesuit-led Catholic Counter-Reformation during the early seventeenth century. In 1640 the Calvinist church in Vilnius was forced to move outside of the city walls and the complete triumph of the Counter-Reformation was only a matter of time after a ban on conversion from Catholicism was implemented in 1668.[14]

The Protestant Swedes were unable to maintain effective control of Poland and rapidly alienated the population. The Lithuanians and Swedes never established a trustworthy relationship, mainly because Lithuanians resented the burden of Swedish military occupation and taxation. An insurgency against the Swedes was launched in Samogitia in April 1656. Muscovy and the Swedes quarrelled over dividing their spoils and in August 1656 Alexis invaded Swedish Livland. The disaster of foreign invasion and war was compounded by a severe plague and famine in 1657–8. This deadly combination of woes in the mid-seventeenth century resulted in the Grand Duchy losing almost half of its population. The number of inhabitants dropped from an estimated 4.5 million in 1650 to 2.3 million in 1670.[15]

The Commonwealth, nevertheless, managed to recover from the military catastrophe, and with the Peace of Oliwa in 1660 the *status quo ante bellum* was basically restored, although Poland–Lithuania gave up its claims to Swedish Livland. After the Commonwealth and Sweden made peace, Muscovy realised that it could not win alone against the Swedes and also signed a peace treaty with the Swedes in 1661, restoring the pre-war situation. The Commonwealth's forces then managed to eject the Muscovites from Lithuania, but with the Peace of Andrusovo in 1667 ceded Kiev and eastern Ukraine and Smolensk. This treaty fixed the border between the two states for more than a century until the first partition of the Commonwealth.

## SWEDISH DOMINANCE AND THE GREAT NORTHERN WAR

Swedish King Gustav II Adolf (ruled 1611–32) created the most efficient military force in Europe and this enabled Sweden to play a decisive role in European politics as the major Protestant power in the Thirty Years'

War (1618–48). In the seventeenth century Sweden essentially established *dominium maris Baltici*, hegemony in the Baltic Sea region. Not only did Sweden control Livland and the entire coastline of the Gulf of Finland, including Ingria (the future site of St Petersburg), after the Peace of Stolbovo in 1617, it also acquired German territories on the southern Baltic coast during the Thirty Years' War. The Swedes attempted to oust the Dutch and English from shipping in the Baltic and obtain control over Russian trade. An important element of this strategy was to build up the city of Narva as the leading centre for trade with Russia.[16]

Although the supreme authority in the provinces of Estland and Livland were the Swedish governors in Reval and Riga, the local German nobility maintained, and even broadened, its privileges. The Swedish Crown recognised the *Ritterschaft* as the single corporate body representing the nobility of the province in Estland in 1584 and in Livland in 1634. Compared to its position in the old Livonian Confederation where it was only one among four estates, the nobility gained considerable power, obtaining the exclusive right of participation in the diet (*Landtag*) of both provinces. The diet appointed a twelve-member council (*Landratskollegium*) whose members enjoyed life-long tenure. Presided over by the Swedish Governor, this council was the highest organ of power in the province. The nobility's privileges were greatest in Estland, where members of the council were not even elected by the *Landtag*, but co-opted by the council itself and the council also served as the highest court in Estland. This system of self-rule institutions, the *Landesstaat*, erected under Swedish rule, with modifications, would govern the Baltic provinces until the twentieth century.

The Swedish state consolidated the formal institutional basis for the Lutheran Church, first in Estland and later in Livland. The Swedish Crown, as a militant Protestant power, followed the admonition of the Lutheran Church that the peasants must be able to read the word of God. As a consequence, the Swedish governors laid great emphasis on developing education, the greatest legacy of the Swedish era. The new Swedish Church Law of 1686 decreeing the establishment of native-language elementary schools in every parish was also applied in Estland and Livland. Bengt Forselius had already established the first teachers' seminary in 1684 in Dorpat, where he prepared 160 Estonian young men as school-teachers. Earlier, Gustav Adolf had founded the first university in the Baltic provinces, the *Academia Gustaviana* at Dorpat in 1632, modelled on Sweden's only university at Uppsala. In contrast to the gains in education, religious bigotry still flourished. The first half of the seventeenth century marked the height of the witch trials during which around 100 men and women were burnt at the stake in the Baltic provinces.[17]

The former lands of the Teutonic Order in Estland became the property of the Swedish Crown, as did later the lands of the Polish king in Livland. Swedish monarchs awarded most of these lands as fiefs to Swedish and German nobles, a practice particularly prevalent under the weak rule of Queen Christina (reigned 1632–54). By the second half of the seventeenth century it became clear that this process deprived the state of much-needed revenue. King Charles XI (ruled 1661–97) reversed this process in the 1680s with a policy of 'reduction', nationalising estate lands to create income for the royal treasury in order to finance Sweden's formidable military machine. A royal commission determined the legitimacy of titles and reclaimed the majority of land for the Crown, five-sixths of the estates in Livland and half in Estland. Revenue from Estland and Livland not only covered the costs of administering these provinces, but in bountiful years provided almost one-quarter of the Swedish state treasury's income.[18] The land-owners formally became Crown tenants, but still remained in charge. The State regulated the relationship between the peasants and the tenants so that the latter could not arbitrarily exploit the former. The tenants were not permitted to sell peasants without land, to take over their lands or to administer corporal punishment. Although the tax and labour burden imposed on the peasants was not eased, peasants were given legal safeguards, including recourse to royal justice in Stockholm.[19] As the peasantry in Sweden had never been enserfed, Charles abolished serfdom on the Crown estates in the Baltic provinces in 1687. To what extent his wish was actually ever implemented is a matter of debate. The 'reduction' was ultimately to prove costly for Sweden since it alienated the nobility. To overcome entrenched resistance among the Livland nobility to its reduction policy, the Crown dissolved the Livland Land Council. Johann Reinhold von Patkul (1660–1707) led the feisty defence of the rights of the Livland land-owners and, for his pains, was sentenced to death *in absentia* by the Royal High Court in Stockholm. In exile, Patkul subsequently helped to forge an international coalition against Sweden.

Of all the periods of foreign domination, only the Swedish one is referred to in the collective memory of Estonians and Latvians as 'good'. The main reasons for this are the introduction of schooling and the reforms which improved the position of the peasantry. The fact that Swedish rule was preceded and followed by calamitous times also played a role in shaping a positive narrative. However, the exaggeratedly positive image of the 'good Swedish era' is a reflection rather of the high hopes at the time than of the reality.[20] The Swedish state's primary objective was to rationalise and make agricultural production more efficient, thus maximising the tax revenue and food stores it obtained from the Baltic provinces. The increased revenue was needed for the maintenance of military forces necessary to defend the newly expanded empire. The efficient governing of this empire required the centralisation and closer integration with Sweden which resulted from Charles XI's imposition of absolutism. The consequences for the peasantry were ambiguous. On the one hand, the estate owners' virtually unrestricted arbitrary whims were curbed and the relationship between lord and peasant was regulated. On the other, the police laws of 1645 in Estland and 1668 in Livland, binding peasants to the estates and stipulating the return of runaway peasants, in effect officially endorsed the practice of serfdom which had in reality already taken shape. Major Swedish reforms, such as the abolition of serfdom on Crown estates and the division of Livland into two administrative districts, corresponding to the ethnic Estonian and Latvian areas, did not have a chance to make an impact since they were announced in the decade before the Great Northern War and did not have sufficient time to be implemented.

Sweden's neighbours sought to curtail her dominance in northern Europe. King Frederick IV of Denmark (reigned 1699–1730), Tsar Peter I of Russia (reigned 1682–1725) and Frederick Augustus, the Elector of Saxony, who also reigned in Poland–Lithuania as Augustus II (1697–1706; 1709–33) hatched an alliance aimed at rolling back the Swedish Empire. They erroneously believed that they could take advantage of Sweden's perceived weakness after the inexperienced 15-year-old Charles XII ascended the throne in 1697. Unexpectedly, Charles turned out to be a brilliant military commander, who believed that the best defence was a strong offence and he immediately took the fight to his enemies. He landed in Denmark in April 1700 and within a fortnight forced Denmark to sue for peace. Charles then crossed to the eastern shore of the Baltic, intending to lift the Saxon siege of Riga, only to find that Augustus had already withdrawn his troops. Instead, he rapidly marched his troops to Narva where they defeated a much larger Russian army in a blinding November snowstorm.

Rather than following up his victory over the Russians, Charles now turned his attention to eliminating Augustus. His successful invasion of Poland failed to deliver the knock-out blow to his opponent and alienated many Poles and Lithuanians in the process. In pursuing the dethronement of his enemy, Charles supported Augustus's Lithuanian opponents, the Sapieha magnate family, who were so much despised by the other Lithuanian nobility that they allowed Russian troops into the country to help them resist the Swedes.[21] For the next seven years Charles's army was mired in Poland, thus allowing Peter to rebuild and modernise his forces and launch devastating raids on weakly defended Estland and Livland. By 1704 only the major cities of Estland and Livland remained under Swedish control. Russian commander Count Boris Sheremetev boastfully reported to Peter, 'there is nothing left to destroy! . . . All places have been emptied and flattened. Men, women and children, as well as horses and cattle, have been taken into captivity by the thousands. Those who could not be taken along, were stuck through or chopped to bits. All of Livland and part of Estland are so empty that places exist only on the map.'[22] Particularly harsh was the treatment meted out to the citizens of Dorpat who on Ash Wednesday 1708 were deported *en masse* to Vologda while their town was systematically razed.[23]

After forcing the abdication of Augustus, Charles finally moved against Peter and mounted an invasion of Russia in 1708. Peter prudently avoided a direct engagement and employed a scorched-earth policy, leaving the invaders desperate for food and supplies at the onset of winter. Charles turned southwards into Ukraine where fields and villages had not been torched. Here he met his nemesis at Poltava on 27 June 1709. Peter's defeat of the weakened and overstretched Swedes was a turning point in European history, marking the beginning of the end of the Swedish Empire and the advent of Russia as a European great power.[24] Charles eluded capture and found refuge in Turkish Moldova where he was forced to cool his heels for five years. In the meantime, Peter returned to the weakly defended Baltic where his army besieged Reval and Riga. The cities and the Estland and Livland corporations of the nobility capitulated in 1710. The Peace Treaty of Nystad in 1721 officially transferred Estland and Livland to Russia. With his new conquests, Peter took the title of 'Emperor of All Russia' and Muscovy generally came to be known as the Russian Empire.

More devastating for the local population than the actual warfare was the plague and famine which followed in its wake in 1709–11. Large swathes of the Baltic countryside were depopulated: 'there was no human voice to be heard for miles and no dog barking or rooster crowing' as one contemporary grimly recorded.[25] Urban areas were the worst affected: perhaps as much as nine-tenths of the population of Reval died in the 1710 bubonic plague. The plague of 1710–11 was almost as devastating further south, where it took the lives of more than a third of the population of the Grand Duchy, striking its Lithuanian areas particularly hard. This demographic catastrophe, made especially devastating by the combined scourges of famine, war and epidemics striking one after the other, had begun with the great famine of 1696–7 which carried off perhaps one-fifth of the peasant population of Estland and Livland. By the second decade of the eighteenth century, the Estonian, Latvian and Lithuanian populations had been reduced to their lowest levels in several centuries. The number of people in the Estonian areas fell to 175,000, in the Latvian areas to 225,000 and in the Grand Duchy of Lithuania to 1,850,000.[26] More than half of the population of Estland and Livland perished during this period, with Courland suffering slightly less.


RUSSIA'S WINDOW TO THE WEST

Peter offered remarkably generous capitulation terms to the Estland and Livland corporations of the nobility and cities in 1710. Not only did they retain their traditional rights, they also recovered privileges abolished by the Swedes – most significantly, the 'reduction' of estates was reversed and the land-owners' estates were restored by the Crown. Peter also upheld the dominant position of the Lutheran Church and the German language. This munificence was to ensure loyalty while the war against Sweden continued elsewhere and Peter also sought to create a 'window to the West'. He permanently altered the physical geography of the Baltic Sea region by boldly founding his new capital, Sankt Petersburg, in 1703 on the swampland where the Neva river flows into the Gulf of Finland. This was accomplished at a fantastic pace during wartime on disputed territory at the cost of the lives of tens of thousands of labourers. In order to carry out his great project of modernising and westernising Russia, Peter needed able administrators with knowledge of the latest European methods. His new Baltic German subjects were ideally suited for the task – during the eighteenth century 3000 Baltic German young men studied in European, mostly German, universities.[27] Between 1710 and 1802, there was no university in Russia's Baltic provinces, since the Swedish Academia Gustavo-Carolina, the future University of Dorpat, was not reopened after the end of the Great Northern War.

The expanding and rapidly developing Russian Empire provided Baltic Germans with almost boundless career opportunities during the eighteenth and nineteenth centuries. The generous policy towards the

Baltic German nobility paid off handsomely as they remained loyal to the Romanov dynasty until the twentieth century. From Peter the Great until the demise of the monarchy in 1917, an astonishingly high proportion (one-eighth) of individuals who served in the top echelons of the Imperial administration were of Baltic German origin.[28] Baltic German nobles were particularly prominent among military officers and the diplomatic corps. Famous Baltic German personalities encompassed people from a wide variety of endeavours, including explorers who led expeditions to uncharted parts of the globe, such as Admirals Adam Johann von Krusenstern (1770–1846), who led the first Russian circumnavigation of the earth, and Fabian Gottlieb von Bellingshausen (1778–1852), one of the discoverers of Antarctica; scientists, such as the founder of embryology Karl Ernst von Baer (1792–1876); and men of letters, such as August von Kotzebue (1761–1819), one the most popular German dramatists of his day anywhere in Europe.

Baltic Germans played an influential role at the imperial court in St Petersburg. The first Empress of Russia, Peter the Great's second wife, Catherine (born Marta Skavronska) (ruled 1725–7), had begun life as a lowly orphaned peasant raised by Ernst Glück, the Lutheran pastor in Marienburg (Alūksne), Livland, who first translated the Bible into Latvian in 1691. Baltic Germans were particularly prominent during the reign of Empress Anna (1730–40), who had been Duchess of Courland before ascending the imperial throne.

The nature of the Baltic German nobility differed from that of the Russian nobility – it was a closed nobility, based solely on birth, rather than on service to the state, as was mostly the case in Russia.[29] In order to protect themselves from being swamped by outsiders, not just Russian nobles but primarily wealthy Baltic German burghers, the *Ritterschaften* compiled an exclusive register (*Matrikel*) of the 'genuine' nobles. Following the earlier example of the Courland nobility (1620), the Livland and Estland *Ritterschaften* established their registers in 1747 and 1756 respectively. On the island of Ösel, administratively separate from Livland between 1731 and 1783, the *Ritterschaft* confirmed its *Matrikel* in 1741. Only a few hundred families in total were matriculated or inscribed in the peerage rolls: initially 115 families in Courland, 127 in Estland, 172 in Livland and 26 on Ösel.[30] Only men from these families enjoyed the right of full participation in running the affairs of their respective provinces. The importance attached to historical legitimacy in the nobility's own self-image was demonstrated by the fact that the registers were compiled in chronological order: first came families who had settled in the province during the Middle Ages, then came those who had arrived in the Polish and Swedish eras and finally those who had arrived most recently under Russian rule.[31] The Baltic German nobility displayed a high degree of particularism, never forming a single, united corporation nor sharing their institutions with the other small group of German colonists, the burghers of the cities.

The supreme decision-making body in each Baltic province, with a broad mandate to decide on 'everything that relates to the rights, interests, and institutions of the corporation [of the nobility] or the welfare of the whole land',[32] continued to be the diet (*Landtag*) of the *Ritterschaft* as developed under Swedish rule. In Estland, the diet consisted exclusively of the matriculated nobles, while in Livland, non-matriculated manor owners and two representatives of the city of Riga also participated, but could only vote on matters of taxation. The diet elected its chairman, the marshal of the nobility (*Landmarschall* in Livland and *Ritterschaftshauptmann* in Estland) who served a three-year period until the convening of the next session of the diet. His most important function was to represent the corporation's interests at the imperial court in St Petersburg.[33] The executive organ was the Council of the diet (*Landratskollegium*), consisting of twelve land councillors (*Landräte*) elected for life by their peers. The administrative head of Estland and Livland was a governor, appointed by the emperor, who more often than not, was a Baltic German nobleman himself. Estland was characterised by Reinhard Wittram as 'the purest land of nobles on earth'.[34]

Under tsarist rule, the landholders enjoyed the greatest leeway with their property, which included their serfs. One contemporary chronicler described Livland as 'the heaven of the nobility, the paradise of the clergy, the gold mine of the foreigners, and the hell of the peasants'.[35] In order to increase the yield from their estates, the land-owners maximised the labour required from the peasants. Although conditions varied from estate to estate, during the long summer an average peasant household had to supply the manor with one workman for two or three days a week, but during the most intensive periods, such as when sowing or harvesting needed to be done, they were pushed to their limits, having to provide four workers (this included women and children) and had to thresh grain during the night.[36] The peasants had no freedom of movement. Binding the peasants to the estates was partly the response of the landlords to the demographic catastrophe of the Great Northern War, which had resulted in an acute shortage of labour in the early eighteenth century. The post-war expansion of the number of manors and the size of their fields at the expense of peasant lands (often depopulated by the war, famine or plague) also contributed to the labour shortage. In the eighteenth century the position of the peasantry sank to its nadir. The infamous declaration written by Livland land councillor Otto von Rosen (1683–1764) in 1739 asserted that not only did the peasants belong entirely to their lords but so did their property. Peasants could be (and in fact were) bought and sold, occasionally even men and women from the same family separately. One contemporary observer pointedly noted in 1777 that Baltic serfs were cheaper than African slaves in the American colonies.[37] Nevertheless, their situation was better than that of serfs in Russia: those in Estland and Livland could sell their surplus produce freely, had recourse to the courts and, until the end of the eighteenth century, were not subject to conscription.[38]

Most of the land was in the hands of the Baltic German nobility, although there were also substantial church and state properties. In addition, many towns also owned estates. In the second half of the eighteenth century, distillation of spirits became widespread and the most important source of income for the manors besides the growing of grain.[39] Most of the surplus grain and spirits were sold in Russia, where there was an increasing demand, particularly in the rapidly growing new capital of St Petersburg. Because the estate owners enjoyed entrenched rights and privileges and had a large supply of free labour at their disposal, they were not inclined to invest in improvements or innovations in agricultural cultivation. Instead, they spent most of their income on luxuries and in constructing grandiose manors in order to maintain the lifestyle expected of their class. This economic upturn coincided with a period of rapid demographic growth. From its nadir in the 1710s, the population of the Baltic provinces and Lithuania more than doubled by the 1790s.

In the hopeless years following the devastation of the Great Northern War, people found solace in a new spiritual message spread by the Moravian Brethren or Herrnhuter movement, which established a seminary in Wolmar in the Latvian part of Livland in 1738. Some landowners saw positive benefits in the movement since it noticeably reduced drunkenness and criminality among the peasantry, thus increasing productivity; others, however, were anxious about the consequences for the social order since the Herrnhuters preached equality between classes and ethnic groups. The Lutheran church hierarchy was particularly alarmed that the Herrnhuters recruited their preachers from among the peasantry, and persuaded Empress Elizabeth (ruled 1741–62) to ban the Brethren in 1743. Although the ban was lifted in 1764, the Herrnhuters gained new momentum only in the early nineteenth century, after the abolition of serfdom. Moravian Brethren had a significant impact on the Latvian and Estonian peasantry, particularly in Livland. Most important was their emphasis on reading, which led to the rapid growth of literacy and, subsequently, to an increase in the number of books published in native languages, one of the first being the complete Estonian-language Bible, published in 1739. Importantly, the Herrnhuters also taught Latvian and Estonian peasants how to self-organise. In some respects, this religious 'awakening', particularly its second wave in the 1820s, presaged the national 'awakening' of the 1860s.[40]

The Herrnhuters brought a personal understanding of the spiritual essence of Christianity to the people for the first time. Conversion by the crusaders had been merely a formal collective political act; the new faith had simply been grafted onto the existing world-view and heathen customs had endured. For example, Midsummer's Eve or the summer solstice, still today the greatest celebration of the year in Estonia and Latvia, took on a nominal Christian sheen as St John's Day. A negative consequence of the Brethren's activities was that it aggressively rooted out surviving old folk customs. Traditional cultural practices, which had survived centuries of foreign domination, were swept aside as remnants of paganism.

Empress Catherine II (the Great) (reigned 1762–96) was the first Russian monarch to interfere in the Baltic nobility's practically unfettered self-rule. In the spirit of the 'enlightened absolutism' of the day, she toyed with the idea of reforming the practice of serfdom. During her tour of the Baltic provinces in 1764, she acquainted herself with the ideas of Livland pastor Johann Georg Eisen von Schwarzenberg (1717–79), who wrote the first abolitionist tract in the region. He, however, remained a voice in the wilderness. In 1783 she introduced an array of administrative and judicial reforms, aligning the practice of the Baltic provinces closer to that of Russia and diminishing the exclusivity of the institutions of the *Ritterschaften* (e.g. giving non-matriculated nobles full voting rights in the *Landtage*) and city councils. The internal customs border with Russia was abolished, the Russian poll tax was introduced and, most worryingly for the *Ritterschaften*, the executive organ of the *Landtage* was eliminated while the post of Governor-General for the Baltic provinces was introduced in Riga. As compensation for disrupting their traditional public institutions, Catherine granted the Baltic nobles unfettered hereditary rights over their private estates, thus further strengthening their control over their serfs. However, most of these measures which sought to modernise and centralise governance were soon reversed by Catherine's son, Paul I (ruled 1796–1801). In 1796 Paul restored the traditional privileges and institutions of the Baltic nobility, but in return compelled Baltic land-owners regularly to provide conscripts for the imperial army from among their peasants.[41]

Until industrialisation and the Russification policy in the final decades of the nineteenth century, few Russians actually moved permanently to the Baltic provinces. Under tsarist rule, the Baltic Germans continued to administer the Baltic provinces as best suited them. The first wave of Russian immigration into the region consisted of Old Believers escaping persecution in Russia in the late seventeenth and early eighteenth centuries. The Old Believers remained true to the original rites and liturgy of the Russian Orthodox Church, rejecting the seventeenth-century state-supported Church reforms. They established separate new communities in the sparsely inhabited eastern borderlands of Livland. The largest number of Old Believers – over 100,000 – fled to the primarily Ruthenian lands of the Grand Duchy of Lithuania during the eighteenth century.[42]

Enlightenment rationalist ideas penetrated into the Baltic region in the latter half of the eighteenth century. A key proponent of Enlightenment ideals in the Baltic littoral was Johann Friedrich Hartknoch (1740–89) whose publishing house in Riga (established in 1765) published most of the notable Enlightenment authors of the region. Hartknoch was also the publisher of some of the most significant works of the great philosopher Immanuel Kant (1724–1804), who spent his entire life in the Baltic littoral, in Prussian Königsberg.[43] Like Hartknoch, many of the major propagators of Enlightenment ideals came from Germany to launch their careers (mainly as pastors or pedagogues) in the Baltic provinces. The greatest of these was philosopher Johann Gottfried Herder (1744–1803), a key initiator of romantic nationalism, who taught at the Riga Cathedral school in the 1760s. Although he only spent five years in the Baltic provinces, his work would become a catalyst for the Latvian and Estonian national awakenings in the nineteenth century. He included Latvian and Estonian folk songs (coining the term) in his groundbreaking collection *Volkslieder* (1778–9), and thus was the first to direct international attention to the existence of these cultures and to make them legitimate subjects of inquiry. Two of his many novel ideas, which would have global revolutionary consequences and implications for the future of the Baltic peoples, were that every nation is unique and has its own inherent value and that thought is determined by language.

An outstanding figure whose contribution to knowledge about the Baltic provinces remains unsurpassed was August Wilhelm Hupel (1737–1819), the pastor of Oberpahlen (Põltsamaa), who, with the help of a network of correspondents, produced three multi-volume series of encyclopaedic surveys on almost all aspects of life in Livland and Estland.[44] Only Johann Christoph Brotze (1742–1823) in Riga came close to Hupel's accomplishment by recording in thousands of drawings almost every monument, building or item of significance in the Baltic provinces. Courland parson Gotthard Friedrich Stender's (1714–96) writings had the most immediate influence on the peasantry and an unmatched impact on the development of Latvian literary language. In addition to immensely popular stories, he compiled a Latvian grammar, dictionary and scientific encyclopaedia, *Augstas gudrības grāmata no pasuales un dabas* (The Book of Great Wisdom of the World and Nature) (1774), which was the first to provide the Latvian peasantry with a wealth of accessible, systematic information. A more fiery and overtly political Enlightenment publicist was Herder's follower, Garlieb Merkel (1769–1850), the son of a Livland pastor, who, in his polemical book *Die Letten* (The Latvians) (1796) and subsequent writings, condemned the Baltic German land-owners for their callous treatment of the Latvian peasantry. Merkel argued that the German crusaders had robbed the natives of their land and was the first to frame the agrarian question as fundamentally a national conflict and make the case for the national rights of the Latvians and Estonians.[45]

## THE DECLINE AND PARTITION OF THE POLISH–LITHUANIAN COMMONWEALTH

The Commonwealth of Poland–Lithuania, the so-called republic of nobles, went against the tide of European history in an era of absolutism during the seventeenth and eighteenth centuries. While neighbouring states were centralising authority in the hands of the monarch, the multitudinous Polish–Lithuanian nobility zealously guarded its 'golden liberties'. The gentry constituted a larger proportion of the population than in other European societies. Around 5 per cent of the population of the Grand Duchy were nobles: approximately 10 per cent in the Lithuanian territories and 3 per cent in the Ruthenian lands.[46] The fact that the king was elected severely circumscribed his powers. The state was hampered in its foreign and defence policies by the nobles' constant fear that the monarch sought to increase his powers at their expense. This suspicion arose almost every time the king requested taxes from the *Sejm* to raise an army for a military campaign. The *Sejm* consisted of three estates: the monarch, the senate and the chamber of deputies. Decisions in the *Sejm*, which met biannually in Warsaw,[47] were reached by consensus. From 1652, the notorious *liberum veto* began to be used with increasing frequency, meaning that a single member's objections could block adoption of legislation and result in a logjam.[48] The *liberum veto* could be suspended only for the duration of a confederation – a league formed by nobles united to support a specific cause. This system also gave ample opportunity for the manipulation of deputies by neighbouring states. Russia, for instance, meddled in Polish–Lithuanian affairs under the pretext of protecting Orthodox believers. The highest offices in the Grand Duchy were dominated by a few magnate families who owned the largest estates and most extensive lands. In the seventeenth and eighteenth centuries these were the Radziwiłł, Chodkiewicz, Sapieha and Pac families. There was constant friction with the lesser nobility, many of whom were landless and resented the domination of a few magnates.

The Vasa dynasty came to an end with the abdication of the childless King John II Casimir in 1668. His plan to place a French candidate on the throne was foiled by the election of Michał Wiśniowiecki (reigned 1669–1673). The Polish nobility preferred to elevate one of their own in order to ensure the monarch's respect for the privileges of the nobility and avoid the danger of absolutism. After Michael I's unexpected death four years later, the popular Polish military commander Grand Hetman Jan Sobieski was elected as John III (reigned 1674–96). Sobieski's military triumphs, most famously the relief of the Turkish siege of Vienna in 1683, however, were not matched by domestic political accomplishments. As other Polish–Lithuanian rulers before and after him, the king failed to overcome the nobles' resistance to his attempts to strengthen the monarchy. In 1697 he was succeeded in a hotly contested election by Frederick Augustus, the Elector of Saxony, who converted to Catholicism and ruled as Augustus II (the Strong). Augustus brought misfortune upon the Commonwealth by embroiling it in the Great Northern War. He was temporarily deposed by the Swedes during 1706–9 and afterwards was dependent on Russian support to keep his crown. Russia was also instrumental in placing his son Augustus III (reigned 1733–63) on the Polish throne after his death in 1733. Both father and son resided mainly in Saxony and devoted most of their energy to turning Dresden into a highly refined artistic, cultural and architectural centre. These decades of largely absentee rule further eroded the author-ity of the monarchy and intensified power struggles among various fractions of the magnates. During the rule of Augustus III, the *Sejm* kept the Commonwealth out of the European alliances and conflicts in which Saxony was embroiled because it feared that the king could strengthen his own position. The result of this rudderless foreign pol-icy was that the Commonwealth became more of an object than a subject of international relations, with neighbouring powers, especially Russia, increasingly influencing the domestic political agenda of the country.[49]

During this time, the Duchy of Courland also fell under increasing Russian influence. Tsar Peter arranged the marriage of his niece Anna Ivanova to Duke Friedrich Wilhelm (ruled 1698–1711) in 1710. The duke, however, died on the return journey from his marriage in St Peters-burg. His widow ascended the Russian throne in 1730 as Empress Anna. She engineered the election of her lover, Ernst Johann Biron (reigned 1737–40, 1763–9), as the new duke after the death of Ferdinand (reigned 1730–7), the last of the Kettler dynasty, in 1737. Enjoying Anna's lavish patronage, the duke's court at Mitau (Jelgava) became a lively cultural centre. At this time, the most magnificent palaces in the Baltic lands, Ruhental (Rundāle) and Mitau, were constructed by the Italian architect Francesco Bartolomeo Rastrelli (1700–71), who also designed the Winter Palace (Hermitage) in St Petersburg. The aspirations of Mitau grew with the establishment of an academic gymnasium, the Academia Petrina, in 1775. Increasingly, the orientation and loyalty of the Courland nobility was torn between Warsaw and St Petersburg.

After the death of Augustus III, Count Stanisław Antoni Poniatowski, who had become a lover of the future Russian Empress Catherine II while serving as a diplomat in St Petersburg, was elected King and Grand Duke Stanisław II Augustus with the support of Russian troops in 1764. The energetic Poniatowksi immediately engaged in wide-ranging reforms, but soon encountered resistance. In 1768 a confederation was formed at Bar by nobles who were opposed to the king's efforts to rationalise gover-nance at the expense of their privileges and to fight growing Russian influence over the Commonwealth's affairs. The Bar Confederates' ini-tial military successes provoked the first partition of the country in 1772, when the neighbouring powers of Russia, Austria and Prussia agreed on each taking slices of the country for itself. The Commonwealth lost almost a third of its territory. In the Baltic region this meant that Inflanty was incorporated into Russia. Humiliatingly, the *Sejm* was pressured by the Austrians, Russians and Prussians into ratifying the partition.

The partition jolted the king and reformers into action in an attempt to remedy the weaknesses of the system of government through limited centralisation and modernisation. One notable success was the creation of Europe's first ministry of education, the National Educational Commission, after the Jesuit Order was liquidated in 1773. However, Russia exercised great influence over Poland–Lithuania, not only through its military might but also through the manipulation of conservative nobles who sought to retain their traditional privileges, and was thereby able to block reforms aimed at strengthening the state. After the first partition, the king was dependent on the support of the Russian ambassador Otto Magnus von Stackelberg (1736–1800), a Baltic German. While Russia was distracted by war with Turkey, the king and reformers used the window of opportunity to press ahead with a radical programme of reforms during the 'four-year diet' (sessions of the *Sejm* traditionally lasted only six weeks) which began in 1788. This culminated with the adoption on 3 May 1791 of a constitution which modernised and centralised the state. The constitution established a parliamentary monarchy with a hereditary monarch, abolished the *liberum veto* and banned confederations. Landless nobles were disenfranchised but city burghers gained citizenship. It also ended the dualistic nature of the state, eliminating Lithuania's independent status by creating a common army, treasury and executive institutions. Lithuanian deputies managed to restore the separate Lithuanian treasury, but their attempt to defend the separate and equal status of the Grand Duchy failed because, on the whole, they also accepted the paramount need to strengthen the state in the face of a mortal external danger.[50]

The Polish–Lithuanian state's attempt to revive itself, however, encountered stiff resistance from many nobles and provoked a Russian invasion of the country in May 1792. Conservative opponents of the reforms allied themselves with Russia and established the Confederation of Targowica. Polish and Lithuanian troops were outnumbered and outclassed by the Russians. Sensing which way the wind was blowing, the king switched sides and joined the confederates to maintain his throne. The reforms were annulled and the old system was restored. Russia's aims, however, went further than the confederates had bargained for: Russia and Prussia together agreed on a second partition of the Commonwealth in January 1793, whereby Russia gained a substantial part of present-day Belarus and Ukraine, with Lithuania losing the palatinate

**Map 4** The partitions of Poland–Lithuania (1772–1795)

Labels on map:

SWEDEN

Reval
ESTLAND
LIVLAND
Pskov
RUSSIA
Riga
COURLAND
INFLANTY
BALTIC SEA
Vitebsk
Smolensk
Kédainiai
Kaunas
Königsberg
PRUSSIA
Vilnius
Danzig
Grodno
Minsk
Poznan
Warsaw
Brest
Pinsk
PRUSSIA
Lublin
Lutsk
Kiev
Cracow
Lvov
Bratslav
AUSTRIA
OTTOMAN EMPIRE

Legend:

1st partition in 1772

2nd partition in 1793

3rd partition in 1795

Commonwealth's border in 1772

Grand Duchy of Lithuania's border in 1772

State borders after the 3rd partition

of Minsk and eastern parts of the Vilnius, Novogrudok and Brest palatinates.

The rapaciousness of Russia and Prussia provoked a desperate uprising (with the king's blessing) led by American War of Independence veteran General Tadeusz Kościuszko (1746–1819) against the Russian occupiers in 1794. Rebellious Lithuanian military units captured Vilnius on 24 April and joined the Polish insurgents' appeal for the restoration of the Commonwealth's pre-partition territory and the constitution of 1791, and the abolition of serfdom. Lithuanian rebels headed by General Jakub Jasinski (1761–94), a Jacobin poet, proclaimed a National Supreme Council of Lithuania in Vilnius, but Russian troops retook the city in August. The insurrection in Poland was crushed within a few months. On 24 October 1795 Russia, Prussia and Austria formally agreed upon the complete partition of the Commonwealth among themselves. All the remaining lands of the Grand Duchy of Lithuania became Russian possessions, with the exception of Suvalkija, the south-western part of the Grand Duchy which was annexed by Prussia. Upon Catherine's command, the king abdicated. Poland–Lithuania was wiped off the map. European monarchs felt little sympathy for the Commonwealth's fate since they viewed the insurrection as being infected by the dangerous republican ideas of the French Revolution.

The 1795 partition also marked the end of the Duchy of Courland which had already for several decades been practically a Russian protectorate, with its rulers spending much of their time in St Petersburg or abroad. The last duke, Peter Biron (reigned 1769–95), was handsomely compensated and given a comfortable pension by Catherine. Most of the Courland nobility gladly transferred their allegiance to the empress, who guaranteed all of their privileges. The Courland nobility's institutions of self-government had developed in a similar fashion to those of Estland and Livland and thus it was logical that within the Russian Empire Courland received the same special autonomy as Estland and Livland and that together the three formed Russia's Baltic provinces. With the final partition of Poland–Lithuania, almost the entire area of the contemporary Baltic states came completely under Russian rule for the first time.[51]

The Commonwealth had been the home of the majority of the world's Jews, with almost two hundred thousand living in the Grand Duchy (more than 5 per cent of its entire population), although less than one third of these lived in the (ethnically) Lithuanian lands.[52] The Grand Duchy's Jews referred to themselves as *Litvaks* and mostly resided in self-governing communities known as *kahals*, which served as their own judicial, educational and taxation bodies. The *kahals* were united under a supreme governing organ, the Lithuanian Jewish Council, which existed from the late sixteenth century until 1764. According to Dov Levin, the Council was one of the 'most formidable autonomous institutions' in Europe.[53] The Jews mostly lived in small towns and were valued for providing essential services as shopkeepers, artisans, innkeepers, commercial agents and pedlars. Jewish merchants had made a living through usury (lending money for interest to the nobles and the Crown, which was forbidden to Christian subjects) and through tax farming (collecting revenue for a percentage of the beneficiary's income).

During the twilight years of the Commonwealth, Vilnius developed a reputation as an important religious and cultural centre for Eastern European Jews, acquiring the moniker of 'Jerusalem of the North'. In a large measure, this was the result of the influence of Rabbi Eliahu ben Shlomo Zalman, known as the Gaon of Vilna (1720–97), a towering figure in Jewish intellectual life.[54] He emphasised the centrality of Torah study for Judaism, and part of his legacy was the establishment of the first *yeshiva*, a college for study of the Torah, by his pupil Rabbi Chaim (1749–1821) in Volozhin in 1803.

# 4

# The Long Nineteenth Century under Tsarist Rule (1795–1917)

Within the Russian Empire, the Baltic provinces and the Lithuanian lands remained distinct from other parts of the empire and from each other. Lithuanians twice rebelled against tsarist Russia while the loyal Baltic German land-owning nobility continued to enjoy self-governing institutions. The agrarian question dominated the era: the serfs were emancipated but the bulk of the peasants remained landless. With the rise of Estonian, Latvian and Lithuanian national movements in the second half of the nineteenth century, the society based on social estates gradually evolved into one divided primarily along ethnic lines. At the same time, the central government implemented measures to integrate the region more tightly into the Russian Empire. The end of the nineteenth century and beginning of the twentieth century witnessed a rapid socio-economic transformation, entailing modernisation, industrialisation, urbanisation and emigration and challenging the existence of the old order. Although the tsarist regime survived the revolutionary upheaval of 1905, its disastrous performance in World War I led to its demise.

## AGRARIAN REFORMS IN THE BALTIC PROVINCES

As elsewhere in Europe, Enlightenment ideas began directly to challenge the status quo in the Baltic littoral in the wake of the French Revolution. Indeed, they even began to influence the thought processes of otherwise conservative imperial policy-makers in St Petersburg. The new Russian tsar, Alexander I (ruled 1801–25), was well disposed towards certain Enlightenment ideals. He re-established the two universities in the region, the German-language Dorpat in 1802 and the Polish-language Wilno (Vilnius) in 1803. Pressure grew for the *Ritterschaften* to introduce measures to improve the lot of the Baltic peasantry, and the *Ritterschaften* found it impossible to avoid discussing reforms to alleviate the inequities of serfdom. A bloody skirmish between 3000 disgruntled Latvian peasants and a tsarist militia at the Kauguri estate near Wolmar in 1802 focused the attention of the imperial government in St Petersburg on the need for change in the Baltic provinces. Afraid that the liberal-minded Alexander I would impose reform from above, the *Ritterschaften* in Estland, Livland and Courland reluctantly drafted new agrarian laws. This improved the situation of the peasants somewhat but the laws were also designed to benefit the land-owners. The reforms of 1802–4, enacted at Alexander's urging, regulated the relationship between land-owners and peasants, banned land-owners from buying or selling serfs, and established local courts where the peasants were represented. The reforms also required the establishment of manorial rolls where all the obligations of the peasants to the lord were recorded. In return, the *Ritterschaften* secured the establishment of a state credit institution to provide loans to cash-strapped Baltic land-owners.[1]

The pressure for significant reform intensified after the peasants were freed by neighbouring Prussia in 1807. However, planned reforms were interrupted by Russia's war with France in 1812. Napoleon's *Grande Armée* swept through Lithuania, and Napoleon resided in the Bishop's Palace in Vilnius for three weeks during the summer of 1812. For a while, Napoleon's creation of the Duchy of Warsaw gave rise to hopes of the recovery of Lithuanian sovereignty. However, such dreams were dashed by the Russian victory. Defeated by the early cold winter and the scorched-earth tactics initially employed by the first Russian minister of war, General Michael Barclay de Tolly (1761–1818), who was a Baltic German, Napoleon and the desperate remnants of his army appeared in Vilnius again in December after their long, calamitous retreat from Moscow. Vilnius and its environs came to resemble a charnel house for tens of thousands of emaciated French troops who froze to death or were killed.[2] Barclay de Tolly went on to command the victorious Russian army which marched on Paris in 1814. Another Baltic German general, Friedrich Wilhelm von Buxhoevden (1750–1811) initially commanded the campaign which brought Finland under Russian rule in 1808–9. In total, more than eight hundred officers of Baltic German heritage led Russian forces against Napoleon – a remarkable contribution, considering their rather tiny population base.

After Napoleon's defeat, Alexander ordered the Estland *Landtag* to renew work on agrarian reform. Legislation abolishing serfdom was adopted first in Estland in 1816, then in the following year in Courland and finally, grudgingly, by the Livland *Landtag* in 1819. The actual emancipation of the peasantry was implemented gradually over more than a decade. Since the reforms introduced contractual relations, there was a need for peasants to have surnames. Peasants had previously been known only by their Christian name and the name of their farmstead. Surnames were assigned by the estate owners or by the parish pastors, who frequently gave German surnames to the Estonian and Latvian peasants. While the peasants gained their personal freedom, the land-owners were released from the responsibility of supporting their tenants in the case of crop failure or other disasters. The manorial lords could no longer directly interfere in the family life of their peasants, but they could still mete out corporal punishment, and personal freedom did not yet include leaving the manor without the land-owner's permission. The legislation confirmed the nobility's ownership of the land; peasants were not given the right to purchase the land that they had farmed for generations, but were now expected to pay rent to the land-owners. In practice, this meant that the peasants had to continue to perform labour duties for the manors. In this sense, the situation of the peasants actually worsened.

The nobility even managed to consolidate its privileges in subsequent years. With the full codification of Baltic corporate law in 1845, the tsar finally recognised the exclusive right of the nobility to own manor lands.[3] This small group of approximately three hundred noble families, together with a larger group of German burghers in the towns, continued to exercise hegemonic control over the native population. By the mid-nineteenth century, such a rigidly stratified society based entirely on status was unknown elsewhere in Europe. The Baltic Germans constituted less than 7 per cent of the total population of the Baltic provinces but dominated all aspects of their political, social, cultural and economic life, both in the countryside and the towns.

There was frequent unrest among the Latvian and Estonian peasantry throughout the first half of the nineteenth century, such as that seen at Jaunbebri in 1841, Veselavska in 1842 and Mahtra in 1858. Typically, these sporadic outbursts occurred immediately after various agrarian reforms had been announced. Peasants believed in the 'good tsar' and thought that the land-owners were concealing or failing to implement new laws promulgated by the tsar to improve their lot. The peasants refused to carry out the most onerous duties and, seeking safety in numbers, gathered together, which almost inevitably led to the land-owners calling in tsarist troops. This resulted in confrontations to disperse the peasants and some of these confrontations were more bloody than others. After harvest failures in the early 1840s, false rumours spread that those accepting the tsar's faith would be granted land, fuelling a spontaneous mass conversion to Orthodoxy among peasants in Livland in the mid-1840s. More than a hundred thousand Estonians and Latvians converted to Orthodoxy. This later caused problems for families because Russian law did not permit reconversion from Orthodoxy.

Continuing peasant unrest persuaded the imperial authorities to prod the *Ritterschaften* to take further steps to address the desperate situation of the peasants. In 1849 Baron Hamilkar von Fölkersahm (1811–56), the atypically far-sighted Livland *Landmarschall*, introduced agrarian reform, the essence of which was the introduction of money rents to supplant *corvée* labour, and the allocation of a certain portion of estate lands for peasants to purchase or lease.[4] Beginning in the 1850s, peasants began to purchase their own land as the *Ritterschaften* released more land for the peasants to purchase. Similar reforms were introduced in Courland and Estland a few years later. With the general emancipation of the peasantry in the Russian Empire in 1861, the stubborn resistance to reform of Baltic land-owners crumbled, although the agrarian order in the Baltic countryside remained on a different basis than in Russia proper until the end of the empire. Russian tsars relied on the Baltic German nobility to ensure social order and were easily convinced by Baltic German dire warnings that reforms could lead to social upheaval and disturbances or even anarchy. The right of corporal punishment was not therefore abolished until 1865. *Corvée* was finally abolished in the Baltic provinces in 1868, by which time most land-owners had finally come around to realising the benefits of the transition to money rents. The peasants were given the right to elect the council members of their own rural townships in 1866, thereby restricting the ability of the estate owners directly to exercise control over local affairs.[5] Although Estonian and Latvian peasants eagerly began to purchase their own land, their means and opportunities were limited. Approximately half of the land (much of it forest) of the Baltic provinces, therefore, remained in the hands of the Baltic German land-owners until the end of the tsarist regime, while more than half of Estonian and Latvian peasants remained landless.[6] A substantial amount of land also belonged to the Crown and the Church.

The tsarist era was the longest period of peace for the Baltic provinces during modern times, allowing demographic recovery and the rapid growth of the population. Nevertheless, the region was not entirely unaffected by war. Swedish troops briefly landed in Estland and a major sea battle took place between Swedish and Russian forces in the Bay of Reval in 1790. During Napoleon's invasion of Russia in 1812, an allied Prussian force occupied Courland. During the Crimean War (1853–6), British and French fleets blockaded the Baltic Sea, bombarded and raided the Baltic coast, and the British even established a temporary base on the island of Nargö (Naissaar), within sight of Reval. A greater impact on lives, however, was the onerous duty, instituted in the Baltic provinces in 1797, of peasant households to provide conscripts for the tsarist army. Service was for a period of 25 years (although the period was later reduced), which was almost a life sentence. Few of these young men returned to their homeland. In 1874 Alexander II abolished the conscription of peasants and instead introduced obligatory military service for all classes: four years for those with an elementary education and two years for those with a secondary education. Estonians, Latvians and Lithuanians served and died for the imperial cause in various wars, such as the Russo-Turkish War (1877–8) and the Russo-Japanese War (1904–5).

## LITHUANIA WITHIN THE RUSSIAN EMPIRE

Although almost the entire territory of the present-day Baltic states passed under tsarist rule with the partitions of the Polish–Lithuanian Commonwealth at the end of the eighteenth century, the status of the Lithuanian lands within the Russian Empire nevertheless differed considerably from that of the Baltic provinces of Estland, Livland and Courland which enjoyed significant autonomy. Inflanty (Latgale), the predominantly ethnic-Latvian northern slice of the Commonwealth which had been part of medieval Livonia, was incorporated into the Russian province (*guberniya*) of Vitebsk.[7] The Lithuanian heartlands of the former Grand Duchy were administered as the Russian provinces of Vil'na (Vilnius) and Grodno.[8] In 1843, their administrative boundaries were redrawn, creating a third province, Kovno (Kaunas), carved out of the north-western part of Vil'na province. The Russian governor-general in Vil'na had responsibility over the three Lithuanian provinces. Nevertheless, the Lithuanian Statute, the legal codex of the Grand Duchy from 1588, initially remained in force. Although Lithuanian nobles received privileges equal to those of the Russian nobility, the role of their institutions of local self-government, the *seimiks*, were restricted. The most fortunate province was Suwałki (Užnemunė), the south-western section of the Grand Duchy of Lithuania, which was annexed by Prussia in 1795 and was subsequently transferred to the Napoleonic Duchy of Warsaw in 1807 and then to the Russian-satellite Kingdom of Poland created by the Congress of Vienna in 1815. Here a more progressive and prosperous Lithuanian peasantry was able to develop because the serfs had already been emancipated by Napoleon in 1808.

Alongside the Poles, Lithuanians rebelled twice against tsarist rule, seeking to restore their Commonwealth. Following the revolt by liberal Polish army officers in November 1830, the Lithuanian gentry organised a rebel force which captured several Lithuanian towns and besieged Vilnius in the spring of 1831. However, this rebel force was easily defeated by the Russian army, who, within a few months, crushed the insurrection in Poland. The tsarist regime responded harshly to the uprising. The constitutional institutions of Congress Poland were dismantled. The University of Wilno, a hotbed of political activity among liberal and patriotic student societies, was closed in 1832. One of the prominent former student activists, who had been arrested and exiled to Russia already in 1823, was the great Polish romantic poet Adam Mickiewicz (1798–1855), whose epic masterpiece *Pan Tadeusz, czyli ostatni zajazd na Litwie* (Lord Tadeusz, or the Last Raid in Lithuania) published in Parisian exile in 1834, begins with the words 'Lithuania, my Fatherland'. Mickiewicz heroicised the Lithuanian pagan past in other poems, notably *Konrad Wallenrod* (1828), about the struggle of the Lithuanians against the Teutonic Knights, and this had considerable resonance among contemporary patriots. Mickiewicz is an example of how the Lithuanian and Polish identities were intertwined.[9] The distinct identity of Lithuania was dealt a further blow when the tsarist authorities replaced the Statute of Lithuania with Russian law in 1840. The name Lithuania disappeared from official documents and imperial authorities henceforth began to refer to the lands of the former Grand Duchy as Russia's North-western Provinces.[10]

The situation of the Lithuanian Jews also deteriorated considerably in tsarist Russia, compared with the rights they had enjoyed in the Grand Duchy. Within the Russian Empire, Jews were restricted to a Pale of Settlement, which roughly corresponded to the borders of the former Commonwealth, and Jews living in rural areas were forced into the towns. Their tax burden increased, they were subject to conscription into military service as of 1827, and they lost formal control over their own communal affairs when *kahals* were abolished in 1844.[11]

**Map 5**  The Baltic lands in the Russian Empire (*c.* 1850)

Russia's defeat in the Crimean War led Emperor Alexander II (ruled 1855–81) to undertake liberalising reforms. Most significantly, Alexander declared the general emancipation of serfs in the Russian Empire in 1861, which meant that Lithuanian and Latgalian peasants also finally gained their personal freedom. Their situation had been in stark contrast to that of the peasants of the Baltic provinces and the Lithuanians living in East Prussia and Congress Poland who had been liberated decades earlier. Alexander also lifted some discriminatory measures and restrictions on the Jews, allowing them to move more freely and participate in municipal life. Henceforth, under certain conditions, the Jews could move outside the Pale of Settlement, leading to the establishment of Jewish communities in Estland and Livland.[12]

Alexander's reforms created an atmosphere of expectancy in the former Commonwealth. Secret societies organised patriotic manifestations in Warsaw and Vilnius. In January 1863, the underground Polish National Central Committee declared an uprising against the tsarist regime and issued a manifesto promising land to the peasants. Subsequently, a revolutionary provisional government for Lithuania was proclaimed. Unlike the previous insurrection, this time the peasants, many of whom were roused by the fiery Lithuanian rebel-leader priest Antanas Mackevičius (1828–63), joined in. However, the small Lithuanian rebel force was defeated by a much larger Russian army in the spring of 1863. Guerrilla skirmishes continued until March 1864 when the last Lithuanian rebel leader Konstanty Kalinowski (Kastuś Kalinoŭski) (1838–64) was captured and hanged. The Russian Governor-General of Vilnius, Count Mikhail Murav'ev (1796–1866), instituted the draconian punishment of rebels, including hundreds of executions and the exile to Siberia of several thousand. In the aftermath of the rebellion, the imperial government implemented policies to tie its recently acquired borderlands more tightly with Russia proper. Among these, the most symbolic was the 1864 ban on the use of the Latin alphabet when writing Lithuanian. The same ban was also applied to Latgalian in Vitebsk province.

The 1863 uprising was the last occasion when Lithuanians joined Poles to fight together for the restoration of their Commonwealth. Henceforth, the paths of Lithuanian and Polish patriots diverged. Lithuanian activists would build a Lithuanian national movement primarily concerned with reducing Polish influence on Lithuanian culture. The development of a Lithuanian national ethos was also rooted in the social conflict between Lithuanian peasants and Polish (or polonised) landlords.

## NATIONAL AWAKENINGS

The development of national movements in the Baltic region can fruitfully be viewed using Miroslav Hroch's three-stage framework of the national movements among small European nations.[13] Hroch's first stage sees the appearance of individual enlighteners for whom the study of the local language and culture is primarily of scholarly interest or simply a pastime. The second phase is the emergence of dedicated activists who embrace and enthusiastically propagate the idea of the existence of a common nation and, in the final phase, the idea spawns a national movement and gains acceptance among the masses.

The first Enlightenment figures to take an interest in the Estonian and Latvian languages and cultures were Baltic German men of letters in the late eighteenth and early nineteenth centuries.[14] They did so in the spirit of recording for posterity languages and cultures which they believed would soon be extinct. It was assumed that the only future trajectory for the Estonian and Latvian peasantry was eventually to assimilate into the German cultural world. Individuals with similar interests gathered together to establish associations or learned societies. Fourteen Baltic German Lutheran clergymen founded the Latvian Literary Society in Riga in 1824 and the Estonian Learned Society was established in Dorpat in 1838. Although both of these pioneering organisations propagated the study of the indigenous language and culture, they naturally conducted their proceedings in German. A similar process took place in relation to Lithuania several decades later, when the Lithuanian Literary Society was founded in 1879 in Tilsit, East Prussia. The founders were also German scholars, one of whom, linguist Georg Sauerwein (1831–1904), in 1879 penned the lyrics of the anthem of East Prussian Lithuanians: 'Lithuanians We Are Born'. Lithuanians in the Russian Empire only managed to establish the Lithuanian Learned Society in Vilnius much later, in 1907.

The high level of literacy among Estonian and Latvian peasants and the rapid development of communications during the nineteenth century, most importantly the spread of newspapers, was a key precondition for the rise of national movements. The first newspaper in the Baltic provinces, the German-language *Ordinari Freytags Post-Zeitung*, was published by Christoph Brendenken (1649–1710) in Reval in 1675. The Great Northern War disrupted publishing in the Baltic provinces, and newspapers did not appear again until half a century later.[15] Publication of native-language newspapers did not begin until the nineteenth century. *Tarto maa rahwa Näddali-Leht* (Tartu Country Folk Weekly) was launched in 1806 but was soon closed down. The first newspaper in Latvian, *Latviešu Avīzes* (Latvian Newspaper), was launched in Mitau in 1822 by Pastor Karl Friedrich Watson (1777–1826) but a rigid censorship policy during the reign of Emperor Nicholas I (1825–55) hampered further progress in publishing. Under the more liberal Alexander II new newspapers appeared which achieved regular publication and wide circulation: the Latvian *Mājas Viesis* (Home Guest) in 1856, edited by Ansis Leitāns (1815–74), and the Estonian weekly, *Perno Postimees* (Pärnu Courier), in 1857, edited by Johann Voldemar Jannsen (1819–90). The latter was the first to address its readers as the 'Estonian people' (*eesti rahvas*), rather than 'country folk' (*maarahvas*), as Estonians referred to themselves. The same year, Juris Alunāns (1832–64), writing in *Mājas Viesis*, proposed the neologism 'Latvia' (*Latvija*) for the territory inhabited by Latvian speakers to replace identification according to province – Courland or Livland.[16] This initial poetic fancy began to acquire political connotations in the 1880s, by which time the term 'Latvia' had been extended to encompass the Latgalians in Vitebsk province, whose identity was still based primarily on their Catholic faith, rather than Latvian ethnicity. This gradual development during the latter half of the nineteenth century was part of the reconceptualisation of the fundamental components of society in the Baltic provinces, as in other parts of Europe, whereby the standard category determining one's belonging shifted from social estate to ethnicity.

A question which vexed the first national activists was the historical origins or roots of the nation. In the era of romantic nationalism, peoples aspiring to nationhood sought to prove their worth by constructing a glorious past. The condescending attitude towards 'ahistorical' nations was summed up by a Baltic German commentator in 1877 who explained why the Latvians did not have a national epic: 'they have never done anything in their past that would be worth singing about, they have no history worth the mention. They have lived only in contact with nature, but they have not reached a level of equality in their contact with other nations.'[17] Unlike Lithuanians patriots who could lionise the prowess of their grand dukes, especially Mindaugas, Gediminas and Vytautas, Latvians and Estonians needed to construct a mythical golden age prior to the foreign conquest by producing their own national epics. Inspired by the example of the Finnish *Kalevala* published in 1835, two Estonian graduates of the faculty of medicine at the University of Dorpat, Friedrich Faehlmann (1798–1850) and Friedrich Kreutzwald (1803–82), compiled the epic *Kalevipoeg* (Son of Kalev), which was published in 1857–61 under the aegis of the Estonian Learned Society. It took three decades more before Andrejs Pumpurs (1841–1902) finally succeeded in creating a Latvian national epic, *Lāčplēsis* (Bearslayer) in 1888. Both tales unfold at the end of the mythical era of ancient liberty. In the latter, the Bearslayer first defeats the Estonian hero, but they then agree to work together for a common purpose in the future against the mortal enemy, the Black Knight – clearly a representation of the German crusaders. The tragic endings of both epics are ambivalent, holding out the possibility that the hero will return to redeem his people.

Many among the first cohort of Estonian and Latvian national activists were born in the 1830s into peasant households and worked as rural schoolmasters or township clerks, but a few managed to become among only the handful of Estonians and Latvians to obtain a higher education. The ideas of the Estonian and Latvian 'national awakening' initially gained new adherents through networks of friends or schoolmates, such as those who had studied together at the teachers' seminary founded in Wolmar in 1837 (moved to Walk in 1849) run by Jānis Cimze (1814–81).[18] Key figures among the 'Young Latvians' leading the Latvian national awakening were Krišjānis Valdemārs (1837–75), Krišjānis Barons (1835–1923) and Alunāns, who studied at the University of Dorpat in the 1850s but found the Baltic German environment stifling. Valdemārs created a scandal at the university, when he placed the sign 'Latvian' on the door of his room.[19] For upwardly mobile Latvians and Estonians, the only conceivable way to make a career was quickly to assimilate into the German-speaking (or, less commonly, Russian-speaking) world and cover all traces of their origin. Led by Valdemārs, these early activists moved to St Petersburg where in 1862, out of the reach of the Baltic German censor, they published the first overtly nationalistic Latvian weekly, *Pēterburgas Avīzes* (St Petersburg Newspaper).

The most prominent figure in the Estonian national awakening was Jakob Hurt (1839–1907), a Lutheran pastor in Otepää (Odenpäh), later in St Petersburg, and one of the first Estonians to obtain a doctorate. Realising that Estonians could never become a great nation in terms of their numbers, he called upon Estonians to become culturally great. Hurt, together with a large network of correspondents, devoted himself to collecting Estonian oral poetry. An even more impressive feat was by Barons and his collaborators who collected and published 220,000 Latvian *dainas* (folk songs). The *dainas* have been characterised as the repository of the Latvian nation's history and wisdom.

All across the Baltic region, there was rapid development of local civil society organisations, epitomised by agricultural improvement associations, temperance unions, volunteer fire-fighters, choirs and musical bands. These various voluntary associations, whose common thread was the impulse for self-help, became the multipliers of the national movement. Two national undertakings in particular helped propagate its ideas: the Riga Latvian Association and the Estonian Alexander School. After several years of obstruction by the local Baltic German authorities, the imperial government approved the establishment of the Riga Latvian Association in 1868. In addition to promoting the interests of Latvian professionals and businessmen, the association did much to encourage the development of Latvian culture, and its headquarters, the Riga Latvian House, served as the base for the national movement. Its example was emulated by similar associations in other towns.[20] In 1862, rural Estonian activists launched a drive to collect funds for the establishment of an Estonian-language secondary school, the Alexander School (named after the tsar who freed the Baltic serfs). Although the goal was modest, the process itself – the creation of a sustainable nationwide network of fund-raising committees – spread the ideas of the national movement to all corners of the land, thus involving people far and wide in the first genuinely national endeavour.[21] Voluntary endeavours such as these also gave Latvian and Estonian activists experience in organisational activity and rudimentary self-governance beyond the tutelage of the Baltic Germans.

The best-known symbol of the convergence of the associational and the national movements were the song festivals. The Vanemuine choral society, established by Jannsen in 1865, organised the first Estonian national song festival in Dorpat in 1869. The first Latvian song festival, organised by the Riga Latvian Association, took place in Riga four years later. These choral song festivals, inspired by the activities of Baltic German choral societies established in the 1830s and 1840s, for the first time brought together large masses of Estonians and Latvians from all across the Baltic provinces and united them with a common purpose and sense of identity. The song festivals rapidly grew in popularity and size. The development of a similar tradition in Lithuania, where the first national song festival was not held until 1924, was impeded by restrictions on secular associations and the print ban.

Opinions diverged among the leaders of the national movements regarding the strategy employed to obtain their goals. These differences have been characterised as a debate between Germanophiles and

Russophiles (or moderates and radicals), but in fact it was simply a question of whether the aims of the Estonian and Latvian national movements would be advanced better through cooperation with progressive elements among the Baltic Germans by protecting the traditional autonomy of the Baltic provinces within the empire or by supporting the centralising policies of the imperial government in order to demolish the remaining privileges of the Baltic Germans. Among Estonians this divide was personified by Jannsen and Hurt and by Köler and Jakobson respectively. Johann Köler (1826–99) was a painter at the St Petersburg Academy of Arts, and Carl Robert Jakobson (1841–82) was the editor of *Sakala*, the first overtly political Estonian newspaper (founded in 1878). Jakobson turned the Baltic German conception of history, based on the crusaders having brought civilisation to the native barbarians, on its head. Developing the ideas first espoused by Merkel, Jakobson spoke in 1868 of a golden age of liberty prior to the conquest which was followed by centuries of servitude and he promised a new dawn for the Estonian nation.[22] This conceptual framework and imagery of light and darkness formed the basis for the Estonian and Latvian national narratives which prevailed in the twentieth century. In the Latvian case, the debate between competing orientations occurred within the Young Latvian movement itself. Valdemārs actively sought the support of imperial officials in St Petersburg and Slavophiles in Moscow to improve economic conditions for Latvians, while his contemporary, teacher Atis Kronvalds (1837–75), emphasised the primacy of Latvian-language schooling in cooperation with liberal-minded Baltic Germans.

A modern ethnonationalism arose among Lithuanians only after the emancipation of the peasantry in 1861 and the crushing of the 1863 insurrection. The imperial government's 1864 ban on the use of the Latin alphabet in writing Lithuanian proved to be ineffective and counterproductive, mainly because a significant number of the Lithuanian national activists were based outside of the Russian Empire. Although the tsarist authorities could keep tight control over Lithuanians in their own realm, they could not hinder activities across the border in the north-eastern area of German East Prussia (Lithuania Minor) where over a hundred thousand Lithuanians lived. Until the ban was lifted in 1904, over four thousand Lithuanian publications were printed in East Prussia, compared to fifty-five published officially by the tsarist authorities using the Cyrillic script. The smuggling and distribution of the banned literature mobilised thousands of Lithuanians and created a social network of dedicated national activists. Almost three thousand individuals, mostly peasants, were caught and punished for smuggling books from East Prussia into the Russian Empire during this forty-year period.[23]

Russian officials were obsessed with combating manifestations of Polish patriotism and their policies towards the Lithuanians were a by-product of that overriding concern.[24] 'Russification' policies actually abetted the growth of a Lithuanian national consciousness because the Russian authorities sought to separate Lithuanians from the Poles as a means of weakening the latter. They simply assumed that the Lithuanians would eventually assimilate into the Russian nation.[25] However, the Russian authorities equated Catholicism with Polish nationalism. Consequently, state discrimination against the Catholic Church unintentionally boosted the Church's moral authority among the Lithuanians by pushing the polonised clergy and Lithuanian peasantry closer together. A key figure in the development of a modern Lithuanian national consciousness was the Bishop of Samogitia, Motiejus Valančius (1801–75), who established not only networks for smuggling and distributing books but also parochial schools where the language of instruction was secretly Lithuanian. Earlier, in 1858, he had established temperance brotherhoods which became a popular social movement and a stimulus for the creation of a national movement. The prime example of the backfiring of the Russification/anti-Catholic policy was the violent dispersal of believers protecting the local monastery church in Kražiai in 1893, which enraged Lithuanian opinion against the tsarist authorities.[26]

The Lithuanian 'national awakening' started more than two decades after the Estonian and Latvian ones. Many of its key figures came from the Suwałki *guberniya* (administratively under Congress Poland) where the peasants had been emancipated in 1808 and where tsarist reforms in 1864 punished the Polish nobles for involvement in the uprising by redistributing their lands to the peasants. These policies created more favourable conditions for the development of a prosperous Lithuanian peasantry who could afford to allow their sons to pursue a secondary education. Although Russian supplanted Polish as the language of instruction in the schools of the Suwałki region, unlike elsewhere, certain subjects were taught in Lithuanian. The gymnasium in Marijampolė (Mariampol) founded in 1866 played a particularly notable role in educating a Lithuanian-language intelligentsia.[27]

One of the graduates of Marijampolė Gymnasium, awarded a stipend to study at Moscow University in 1873, was Jonas Basanavičius

(1851–1927), who later became revered as patriarch of the Lithuanian national movement. Basanavičius was inspired by the Czech national movement while briefly employed in Prague. He launched the first secular Lithuanian newspaper, *Aušra* (Dawn), in 1883, published in East Prussia. Although it was only appeared for three years, it was extremely influential. Remarkably, Basanavičius guided the Lithuanian national awakening from abroad while working for more than two decades as a medical doctor in Bulgaria, returning to Lithuania only in 1905. He wrote passionately on Lithuanian history and culture, eventually succeeding in imbuing a new sense of self-identity in his compatriots. Unlike the major leaders of the Estonian and Latvian national awakenings, Basanavičius lived to participate in the establishment of statehood.

Secular nationalists (as opposed to the conservatives associated with the Catholic Church) formed a circle around *Varpas* (The Bell) which was founded in 1889 and published in East Prussia and was the first journal to deal with political and socio-economic issues. Launched by Vincas Kudirka (1858–99), also a physician from the Suwałki region, *Varpas* encouraged self-improvement and urged Lithuanians to transform themselves from peasants into a modern nation by entering urban trades and professions. In the urban areas of the Lithuanian lands in 1897, the mother tongue of the population was 42 per cent Yiddish, 24 per cent Polish, 22 per cent Belarusian or Russian, and just 8 per cent Lithuanian.[28] As these figures illustrate, Lithuanian and Jewish social structures were rather dissimilar. Jews dominated the Lithuanian economy: they owned most of the enterprises but also comprised the majority of the fledgling industrial proletariat, while few Lithuanians could be found in either category. The two ethnic groups had the potential to complement each other, since both struggled against the restriction of their rights under the tsarist regime and were suspicious of the Poles. However, the fact that their national movements evolved in parallel militated against their having a common cause.[29] Jewish Zionism, which propagated emigration to Palestine, was indifferent to the Lithuanians and so were the other strands of Jewish political activism which advocated for Jewish rights and social egalitarianism in an area wider than just the Lithuanian lands. The appeal by Lithuanian leaders, such as Kudirka, for Lithuanians to break out of the peasant mould and take up vocations in the towns traditionally in the hands of the Jews (commerce, crafts, the free professions and industry) led to competition and tension between the two groups.

## RUSSIFICATION AND MODERNISATION

After the Polish–Lithuanian uprising of 1863, the Russian government contemplated measures which would bind the western borderlands of the empire more tightly to Russia. The traditional privileged anomalies within the empire, such as the self-governing institutions of the Baltic Germans in the Baltic provinces, came to be seen as archaic, particularly by Slavophile nationalists. In 1868, Slavophile publicist Yuri Samarin (1819–76) called for the curtailment of the autonomy enjoyed by the Baltic provinces and their closer integration with Russia. The Baltic Germans' response, characterised by Dorpat history professor Carl Schirren's (1826–1910) polemic reply in 1869, was to 'stand fast' and 'to hold out' against the encroachments to their inalienable rights that had been confirmed by Peter the Great and subsequent tsars.[30] After the unification of Germany in 1871, Slavophile Russian nationalists increasingly questioned the loyalty of the Baltic Germans. As modern ethnonationalism came to predominate in late nineteenth-century Europe, the privileged status of the Baltic Germans, based on their traditional class identity, came under threat. The Baltic German nobility had no viable alternative but to continue to stress its absolute loyalty to the Romanov dynasty. As long as their talents and service were highly valued by the tsars, their position of dominance remained secure.

Under Emperor Alexander III (ruled 1881–94), the state took a more active role in the affairs of the Baltic provinces in what has conventionally been labelled a 'Russification' campaign, although this term implies a greater degree of coherence in policy formulation than actually existed. In 1882, the emperor dispatched Russian Senator Nikolai Manasein (1835–95) to the Baltic provinces of Livland and Courland to conduct a wide-ranging review of their administration. His mission raised the hopes and expectations of the Estonians and Latvians, who presented him with 20,000 petitions. These echoed the demands of the Great Petition presented by delegates from 17 Estonian societies to the tsar in 1881.[31] Most of the requests dealt with the problems of agrarian reform: practical measures to improve the economic lot of the peasantry and a reduction of the influence and control that the land-owners exercised over them. The petitioners wanted the Baltic German *Landtage* to be replaced with more inclusive Russian *zemstva* (local government assemblies) and the administration of the Baltic provinces to correspond to the areas of Latvian and Estonian inhabitation. They asked for the introduction of Estonian- and Latvian-language schooling, and, in general, called for a greater role for the imperial administration, in order to curtail the dominance of the *Ritterschaften*. Manasein's report to the emperor claimed that Germanisation of the Estonians and Latvians was the greatest danger to be combated. Subsequently, in 1885, the imperial government acted upon Manasein's recommendations by appointing new Russian governors in Estland, Livland and Courland (the previous governors had usually been Baltic Germans) and by introducing Russian as the official language.

The imperial government's 'Russification' policy in the Baltic provinces had two main thrusts: cultural and administrative.[32] The education system became one of the main battlegrounds for cultural Russification. Russian became the language of instruction in Baltic schools by the end of the 1880s. In 1893, the German-language Dorpat University became the Russian-language Yur'ev University (as did the name of the town itself). The Russian Orthodox faith began strongly to be propagated. Ostentatious Russian Orthodox churches were constructed in prominent locations in all the major Baltic cities at the end of the nineteenth or beginning of the twentieth century. Imposing monuments were erected to the conquerors, Peter the Great in Reval and Riga (1910) and Catherine the Great in Vilnius (1904), as signs of local loyalty to the Romanov dynasty. Both the Baltic Germans and the Russian authorities believed that the Estonians and Latvians had no future or potential as nations and would surely be assimilated. The question for them was only whether Estonians and Latvians would eventually become Germanised or Russified.

The Russification campaign was in part an effort to ensure that the Estonians and Latvians would not be absorbed into the German cultural space, a concern which arose after the unification of Germany in 1871. However, these measures were imposed two generations too late to succeed in their goal of assimilating Estonians and Latvians into the Russian cultural orbit because the Estonians and Latvians had already experienced a national awakening and managed to reach a level of maturity and self-confidence which resulted in the creation of their own public sphere resistant to the pressure of Russian culture. If anything, cultural Russification only served to heighten the Estonian and Latvian sense of national identity.[33] Russification, however, did diminish the real danger of Germanisation by emancipating Estonians and Latvians from Baltic German tutelage. Learning Russian opened professional opportunities for them in the wider empire, especially in the agricultural sector. Previously, upwardly mobile Estonians and Latvians, particularly in the cities, had adopted German manners and the German language and had distanced themselves from their peasant roots. Even the first generation of nationalist activists in the mid-nineteenth century communicated with each other in the more sophisticated German language, the medium through which they could conduct intellectual debate. After all, the modes of building civic activism and self-improvement on the part of Estonians and Latvians followed German models.[34]

Estonian and Latvian secular literature burgeoned in the wake of the national awakenings. The output of Estonian- and Latvian-language publications grew exponentially, particularly in the final decades of the nineteenth century, despite the Russification policies.[35] The development of a reading public and a national intelligentsia was aided by widespread literacy – the literacy rate in the Baltic provinces was significantly higher than in any other region of the Russian Empire, with the exception of the Grand Duchy of Finland. According to the 1897 census, 96 per cent of Estonians and 92 per cent of Latvians in the Baltic provinces were able to read. The ability to read was remarkably evenly spread throughout Estonian and Latvian society: the literacy rate in the countryside was almost the equivalent of that in the towns, and slightly more women than men could read. While the Estonian and Latvian literacy rate matched that of the Baltic Germans (95 per cent), the latter were by far the most highly educated ethnic group within the empire. Literacy and the extent and quality of the education system was clearly linked with religious confession, since only 58 per cent of the Catholic Latvians in Latgale (Vitebsk province) and 48 per cent of Lithuanians could read. Nevertheless, Catholics had a significantly higher level of literacy than Orthodox believers in the empire as only 29 per cent of Russians could read.[36] Sixty-five per cent of Jewish men could read but only 37 per cent of Jewish women were able to do so.[37]

After the romantic patriotism of the national awakening period, exemplified by Estonian poetess Lydia Koidula (1843–86) and Latvian poet Auseklis (Miķelis Krogzemis) (1850–79), Estonian and Latvian authors developed realism in prose and drama. An important milestone was the first Latvian novel *Mērnieku laiki* (Time of the Surveyors) by brothers Reinis (1839–1920) and Matīss (1848–1926) Kaudzīte, which was published in 1879. By the end of the century, psychological or critical realism, dealing mainly with conflicts in rural communities, was mastered by Latvian Rūdolfs Blaumanis (1863–1908) and Estonian Eduard Vilde (1865–1933). At the turn of the century, the Latvian poets and playwrights, husband and wife, Rainis (Jānis Pliekšāns, 1865–1929) and Aspazija (Elza Rozenberga, 1865–1943) embraced symbolism and spearheaded modernism. Aspazija's works also espoused female emancipation. These developments in literature were accompanied by efforts to standardise the orthography and expand vocabularies so that these peasant languages could express more abstract concepts.

Similar developments took place several years later in Lithuania. The great bard of the Lithuanian national awakening, Maironis (Jonas Mačiulis, 1862–1932), published his first poem in *Aušra* in 1885 and his volumes of poetry, *Pavasario balsai* (The Voices of Springtime) and *Jaunoji Lietuva* (Young Lithuania), heralding the national renaissance, a decade later. The flourishing of Lithuanian literature, however, was delayed until after the press ban was lifted in 1904.

Estonians, Latvians and Lithuanians also aspired to professional heights in other creative arts. The turn of the century saw the emergence of visual artists who laid the foundations for national schools of painting: Latvian Jānis Rozentāls (1866–1916), Estonian Ants Laikmaa (1866–1942) and Lithuanian Mikalojus Čiurlionis (1875–1911), who was also a highly-talented composer. Estonian and Latvian amateur theatre troupes, first established in the 1860s and 1870s, were transformed into professional theatre companies at the beginning of the twentieth century.

The administrative dimension of Russification was more successful, and more welcomed by Estonians and Latvians, than its cultural aspects. The imperial authorities sought to harmonise administrative structures throughout the empire in their bid to modernise the country. Russification eliminated many of the archaic anomalies of the Baltic provinces, thereby reducing the special privileges of the Baltic German land-owners and burghers and creating new opportunities for the indigenous peoples. The Baltic Germans came under pressure from both above and below: the government strove to standardise administration throughout the empire, while the Estonian and Latvian masses increasingly demanded that their voices be heard. Reforms of fundamental importance were the replacement of the traditional Baltic judicial system with Russian court procedures and the reallocation of the police system under the imperial Ministry of the Interior in 1888–9, creating a more impartial system than the previous one, which had been strongly under the influence of the local Baltic German land-owners.[38] However, access to the justice system became more difficult for the peasants because most did not understand Russian, the new official language.

Estonians and Latvians were able to challenge the Baltic German monopoly of power for the first time as a result of the introduction in 1877 of a new municipal law which harmonised the regulations concerning towns in the Baltic provinces with the Russian municipal statute of 1870. This broke the power of the narrowly based Baltic German urban oligarchy by widening the franchise considerably, although property qualifications remained. The first breakthrough came in 1897 when Latvians won power in Wolmar (Valmiera). The greatest achievement was the victory of a joint Estonian–Russian electoral list in Reval in 1904. German–Russian electoral cooperation, however, kept the Latvians from office in Riga until World War I.[39]

Unlike the Russification implemented later by the Soviet regime, tsarist policy did not entail colonisation. Certainly, there was the presence in the Baltic region of Russians involved in the imperial bureaucracy and military, as well as growing numbers of Russian industrial workers. However, this was not comparable to the massive influx during the Soviet period. In fact, Russification also targeted the majority of Russians already present in the Baltic countryside and was not necessarily welcomed by them. The Russian Old Believers who had settled in the Baltic region in the eighteenth century were subject to discrimination and attempts to convert them to state-sponsored Orthodoxy. Nevertheless, the Old Believers clung stubbornly to the 'true faith' and were inherently distrustful of the governmental authorities.

The first general census in the Russian Empire in 1897 revealed that the population of Estonia (Estland and the northern half of Livland)[40] numbered 960,000, of which 91 per cent were Estonian, 4 per cent Russian and 4 per cent German by nationality. The population of Latvia (Courland, the southern half of Livland, and Latgale) had grown to 1,930,000, with an ethnic composition of 68 per cent Latvian, 12 per cent Russian or Belarusian, 7 per cent Jewish and 6 per cent German. Of the 2,670,000 people inhabiting the Lithuanian lands, 58 per cent were Lithuanian, 15 per cent Russian or Belarusian, 13 per cent Jewish, and 10 per cent Polish.[41]

At this point, the Baltic provinces and the Lithuanian lands were experiencing large-scale outward migration since population density increased significantly but most peasants remained landless. Following the new internal passport regulations of 1863, allowing peasants to move within and outside of the Baltic provinces, and the famine of 1867–8, there was substantial emigration by Estonian and Latvian peasants eager to find land and freedom (from Baltic German domination) in the east, mostly to the adjacent Russian provinces and central Russia, but also much further to Siberia, the Crimea and the Caucasus. The imperial capital of St Petersburg also attracted huge numbers of migrants of all classes from the Baltic provinces who sought better employment opportunities. By the outbreak of World War I, more than two hundred thousand Latvians and a slightly smaller number of Estonians lived in the Russian Empire outside of their homeland.[42]

Since Lutheran migration into Russia was encouraged but Catholic and Jewish migration was hindered, the pattern of emigration from the Lithuanian lands differed from that of the Baltic provinces. Unlike the Estonians and Latvians, but similar to the Poles, large numbers of Lithuanians moved to the USA. Lithuanian emigration started in the wake of the 1867–8 famine and the introduction of obligatory military service in 1874. It was easier for the Lithuanians to leave the Russian Empire illegally because they could slip across the border into German East Prussia. In the USA, Lithuanians worked in the coalmines of Pennsylvania, the slaughterhouses of Chicago and the steelworks of Pittsburgh. The first Lithuanian-language newspaper was published in the USA in 1879, four years before *Aušra*, and the first original Lithuanian-language theatre play was performed there in 1889, ten years earlier than in Lithuania. Almost a quarter of Lithuanians migrated, proportionally one of the largest European emigrations. Between 1899 and 1914, the most intense period of emigration, 250,000 Lithuanians arrived in the USA.[43] Several of the Lithuanian Jews who moved to the USA would later become world famous: entertainer Al Jolson (1886–1950), violinist Jascha Heifetz (1901–87), abstract painter Mark Rothko (1903–70)[44] and anarchist Emma Goldman (1869–1940).

The latter half of the nineteenth century was a period of rapid socio-economic transformation and modernisation. A revolutionary development which increased the speed of communications was the advent of the telegraph, the use of which spread through the Baltic region in the 1850s. A key catalyst for industrialisation and urbanisation was the arrival of the railroad in the Baltic region in the 1860s. The construction of the St Petersburg–Warsaw line to connect the imperial capital with Europe reached Dünaburg (Daugavpils) in 1861 and Vilnius in 1863. The first internal railroad line in the Baltic was built in 1862 to connect Riga with this major line at Dünaburg. Reval was connected with St Petersburg in 1870.

Improved transportation and economic development stimulated urbanisation. Riga's population multiplied exponentially, growing five-fold in less than fifty years: from 102,000 in 1867 to 282,000 by 1897 and 507,000 by 1913. The other major Baltic cities remained in Riga's shadow: in 1897 Vilnius had 155,000 inhabitants and Reval had just

60,000. Since most of the new residents of Riga were peasants from the countryside, the ethnic composition of the city also changed swiftly: from 43 per cent German, 25 per cent Russian, 24 per cent Latvian and 5 per cent Jewish in 1867 to 42 per cent Latvian, 26 per cent German, 17 per cent Russian and 7 per cent Jewish in 1897.[45]

Riga became the empire's third largest industrial centre (after St Petersburg and Moscow) as the Russian government embarked on an ambitious programme of industrial expansion in the 1890s. The major industries in Riga were mechanical engineering, metalworking and chemicals. The giant Russo-Baltic Wagon Factory in Riga was a leading producer of railway carriages and pioneered aeroplane and automobile manufacturing in the Russian Empire. More than a quarter of Russia's trade flowed through the Baltic ports, the largest of which was Riga, followed by Reval. They mainly exported Russian flax, wheat, timber and hides to Europe and imported cotton, steel, coal, industrial machinery and fertilisers. Riga became the world's leading port for timber exports.[46]

This rapid economic growth necessitated training in new skills. To meet the needs of the new economy, the city of Riga and the Livland *Ritterschaft* financed the establishment of the German-language Riga Polytechnic in 1862, the first multi-branched polytechnical institute in the Russian Empire. One of its instructors, future Nobel Prize winner Wilhelm Ostwald (1853–1932), a Riga native and graduate of Dorpat University, invented the process leading to the mass production of fertilisers and was one of the founders of physical chemistry.

The increased wealth and population spawned cultural vitality. Riga became a cosmopolitan centre which attracted talented individuals from all over the empire and the German-speaking world. Richard Wagner (1813–83) began writing his first successful opera (*Rienzi*) while working as music director of the Riga Theatre in the late 1830s. The future Oxford philosopher Isaiah Berlin (1909–97), the son of a Riga timber merchant, spent his early childhood years in a magnificent Art Nouveau house designed by architect Mikhail Eisenstein (1867–1921), the father of the future pioneering Soviet film director Sergei Eisenstein (1898–1948) (also born in Riga). The architectural face of Riga was transformed: medieval town walls were torn down and parks and wide boulevards were constructed.

In the Estonian areas, textile manufacturing was the largest industry. The Kreenholm Cotton Manufacture, which was founded in 1858 at Narva and which at its height around 1910 employed 10,000 workers, was one of the largest in the world. Reval experienced a substantial industrial expansion when, during the arms race leading up to World War I, the Russian government established three shipyards for the purpose of building warships for the Imperial Navy. Although the tsarist government embarked on a massive construction programme of concrete fortifications around Kovno to defend the empire's western front, the development of large-scale industry in Lithuania lagged far behind that in the Baltic provinces. Most of the new industries in the Baltic region produced goods for the domestic Russian market; there was very limited export of manufactured goods.[47]

## THE REVOLUTION OF 1905 AND WORLD WAR I

Rapid economic and social change and the emergence of a new urban proletariat inevitably had political repercussions. The Latvian 'New Current' emerged in the late 1880s, led by Rainis, Pēteris Stučka (1865–1932), Jānis Jansons-Brauns (1872–1917) and Miķelis Valters (1874–1968). It introduced German Marxist social critique into the Baltic provinces and challenged the right of the older generation of Latvian nationalists to speak in the name of the people. Stučka and Jansons-Brauns were among those who founded the Latvian Social Democratic Workers' Party in 1904.[48] Although underground, the party was highly organised and attracted a substantial following. A Lithuanian Social Democratic Workers' Party had actually been founded earlier in 1896, but initially consisted primarily of ethnic Poles, one of whom, Felix Dzerzhinsky (Feliks Dzierżyński) (1877–1926), would later be the creator of the *Cheka* (Soviet secret police). In Vilnius in 1897 Jews established their own socialist party for the entire empire – the General Jewish Labour Union of Lithuania, Poland and Russia, known as the *Bund*. A branch of the Russian Social Democratic Workers' Party was established in Reval in 1902; Mikhail Kalinin (1875–1946), the future head of state of the USSR, was one of its founders. Estonians, however, were slower to take up socialist slogans than their southern neighbours.

Socio-economic inequities and long-standing grievances against the tsarist regime exploded into revolutionary upheaval in the midst of the disastrous Russo-Japanese war. Following 'bloody Sunday' in St Petersburg on 9 January 1905, when the imperial guard mowed down peaceful demonstrators, solidarity strikes broke out in the larger Baltic cities, and a few days later 56 demonstrators in Riga were killed in a similar tragedy. During the following months, Latvian towns and rural areas witnessed more strike activity than any other part of the empire. In October, a general strike paralysed the empire, including the Baltic region. Troops killed 94 peaceful demonstrators in Reval as well as five strikers in Vilnius. In an effort to quell the unrest within the empire, Tsar Nicholas II (reigned 1894–1917) hesitantly promised political liberalisation. However, the tsar's October Manifesto fuelled further demands. Political fermentation gripped the major centres of the empire as the authorities lost control over the situation. Two months of frenzied political activity ensued, involving the formation of embryonic political parties and labour unions. The Latvian Social Democratic Workers' Party achieved broad appeal (having 18,000 members at this point) and played the leading role in directing the campaign against the autocratic regime and Baltic German hege- mony in Courland and Livland. Numerous meetings issuing political demands were held across the Baltic region, culminating in November when the first Estonian, Latvian and Lithuanian nationwide congresses were convened, with delegates representing local authorities and various associations from all parts of the Estonian, Latvian and Lithuanian lands. An all-Estonian congress was convened in Dorpat by Jaan Tõnisson (1868–1941?), editor of the daily *Postimees*, which split into two separate meetings: moderate and radical. Two all-Latvian meetings were held in Riga: the Schoolteachers' Congress and the Congress of Rural Delegates. Basanavičius initiated the Lithuanian congress in Vilnius which was held in December, attended by 2000 delegates, and came to be referred to as the 'Great *Seimas*' (Great Diet).[49] For the first time, Estonians, Latvians and Lithuanians asserted their right to decide their own affairs instead of them being decided by the Baltic German and Polish nobilities who had hitherto monopolised the right to speak on behalf of their shared homelands. Although the resolutions adopted by these congresses had different emphases, they had many common demands: democratic elections, the abolition of censorship, autonomy corresponding to ethnographic boundaries, the end of Russification policies, native-language schooling, land reform and the abolition of the remaining privileges of the land-owners. In a limited way, the people themselves had already begun to implement these resolutions directly during the heady 'days of freedom' – Latvians and, to a lesser extent, Estonians and Lithuanians elected leaders from among themselves to replace tsarist officials in local administration.

The violent climax of the revolution, initiated by radicalised Riga workers, unleashed an orgy of pent-up class hatred – the torching of manor houses in the countryside and the lynching of Baltic German clergymen. Latvian peasant bands overwhelmed the forces of authority and even seized control of some provincial towns. Encouraged by the Latvian example, Estonians went on a week-long rampage of looting and burning manors in December. By the end of 1905, the tsarist regime recovered its nerve and imposed harsh retribution. Military punitive expeditions were dispatched to the Baltic provinces and 1315 individuals were summarily executed. More executions were carried out in the Baltic provinces than in any other region of the Russian Empire. Several thousand Latvians and Estonians who were suspected of involvement in the disturbances were subjected to corporal punishment, arrested and/or exiled to Siberia, while a similar number fled to Europe or America.[50] Subsequent years witnessed the increased emigration of Estonians and Latvians to the open spaces of Russia. Martial law remained in force in the Baltic provinces until 1908. The vehemence of revolutionary activity among the Latvians, and the corresponding lack of it among the Lithuanians, is mainly explained by the high level of industrialisation and the emergence of a large urban proletariat.

The events of 1905–6 were a watershed for the Baltic provinces and left a bitter legacy and an insurmountable divide between the ruling Baltic German elite and the Latvians and Estonians.[51] Any remaining illusions among progressive Baltic Germans and moderate Estonians and Latvians about the viability of any compromise reform programme were shattered. The gap between them was too wide to be bridged; suspicion, mistrust and resentment were simply too strong. The Baltic Germans entrenched themselves further while Estonians and Latvians increasingly looked to revolutionary means to achieve social justice. The failed revolution witnessed unprecedented political mobilisation and raised expectations. Class and national interest had previously been intertwined, but from this point forward two ideological currents diverged: one prioritising the interests of the working class; the other emphasising national goals.

The major gain from the revolution was the convening of the State Duma (parliament) by the emperor in St Petersburg in 1906. Although the duma had an indirect and limited franchise which favoured wealthier property owners, it provided the first experience of professional politics for Estonians, Latvians and Lithuanians, and the opportunity to network with representatives of other parts of the empire. In the duma, Estonian, Latvian and Lithuanian deputies aligned themselves with liberal and left-wing Russian parties and with representatives of non-Russians. The main issue was the need for further agrarian reform. Several of the men elected to the duma, such as Tõnisson, Jānis Čakste (1859–1927) and Martynas Yčas (1885–1941), would later play a role in the creation of independent Baltic states. However, feeling more secure, the tsarist regime dissolved the Second Duma in June 1907 and partly rescinded its democratic concessions. As a result of a new reactionary duma electoral law, the majority of representatives from the Baltic and Lithuanian provinces in the Third (1907–12) and Fourth (1912–17) Duma were Baltic Germans or Polish and Russian land-owners, whereas in the First and the Second Duma almost all of them had been ethnic Estonians, Latvians and Lithuanians.[52] Jewish deputies were elected to the duma from Kovno and Courland as a result of electoral coalitions with Lithuanians and Latvians.

Arguably, the most important development in the Russian Empire in the years immediately following the failed revolution was the agrarian reform of Prime Minister Pyotr Stolypin in 1906, which encouraged the consolidation of scattered plots of land into individual peasant homesteads. As a result, the pattern of land tenure in the provinces of Vil'na and Kovno as well as in Latgale came to resemble more closely that already existing in the Baltic provinces. The first decades of the twentieth century also witnessed the remarkable spread of the cooperative movement among the peasantry in both the Lithuanian lands and the Baltic provinces.[53]

The assassination of Austrian Archduke Franz Ferdinand in Sarajevo on 28 June 1914 precipitated a chain of events which led to the outbreak of World War I. On the Eastern Front, the fighting began when the Russian army advanced across the German border towards Königsberg in August 1914. The Baltic nations experienced the impact of the war differently: Lithuanian territory was occupied by Germany for the duration of most of the war, while Estonian soil was untouched by military action until almost the final year of the war. Latvians suffered most grievously since the front line ran through the middle of their land during most of the conflict. Baltic Germans found themselves in an uncomfortable predicament since in the new highly charged atmosphere of Russian nationalistic fervour – when even the name of the capital was changed from its German name to the Russian Petrograd – persons of German heritage came under suspicion. The Baltic Germans, however, had no option other than to maintain their traditional loyalty to the Romanov dynasty. Indeed, it was a Balt, General Paul von Rennenkampf (1854–1918), who led the Russian First Army's invasion of East Prussia.

After the bitter memories of 1905, the Latvians were most enthusiastic about fighting the Germans, whom they identified with the Baltic Germans. Tens of thousands of Estonians, Latvians and Lithuanians were conscripted into the tsarist army. The Latvians also suffered the greatest casualties, most notably soldiers of the Twentieth Corps of the Russian First Army, which endured huge losses in East Prussia in early 1915. By September 1915 the Germans had pushed the Russian forces back and managed to overrun Lithuania. The front line settled along the Daugava river, south of Riga. Although German military occupation was harsh, it probably spared the lives of thousands of Lithuanian young men who would otherwise have been conscripted into the tsarist army.

Ahead of the German advance, the tsarist government dismantled and evacuated factories and their workers to the Russian interior. Thirty thousand railway cars full of industrial equipment, machinery, and materials made of valuable metals, such as copper roofs, departed from Riga in 1915.[54] Even the Riga Polytechnical Institute was evacuated to Moscow in 1915, along with Reval-born architecture student Alfred Rosenberg (1893–1946), the future chief ideologue of the Third Reich. One-third of the entire Latvian population (800,000), the bulk of whom were from Courland, abandoned their homes. Among those forcibly uprooted were the Jews of Courland, whom the tsarist authorities suspected of sympathising with Germany.[55] Three hundred thousand people fled or were evacuated from Lithuania to the interior of Russia. With the refugees living in difficult circumstances and scattered around the major cities of western Russia, Lithuanians and Latvians created their own relief organisations. The Lithuanian Committee to Assist the Victims of the War, headed by Yčas, and the Latvian Central Committee for Refugee Relief also served as political training grounds for future national activists.

With the enemy at the gates of Riga in 1915, the Russian military command made an exception to its policy of precluding national units and authorised the formation of Latvian rifle regiments. These proved hugely popular – 130,000 Latvian young men eventually enlisted, and the Latvian riflemen displayed exceptional courage and determination in defending their homeland. Their sacrifices, however, were squandered by inept Russian military leadership, which led to a general disillusionment with the tsarist regime among the Latvians.

# 5

## The Short Era of Independence (1917–1939)

In the wake of the revolution in 1917, Russia's descent into civil war after the Bolshevik seizure of power and Germany's defeat in World War I, Lithuanian, Estonian and Latvian national leaders seized the opportunity to proclaim independent states. After successfully fending off external aggressors and obtaining international recognition, these new republics created progressive democracies and egalitarian societies, with remarkable achievements in land redistribution, education, and cultural autonomy for minorities. Liberal democracy eventually succumbed to authoritarian rule, which had considerable popular support. While the Smetona, Päts and Ulmanis regimes successfully promoted economic and cultural development, they were unable to find a durable solution for their nations' security.

### THE RUSSIAN REVOLUTION AND GERMAN OCCUPATION

Russia's military campaigns in World War I were a series of colossal disasters which eventually turned into public anger at the incompetent autocratic government. Nevertheless, the sudden collapse of the regime and the abdication of Tsar Nicholas II on 2 March 1917[1] came as a surprise. Estonians, Latvians and Lithuanians reacted by immediately reviving their demands from 1905 for majority rule and presented these to the newly established Russian Provisional Government in Petrograd. After 40,000 well-disciplined Estonians pressed their case with a protest march in Petrograd, the provisional government agreed on 30 March to dismantle the archaic governing institutions of the Baltic German nobility and to merge the northern half of Livland with the province of Estland, creating a single administrative unit which corresponded to the ethnographic distribution of Estonians. For the first time, ethnic Estonians and Latvians were placed in charge: the Russian Provisional Government appointed the Mayor of Reval, Jaan Poska (1866–1920), as commissar for Estonia and the Mayor of Riga, Andrejs Krastkalns (1868–1939), as commissar for Livland. To replace the Baltic German *Landtage*, Poska proclaimed elections to an Estonian Provincial Assembly (*Maanõukogu*) which convened in July. Its composition was split almost equally between socialist and non-socialist parties. The Livland Provincial Assembly election in September was a triumph for the Latvian Bolsheviks, who won 63 per cent of the vote.

The power of the provisional authorities was challenged by the soviets (revolutionary councils of workers, soldiers and sailors) which sprang up in the major cities of the empire. The soviets grew increasingly vocal and they came to be dominated by the most radical Marxist party, the Bolsheviks, led by Vladimir Lenin. Since the soviets mainly represented the industrial proletariat and military personnel, the Latvian and especially the Estonian soviets contained a high proportion of Russians. Following the Bolshevik seizure of power in Petrograd on 26 October 1917, Estonia and the unoccupied Latvian areas immediately came under local Bolshevik control. Few believed that the Bolsheviks would be able to rule for long, and the forthcoming Russian Constituent Assembly was still expected to determine the shape of the future democratic Russia.

The Bolshevik seizure of power, coupled with the looming threat of German full military occupation – Riga fell on 22 August – provided the impetus for independence. The Estonian and Latvian political goal – democratic autonomy within a democratic Russian federation – no longer appeared realistic or desirable. On 15 November the Estonian Provincial Assembly declared itself the supreme authority in Estonia, and a few days later the newly formed Latvian Provisional National Council, uniting the non-Marxist Latvian political forces, met in Valka and declared itself the sole legitimate representative of the Latvian people. At the same time, a democratic bloc, led by Social Democrats but including key members of the newly formed Peasants' Union, such as Kārlis Ulmanis (1877–1942), worked in German-occupied Riga for the principle of Latvian self-determination.

Elections to the Russian Constituent Assembly in November demonstrated strong support in the Baltic provinces for the Bolsheviks, who won 40 per cent of the vote in Estonia and 72 per cent in unoccupied Latvian Livland. Indeed, the Bolsheviks were more popular at this point among the Latvians than any other nationality; in the Russian Empire as a whole the level of support for them was three times less. Several factors account for the popularity of Bolshevism among Latvians: the high degree of industrialisation; the intensity of the revolution of 1905 and its bitter legacy; the intertwining of class and ethnic conflict, and the dislocation by the war of hundreds of thousands of Latvians – an experience which undoubtedly served to radicalise political views. The Bolshevik slogan 'Peace, land, and bread!' had tremendous appeal. While other Russian political parties also promised land and bread, only the Bolsheviks also promised an immediate end to the war. This resonated powerfully among the Latvians through whose homeland the front line ran. Furthermore, the Bolsheviks were the best-organised Latvian political party; they were not simply one faction among the socialists as in Russia, but predominated the Latvian left.[2]

When the Constituent Assembly convened in Petrograd in January 1918, it was immediately shut down by the Red Guards, a step which precipitated Russia's descent into a bloody civil war. The Estonian and Latvian Bolsheviks introduced further measures liquidating the old regime, but alienated many by demonstrating their intolerance of other political forces. The Latvian Bolsheviks managed to gain the approval of Petrograd for the unification of Latgale with Livland and Courland and the official use of the Latvian language. Bolshevik rule, however, had little time to consolidate itself in Estonia and Livland before the advance of the German army forced the Bolsheviks to abandon Livland and Estonia entirely in February 1918. The Salvation Committee, the three-man executive of the Estonian Provincial Assembly, headed by Konstantin Päts (1874–1956), used the brief window of opportunity on 24 February ahead of the arrival of the German army in Tallinn (Reval) to issue the proclamation of Estonian independence.

The German military occupation was harsh, exploiting the local economies for the needs of the war effort. Although the duration of the German occupation of Lithuanian territory was longer than in the Baltic provinces, it was, nevertheless, more conducive to native aspirations in the former because the interlocutors for the occupiers in Lithuania were the local leaders of the national movement, not reactionary Baltic German barons.[3] After the revolution, the Russian Provisional Government had rejected the appeal by Lithuanian political leaders in Petrograd for a promise of Lithuanian autonomy. The Germans decided that it would be advantageous to allow Lithuanian leaders to meet and organise themselves. This was consistent with their goal of weakening

Russia, which had already been greatly advanced by their facilitation of Lenin's return to Russia in April 1917. A conference of 222 Lithuanian delegates met in Vilnius on 18–22 September 1917 and elected a 20-member Council of Lithuania (*Lietuvos Taryba*), headed by Antanas Smetona (1874–1944). The members of the *Taryba* had to walk along a political tightrope: they needed to work with the German occupation authorities in order to advance the Lithuanian national cause but, by doing so, they constantly risked being viewed as collaborators by the population. On 11 December the *Taryba* adopted a resolution establishing a Lithuanian state closely linked with Germany. The Germans wanted to use Lithuanian self-determination as a bargaining chip in the peace negotiations with the Russian Bolsheviks which began a few weeks later at Brest-Litovsk. Left-wing members withdrew from the *Taryba* in protest but rejoined upon a new public declaration of full-fledged independence on 16 February 1918. Although Germany rejected this declaration, in March it recognised Lithuania's independence on the basis of the December resolution, but did not relinquish its control over the country. Kaiser Wilhelm II (reigned 1888–1918) and the German military high command sought to bind Lithuania to Germany through a personal union with the Prussian royal family. However, the Lithuanians sought to stymie this plan by following the friendly advice of Matthias Erzberger (1875–1921), a leader of the Catholic Centre Party in the German *Reichstag*, to invite a favourably disposed Catholic German royal to be their king. In July, the *Tarbya* elected Wilhelm, the Duke of Urach and Count of Württemberg (1864–1928), to be crowned King Mindaugas II, although the German government never approved this decision.

Lenin was willing to trade large swaths of Russian territory in the west in exchange for halting the war with Germany. He coldly calculated that consolidating the power of the Bolsheviks in the Russian heartland against all challengers was the greatest priority. Germany and the Bolsheviks signed the Brest-Litovsk peace treaty on 3 March 1918 whereby Russia ceded most of its territory occupied by Germany, including Lithuania, Courland, Riga and the Estonian islands. Germany undertook to determine the final status of these areas in accordance with the wishes of the inhabitants. On 27 August, in a supplementary accord, Russia also renounced its sovereignty over Estonia and Livland. Lenin saw the territorial concessions to Germany as temporary since he fully expected the revolution soon to spread into Germany itself.

The Entente powers sought to thwart German claims to the region as well as to counter the Bolsheviks. Thus the petitions for *de facto* recognition, forwarded by delegates sent by the Estonian Provincial Assembly in early 1918, found a favourable reception in London and Paris. The British and French governments recognised the Estonian Assembly in May 1918 as the provisional *de facto* government and in October the British accorded similar recognition to the Latvian Provisional National Council. The future status of the Baltic provinces was thus transformed into an international issue to be decided at the peace conference at the end of the war, rather than just an internal Russian matter.

The German military command who administered the occupied territories viewed the Baltic provinces as a future natural part of the German *Reich*. After the Bolshevik coup, the Baltic Germans had forsworn their loyalty to Russia. In response, the Bolsheviks had declared them to be outlaws. The German nobility in Estland and Livland joined their brethren in Courland, which had been occupied by Germany earlier, in attempting to turn back the clock to the pre-Russification era of the mid-nineteenth century. They believed that they could resume their natural hegemony and rule without reference to the wishes of the majority. To strengthen their position, they planned to encourage the settlement of colonists from Germany. The *Ritterschaften* convened a joint Estland, Livland and Ösel *Landesrat* (council) with some token Estonian and Latvian representatives, which in April 1918 appealed to the Kaiser to create a Baltic Duchy dynastically linked with the Prussian royal family.[4] The plans of the reactionary Baltic German nobles and the military command, however, were dashed by the outbreak of revolution in Germany, the abdication of the Kaiser and the conclusion of the armistice on the Western Front on 11 November 1918.

The imminent collapse of German power accelerated the pace of change. As early as 2 November, the Lithuanian *Taryba* annulled the election of the king and created a three-man presidium chaired by Smetona to head the state. On 11 November, it appointed the first government led by Augustinas Voldemaras (1883–1942). On the same day, the Estonian Provisional Government was formed, with Päts as its head. A Latvian National Council, comprised of all political forces except the Bolsheviks, was established on 17 November 1918. Čakste was elected chairman and Ulmanis was charged with forming a provisional government. The following day, the council declared Latvian independence. Nevertheless, actual power in Riga initially rested in the hands of August Winnig (1878–1956), the new German provisional government's representative in the Baltic provinces, since the German Eighth Army remained the only organised military force in the region.

## THE WARS OF INDEPENDENCE

Within a few days of the end of World War I, the German occupation authorities handed over power to the freshly formed Estonian, Latvian and Lithuanian provisional governments. In the terms of the Armistice, the Entente stipulated that Germans troops should remain in the Baltic as a bulwark against the spread of Bolshevism. The German government likewise also viewed the Baltic as the front line in preventing Bolshevism from reaching Central Europe. Desperate for disciplined troops, the Ulmanis government agreed to German military support in exchange for citizenship and property rights for German volunteers fighting for the Latvian cause – an agreement which initially made the Ulmanis government look suspect in the eyes of most Latvians. The regular German troops mostly returned home and were replaced by volunteer freebooters (*Freikorps*) and by a local Baltic German *Landeswehr* militia.

The new native governments faced the herculean task of creating state institutions from scratch and recruiting national armies among war-ravaged populations. Few believed that they would succeed. Militarily, the Estonians were in the best starting position since the men of the Estonian national regiment, which had been formed in the spring of 1917, had remained loyal to the underground Estonian Provincial Assembly. The Latvians had the most battle-hardened units, but after the Germans occupied Livland these had retreated into the Russian interior where they fought ferociously in the service of the Russian Bolshevik government in the Russian civil war during 1918. The Latvian riflemen had arguably changed the course of world history in July 1918 when they alone prevented the Socialist Revolutionaries from toppling Lenin's Bolshevik regime in Moscow. They were eager to return to Latvia as liberators of their country from the German yoke. In their eyes, Ulmanis' government was too closely linked to the Germans. In Lithuania, Voldemaras focused his energy on preparing the Lithuanian case for the Paris peace conference rather than on creating an army. All three national governments faced great difficulties in obtaining not only weapons, arms and equipment for the few troops they had but also basic necessities for the civilian population.

With German capitulation to the Entente powers, the Bolshevik Russian government immediately declared the Brest-Litovsk Treaty void and set about reconquering abandoned territories of the Russian Empire. Lenin and his comrades sought to spread the proletarian revolution and dreamed of linking up with revolutionary workers in Germany. For them, the world revolution was not an abstract idea to be realised sometime in the future, but something to be achieved over the following few years, if not months. The route from Petrograd to Berlin went through the Baltic. The advance on the West, with the initial thrust directed at Riga, was spearheaded by the Latvian riflemen, the most disciplined soldiers in the Red Army. Their commander, Colonel Jukums Vācietis (1873–1938), even served as the first head of the Red Army in 1918–19. Several other Latvians, such as Jēkabs Peters (1886–1938) and Mārtiņš Lācis (1888–1938) worked in the *Cheka* (secret police), helping to lay the foundations of the Bolshevik regime in Russia.

As soon as the Red Army invaded Estonia, Latvia and Lithuania at the end of 1918, Soviet governments, headed by local Bolsheviks Jaan Anvelt (1884–1937), Stučka, and Vincas Mickevičius-Kapsukas (1880–1935) respectively, were proclaimed on the territory they controlled. By the beginning of 1919 the Bolsheviks held the eastern halves of Estonia and Lithuania and all of Latvia except Liepāja. Soviet power was most entrenched in Latvia where it lasted longest and had the broadest local support. Its leader, Stučka, belonged to the top echelon of the All-Russian Bolshevik Party, and was later an author of the Soviet constitution and the USSR's chief justice. The Soviet Lithuanian government established in Vilnius was merged with the Byelorussian one in February 1919, forming the Lithuanian–Byelorussian SSR (Litbel), following the tsarist administrative tradition of the North-western Provinces.

The Bolsheviks rapidly alienated many of their initial supporters with their policy of terror, aimed primarily at businessmen and the clergy but also at anyone who was suspected of opposing them. The economic situation was dire but their policies and incompetence created more chaos and resentment and even hunger in the cities. They were not interested in building up state institutions since they viewed independence as a bourgeois concept which would shortly be swept away by world revolution. Perhaps the greatest mistake of the Estonian, Latvian and Lithuanian Bolsheviks was their agrarian policy. The Bolsheviks immediately proclaimed the nationalisation of the land, with large holdings to be collective farms and smaller holdings to be leased. This was contrary to the Baltic dream of every peasant owning his own family farm.

The Estonian, Latvian and Lithuanian national governments were more attuned to the aspirations of the people. Their promise of land for all those who enlisted in the national forces provided a powerful incentive for young men to fight for their country.[5]

Soviet rule did not last long. The Estonians, aided by Finnish volunteers and a British naval squadron, were the first to turn the Red tide. The Bolsheviks were within 35 kilometres of Tallinn when the Estonian counteroffensive, led by the politically and diplomatically astute 35-year-old supreme commander, General Johan Laidoner (1884–1953), began in January 1919.[6] By spring, Estonian territory had been cleared of the enemy. In the south, German troops blocked the advance of the Red Army towards Kaunas to where the Lithuanian government had evacuated in January 1919. The Polish army drove the Bolshevik Litbel government from Vilnius in April. This gave the Lithuanians time hastily to organise their own military forces, which managed to clear ethnically Lithuanian territory of the Bolsheviks by the summer and also thwart further Polish designs on Lithuania.

The Bolsheviks were only prevented from completely overrunning Latvia by the German *Freikorps*. The alliance of expedience between the Germans and the Ulmanis government came to an abrupt end in April 1919 when the *Freikorps* toppled the Latvian provisional government based in Liepāja and created a puppet government headed by the Latvian Lutheran pastor and popular writer Andrievs Niedra (1871–1942). Ulmanis found refuge on a British warship anchored in the harbour.

In spring 1919, the Reds were pushed back into Latgale by the Germans advancing from the west and the Estonians from the north. The lines of the two ostensibly allied armies met near Cēsis (Wenden) in June 1919. The Estonians refused to allow the Germans to advance northwards. Fresh memories of German military occupation gave the Estonians good reason to suspect their ultimate aims. In the hard-fought battle which ensued, the Estonian army, including Latvian volunteer units, routed the Germans. This highly symbolic victory would later be celebrated by the Estonians as Victory Day, historic revenge for '700 years of slavery'. The Estonians were eager to press their advantage, but the Entente, interested in maintaining a united anti-Bolshevik front, brokered a truce, obliging the Germans to withdraw to Courland and enabling the Ulmanis government to return to Rīga.

This was not, however, the end of the involvement of German troops in the Baltic region. Together with fresh German volunteers and former

Russian prisoners of war (POWs) sent from Germany, the *Freikorps* was reformed in the summer of 1919 in Courland into a bizarre force named the Russian Volunteer Western Army, under tsarist officer Count Pavel Bermondt-Avalov (1877–1974). Their leaders dreamed of restoring tsarist rule in Russia which in turn would help revive the German monarchy and enable Germany to defy the Entente powers. They were disowned by the democratic German government. The Bermondtists attacked Rīga from the rear in October. Only with substantial losses (and the help of British naval guns) were the Latvians able to repulse them and drive them from Latvian territory. The Bermondtists then became the problem of the Lithuanians, who, together with Entente pressure, succeeded in expelling them to German East Prussia by the end of the year. The bloody (mis)adventures of the German *Freikorps* were later heavily romanticised and several participants became influential figures in the Nazi Party in Germany during its formative years.[7]

While the Baltic states were fighting for their independence, the Russian civil war between the Bolsheviks and the Whites raged on a much grander scale. The North-Western Russian White Army, led by General Nikolai Yudenich (1862–1933), used Estonia as a staging area for its attack on Petrograd. The British encouraged the campaign and pressured Yudenich into a grudging recognition of the Estonians' right to self-determination, although the Russian Whites sought to keep the empire intact. Having already secured their own territory, the Estonians were not enthusiastic about intervening in the Russian civil war, but the Entente powers dangled the carrot of international recognition of Estonian statehood to ensure Estonian military support for Yudenich's army.[8] In September 1919, the hard-pressed Bolsheviks offered to begin peace negotiations with the Baltic governments, but only the Estonians were in a position to begin preliminary talks. However, in October the North-Western Russian White Army, supported by the Estonians, launched its offensive to topple the Bolshevik regime. When the offensive faltered at the gates of Petrograd, the Red Army chased the Whites back into Estonia. Although most of the Whites were disarmed and interned by their erstwhile Estonian allies, this did not stop the Bolsheviks from launching an offensive against Estonia. During November and December 1919, in the bloodiest engagements of the Baltic wars of independence, the Estonian army prevented the numerically superior Red Army from advancing across the Narva river. In the meantime, peace negotiations with Soviet Russia had begun and the stubborn defence of their territory enabled the Estonians to secure favourable terms. Lenin put a brave face on the failure to defeat the Estonians by claiming that the Tartu Peace Treaty signed on 2 February 1920 breached the 'imperialist' blockade of Soviet Russia. Estonia and Soviet Russia became the first countries to recognise each other's existence.

The final phases of the Baltic wars of independence were influenced by the Polish–Soviet war. In January 1920 the Polish army helped Latvia to win Latgale, thus completing the unification of ethnically Latvian lands. A peace treaty was concluded on 11 August 1920 whereby Russia renounced all sovereign rights over Latvia in perpetuity. Lithuania had signed a peace treaty with the Soviets a month earlier on 12 July. The Bolsheviks recognised the Lithuanian claim to Vilnius (under Polish control at the time) and the Lithuanians agreed to the entry of the Red Army on to Lithuanian territory in the case of a Russian conflict with Poland. The Soviet government made use of this provision just two days later when its troops occupied Vilnius in the context of the Russo-Polish war in which Lithuania was officially neutral. Soviet forces handed Vilnius back to the Lithuanians in August after the Red Army's advance had been halted before the gates of Warsaw. While pursuing the Bolsheviks eastwards, Polish troops under the command of General Lucjan Żeligowski (1865–1947) seized Vilnius on 9 October and proclaimed a Republic of Central Lithuania. Although officially disowned by the Polish government, Żeligowski was acting on orders from the Polish leader Marshal Józef Piłsudski (1867–1935), who was from a Lithuanian noble family and believed in the restoration of the old Commonwealth within its historic boundaries.[9] In Piłsudski's romantic vision, Vilnius could belong to Lithuania if Lithuania itself were part of a federation with Poland. Federation with Poland, however, was anathema for Lithuanian nationalists. The Lithuanian army resisted Żeligowski's attempt to advance further and an armistice between Lithuania and Poland was signed on 29 November 1920.

Piłsudski's ideals belonged to a bygone era and were incompatible with the twentieth-century dominance of ethnic nationalism. For modern Polish nationalists, Lithuanian statehood was tolerable only if it was narrowly confined to its ethno-linguistic borders.[10] On the issue of Vilnius, both sides had strong arguments. For the Lithuanians, Vilnius was their ancient capital. On the other hand, the majority of the city's residents were Polish and Jewish. It was an important site not just for Lithuanian and Polish culture but also for Jewish and Belarusian culture. Vilnius changed hands six times between the Germans, Lithuanians, Poles and Russians during the two years of conflict after World War I.

Agreeing on borders between the newly independent Baltic states was less problematic, since they followed the approximate ethnographic frontiers. The main bone of contention in the former province of Livland was the central town of Valga/Valka, a major railway junction. Estonia and Latvia needed British mediation to settle their dispute over how to draw the borderline through the town. A British military mediator also fixed the final Latvian–Lithuanian border.

Although the wars of independence had been won, international recognition did not follow immediately because the Entente powers, particularly the USA, continued to hope for a White victory in the Russian civil war and were loath precipitously to jeopardise Russian territorial integrity. The Entente powers[11] finally granted Estonia and Latvia *de jure* recognition on 26 January 1921. All three Baltic countries became members of the League of Nations in September, but *de jure* recognition of Lithuania by Britain and France was delayed for almost two years (20 December 1922) owing to the Vilnius dispute. However, few outside observers expected the newly independent states to survive for long and most predicted that they would sooner or later be reintegrated into the Russian realm. In the short term, the Balts were to prove the pessimists wrong.

In the historical literature the formation of the Baltic states is frequently attributed to the Versailles Treaty; statehood often appears as a gift of the Entente powers wanting a *cordon sanitaire* or buffer zone against Bolshevik Russia. In fact, the peacemakers in Paris in 1919 had faint interest in or knowledge of what was happening in the Baltic region. No one favoured the establishment of these independent states except the Estonians, Latvians and Lithuanians themselves. The conflicts in the Baltic region were viewed as peripheral elements of the wider Russian civil war. The Entente powers, particularly the USA and France, preferred to maintain the territorial integrity of the Russian Empire and supported the Russian Whites whose principle was 'Russia one and indivisible'. Among the many ironies and contradictions in this confusing and complex series of conflicts, where coalitions were fluid and alliances changed overnight, was that the wars of independence were fought partly in alliance with the Russian Whites against the Russian Bolsheviks, who, in the end, were the only ones willing to recognise the right to self-determination of the Baltic nations because they expected that world revolution would soon make nation-states irrelevant.

## FROM DEMOCRACY TO AUTHORITARIANISM

Having successfully fought to gain their independence, the Baltic states faced the challenging task of state-building. A constituent assembly had already been elected in Estonia already during the war in April 1919 and a constitution had been adopted the following year. As fighting continued longer on their territories, the process was slower in Latvia and Lithuania, where the constituent assemblies convened in 1920 and completed their work in 1922. The constitutions adopted by the three Baltic states were inspired by the same impulse – the liberating ideals of the February revolution and a reaction against the autocratic tsarist regime. They were strongly influenced by the most modern and progressive example – the German Weimar constitution – but also by those of the French Third Republic and even the direct democracy of Switzerland. All three were highly suspicious of a strong executive and therefore vested power in the representatives of the people: legislative assemblies. Presidents were elected by the parliaments and given only symbolic powers. The Estonians did not even create a head of state, but provided for the chairman of the parliament to fulfil that function. The unicameral legislatures, the Estonian *Riigikogu*, Latvian *Saeima* and Lithuania *Seimas*, were elected for three years. Women were given the vote, something not yet common in Europe.

The Estonian and Latvian political party systems were similar, with three large blocs of parties: the socialists on the left, the agrarians on the right, and a variety of smaller parties in the centre. The Communist Party, which fought against the establishment of the republic in the war of independence, was banned. Nevertheless, communists were usually present in the parliaments by means of various electoral front organisations. While there was significant residual support for the Bolshevik cause in the immediate post-war period, the unsuccessful putsch which had been sponsored by Soviet Russia in Tallinn on 1 December 1924 dispelled the illusions of many of their Baltic sympathisers. Additionally, national minorities – Germans, Russians, Jews, Poles and Swedes – formed their own political parties and, in the case of Russians and Jews in Latvia, several rival parties. Ethnically based parties played the largest role in Latvia but, despite the prominence of several individual parliamentary deputies, they remained marginal and rarely participated in government formation.

The Estonian and Latvian party systems followed similar dynamics. In the early years of the republics, the Socialists were the largest party.

However, the sweeping reforms, such as the land reform, introduced by the Socialist-dominated Estonian and Latvian constituent assemblies, appeased most of the main grievances of the masses and resulted in a subsequent decline in support for left-wing parties. The newly created property-owning class naturally supported less radical measures. The reverse trend was the case for the agrarians who eventually formed the largest bloc, consisting of two main parties, the Farmers' Union and the smaller New Farmers, representing those who received land through the land reform. The Farmers' Union had the most experienced cadre of national leaders and most often provided the heads of governments, such as the multiple-serving Päts in Estonia and Ulmanis in Latvia. The various parties of the centre – most importantly Tõnisson's People's Party in Estonia and the Democratic Centre Party in Latvia – were usually well represented in the government, as their support was crucial for coalition formation. The latter supplied Latvia with two presidents, Čakste (1922–7) and Gustavs Zemgals (1871–1939; president 1927–30). Among the smaller parties, the Christian Peoples' Party in Estonia and the Christian Nationalists in Latvia, who championed the interests of the Lutheran Church, also had a significant presence.[12]

Governments typically lasted less than a year, and the parliament, particularly the Latvian one, was highly fragmented. As proportional representation was employed in elections and there was no threshold for obtaining seats, the majority of the parties represented in the *Saeima* held just one seat. Forming governing coalitions in Latvia and Estonia was rendered difficult by the ideological reluctance of the largest party, the Socialists, to share responsibility in any 'bourgeois' cabinet. Despite the apparent teething problems of these young democracies in Estonia and Latvia, government policy was nevertheless quite stable and effective.

Parliamentary democracy in Lithuania lasted only until 1926. The three major political forces were the Christian Democrats, the Populists and the Socialists. The largest party, the Christian Democrats, represented the mass of the conservative peasantry and emphasised the values of the first, rather than the second, part of their party name. One of their leaders, Aleksandras Stulginskis (1885–1969), served as head of state from 1920–6. The Populists had a similar electoral base but were secular in their orientation. Unlike in Estonia and Latvia, the Socialists, whose core supporters were usually from the urban working class and intelligentsia, were the weakest of the three main parties. The national minorities, the Jews and the Poles, also had their own parties whose representatives were elected to the *Seimas*.

The Christian Democrats dominated the political system in Lithuania – they were the only party in the Baltic states ever to obtain an absolute majority in a parliamentary election, and they governed continually until 1926. This led to corruption and the abuse of power, but the greatest blow to their popularity was their inability to prevent the Vatican's decision to recognise Polish jurisdiction over the Vilnius diocese in 1925. After the May 1926 elections the Christian Democrats remained the largest party, but the other parties managed to form a coalition which excluded them from office. The new government immediately began to reverse the Christian Democratic government's policies: restrictions on civil liberties were removed, political prisoners (mainly communists) were amnestied, the Polish minority was allowed to establish native-language schools, a mutual assistance treaty was signed with the USSR, and military expenditure was reduced. For the mass of patriotic, conservative, Catholic peasants, who formed the bulk of the population and of the supporters of the Christian Democrats, these measures were unpalatable. The most fateful step was probably the reduction of the size of the officer corps, since this resulted in junior officers forming a plot against the government.

On 16 December 1926 the military conspirators seized key government buildings and took the political leadership into custody. Their action was probably inspired by the example of Piłsudski who carried out a coup d'état in Warsaw in May 1926. The officers did not seize power for themselves, but looked to Smetona and Voldemaras to provide political leadership. As the republic's first head of state and of government, respectively, they were highly regarded figures. Both men were critical of Lithuanian democracy, but had remained out of parliament, lecturing at the university in Kaunas until the 1926 election when their Nationalist Union (*Tautininkai*) won three seats. President Kazys Grinius (1866–1950) was not fooled by the conspirators' claims of an imminent communist coup, but he finally yielded to pressure to resign after Smetona swore to uphold the constitution.

The transfer of power proceeded peacefully and legally; on 19 December the parliament elected Smetona as president and subsequently confirmed Voldemaras as prime minister. The Socialists and Populists made the mistake of boycotting the session while the Christian Democrats threw in their lot with the conspirators because they desperately sought to oust the government which was rapidly reversing their policies. The Christian Democrats were confident that new elections would eventually return them to office. Smetona and Voldemaras, however, had no intention of relinquishing the reins of power. In April 1927 Smetona dissolved the parliament and the Christian Democratic ministers resigned from the government. The Christian Democrats only broke irrevocably with Smetona in November when they finally realised that he had no intention of holding elections.[13] From this point onwards, Lithuania can clearly be characterised as an authoritarian regime.

Parliamentary democracy came under threat in Estonia and Latvia as a result of the world economic depression, whose full force hit the Baltic states in 1931. The situation heightened political tensions as the parliamentary parties were unable to deal effectively with the economic crisis. The panacea appeared for many to be the establishment of a strong presidency. Päts had long pleaded for Estonia to introduce a presidency, but the issue became salient only when the Central League of Veterans of the Estonian War of Independence (known as the Vaps movement), initially a lobby group for veterans' interests, took up the cause. Led by the young, charismatic and ambitious lawyer Artur Sirk (1900–37), the Vaps movement became increasingly engaged in politics and took on the appearance of a fascist-type organisation. Their appeals for an end to political corruption and a renewal of the patriotic spirit of solidarity and national unity resonated with the public, making them the largest and most dynamic political force in Estonia by 1933. Like their inspiration, the Finnish Lapua movement, they brought pressure on the parliament to act. Within the space of little more than a year, three national referenda on constitutional amendments, proposing the introduction of a presidency, were conducted. The first two constitutional amendment bills were presented by the parliamentary parties and were championed by both Päts and Tõnisson. However, these were not radical enough for the Vaps and were also opposed by the Socialists, who feared an increase in executive power. After these failed, a third national referendum was held in October 1933 on the initiative of the Vaps movement (which had gathered the requisite number of citizens' signatures). Their constitutional amendment bill creating a strong presidency and reducing the powers and size of the parliament was approved by 73 per cent of the voters. As a result, new presidential and parliamentary elections were set for April 1934. Momentum appeared to be on the side of the Vaps who triumphed in the municipal elections in January 1934 as political campaigning reached an unprecedented level of intensity. However, on 12 March 1934 Prime Minister Päts and his fellow presidential candidate, retired General Laidoner, declared a state of emergency, arrested the leaders of the Vaps movement and postponed the elections. Päts justified his actions by claiming that they had saved democracy from the threat of fascism and prevented civil disorder, and he obtained the support of all the political parties in parliament for a six-month state of emergency. The Socialists genuinely feared the Vaps movement, while the other parties were relieved that a dangerous competitor had been eliminated.[14]

Two months later, Latvian Prime Minister Ulmanis emulated the events in Tallinn. Like Päts, Ulmanis advocated constitutional reform to give greater powers to the president, naturally seeing himself as the man best suited for the office. However, other political parties remained justifiably suspicious of his intentions. Their rejection of his proposed 'necessary' reform gave Ulmanis an excuse to portray himself as a patriotic statesman battling special interests, particularily those of the national minority parties, and a pretext for sweeping away the unresponsive parliament altogether. On 15 May 1934 Ulmanis declared a state of emergency. Ulmanis also justified his action as being necessary to counter the threat of extremist forces, although this was less plausible in the Latvian case.[15] The chief fascist organisation among Latvians, the Thunder Cross (*Pērkonkrusts*), was more radical than the Estonian Vaps but had much less popular appeal. Its leadership consisted primarily of university-educated Latvian young men whose frustration was channelled at the Germans and Jews who dominated the urban professions and commerce in Rīga. Ulmanis' main blow was actually directed against the left; among those arrested was Dr Pauls Kalniņš (1872–1945), the Socialist chairman of the *Saeima*. Päts and Ulmanis relied on the police, army and civil guard in carrying out their coups, both of which were bloodless and provoked little protest.

Once Smetona, Päts and Ulmanis had obtained power, they showed little inclination to relinquish it. Martial law, with its accompanying censorship and restrictions on civil liberties, was repeatedly extended and remained in force until 1940. Political parties were disbanded. The *Tautininkai* became the official state party in Lithuania. Päts created the Fatherland Union as a prop for his regime and successfully co-opted leading figures from other parties, while Ulmanis saw no need for any political organisation.

Smetona consolidated his power by promulgating a new constitution in May 1928, the main feature of which was a strong presidency with a seven-year term.[16] The president was no longer to be elected by parliament, but by an electoral college whose delegates were mainly appointed by the administration. Smetona was duly re-elected in 1931 and 1938. In 1929 Smetona dismissed the increasingly ambitious prime minister,

Voldemaras, whom he viewed correctly as a rival, and replaced him with his brother-in-law, economist Juozas Tūbelis (1882–1939).

Perhaps reflecting his background as a lawyer, Päts respected legal niceties to a greater extent than did Ulmanis. In 1937 Päts convened a national assembly to draft a new constitution which came into force in 1938. Although Päts claimed that this new constitution strode a middle path between the liberal 1920 constitution and the authoritarian 1933 constitution, in practice all the levers of power remained in his hands. Despite rigging the rules in his favour, Päts nevertheless allowed competitive parliamentary elections to be held in 1938 and the opposition obtained a significant number of seats. Ulmanis was the most unabashed dictator of the three – he did not permit any elections at all. Ulmanis was content to merge the offices of prime minister and president in his own person after President Alberts Kviesis' (1881–1944) term expired in 1936. Smetona, Päts and Ulmanis justified their continued dictatorship by claiming that the parliamentary system had failed and that the political parties were not mature enough for democracy.[17]

Apologists for the three regimes later observed that all around them in Central and Eastern Europe, with the exception of Finland and Czechoslovakia, democracies succumbed to dictatorships during the inter-war period. By the end of the 1930s parliamentarism appeared to be destined for the dustbin of history and new authoritarian models of rule of the fascist or communist type appeared to be the trend of the future. Furthermore, it was claimed that since the Baltic states were located in a tough neighbourhood between the two most brutal and aggressive totalitarian states, Nazi Germany and the Soviet Union, they required strong national leadership and unity. Although government instability was indeed endemic during the parliamentary era, these retroactive justifications overlook the remarkable achievements in state-building made during the 1920s. Had it not been for the personal ambitions of Smetona, Päts and Ulmanis, democracy could probably have survived.

The typical pattern in Central and Eastern Europe after the Nazi seizure of power in Germany in 1933 was for the conservative elites to form an authoritarian regime to neutralise the challenge from the populist radical right of the younger generation. Although these regimes borrowed some of the external trappings and style of fascism, they were certainly not 'fascist' as Soviet propaganda claimed. Following the fashion set by Italian dictator Benito Mussolini, they experimented with creating corporatist chambers to replace parliamentarism and political parties as representative bodies. Nevertheless, all three Baltic dictators explicitly rejected fascism and claimed to be developing a system of rule based not on foreign models but on indigenous needs, since liberal democracy was allegedly not suited to the national character. Smetona, Päts and Ulmanis saw themselves not as modern dictators but as paternalistic masters of the farmstead (which in their case was the entire country). Ulmanis unabashedly proclaimed himself *Tautas Vadonis*, leader of the nation. Smetona fancied himself as a philosopher, claiming to read Plato daily. The military was a key prop for their regimes and they lavished attention on their armies which were overstaffed with generals.

There was little opposition to the authoritarian regimes because Smetona, Päts and Ulmanis were widely respected as the fathers of their nations' statehood. Päts and Ulmanis had been the leaders of the agrarian parties which represented the largest segment of the population and they were also fortunate in their timing, seizing power just when the economy was beginning to recover from the low point of the depression. Their policies of state intervention – extending credit to farmers, encouraging industrial development and building public works – promoted economic growth. Few yearned for the return of what was perceived to be fractious, inefficient parliamentary democracy, and the desire for strong leadership remained popular. The authoritarian regimes appropriated many of the popular ideas of the radical right, championed affirmative action for the titular ethnic group, and were ardent promoters of the Estonian, Latvian and Lithuanian national cultures. The only notable opposition to the authoritarian regimes came from the underground radical right, who plotted against the government. These young nationalists were impatient with Smetona, Päts and Ulmanis, whom they saw as too tolerant of the national minorities and corruption and not strident enough in their authoritarianism. The most serious opposition to Smetona came from the younger members of his own Nationalist Union who, along with Voldemarists and the radical right Iron Wolf, regarded Smetona as too soft. Criticism of the authoritarian regime also originated from Catholic and Christian Democratic circles in Lithuania (the membership of various Catholic civil-society associations outnumbered those of state-sponsored nationalists),[18] left-wing socialists in Latvia and liberal intellectuals in the Estonian university town of Tartu. The only use of violent force by any of the three regimes occurred in Lithuania in 1935 when the suppression of a farmers' strike resulted in several deaths. After suffering foreign-policy humiliations at the end of the 1930s,[19] Smetona and Päts both made some limited concessions to the opposition by bringing a few representatives of the democratic era political parties into the government.

## ECONOMIC, SOCIAL AND CULTURAL PROGRESS

The most pressing question for the newly created states, resulting in the most far-reaching legislation, was land reform. The urgency of the issue is demonstrated by the fact that the constituent assemblies all enacted land reform even before they adopted the constitution and the Estonian Constituent Assembly had already adopted the land reform act in October 1919 while the war of independence still raged. Land reform legislation was adopted in Latvia a year later (September 1920) and in Lithuania in April 1922. During the wars of independence the Estonian, Latvian and Lithuanian provisional governments had promised land to those who fought for the national cause. Ownership of their own family farmstead was the dream for most Estonian and Latvian peasants, who harboured centuries-old resentment of the Baltic Germans whose ancestors had 'stolen' their land. The redistribution of land also served the purpose of undermining support for the Bolsheviks.

In the pre-war Baltic provinces, manors possessed almost half of the land, and the average size of an estate was over two thousand hectares, a vastly larger area than the average peasant farm of less than 30 hectares. The disparities were not as great in Lithuania where manors possessed about one-quarter of the land and their average size was only one-fifth of that in the Baltic provinces.[20] The republics expropriated the lands of the large estate-owners and the Church, and established a state land fund for the redistribution of the land among the peasantry. Although the broad outlines of the land reform were similar, there were significant differences between the three countries. The Estonian and Latvian reforms allowed estate-owners to retain only 50 hectares, while the Lithuanian reform was less radical, allowing estate-owners to retain up to 150 hectares of land (initially 80 hectares). In Estonia 94 per cent of estate land was confiscated, in Latvia it was 84 per cent and in Lithuania it was 77 per cent. The compensation provided to the former land-owners was only a fraction of the real value of their property and the Latvians decided not to grant any compensation at all. The national governments awarded choice properties to those who were decorated for bravery in the independence wars or for outstanding services to the state, although the vast majority of peasants who wanted land received a plot. As a result of the redistribution, the total increase of peasant–owned land in Estonia was 69 per cent, in Latvia it was 54 per cent and in Lithuania 17 per cent. The peasants were given the land at well below the market value and allowed several decades to repay the state loan.[21]

The redistribution of land had major socio-economic consequences: overnight an Estonian, Latvian and Lithuanian agrarian middle class came into being. Prior to the land reform the majority of the rural population had been landless. In Latvia, 61 per cent of the rural population was landless in 1920; by the end of the reform in 1937 only 18 per cent were landless. The plots of redistributed land were relatively small: the average size of the 54,500 new farms created in Latvia, for example, was 17 hectares.[22] The land reform in the Baltic states was more radical, far-reaching, equitable and successful than in the other new states of eastern Europe which faced similar problems. As a result of the land redistribution, the Baltic states became among the most egalitarian societies in Europe. After the reforms, large landholdings of over a hundred hectares accounted for only 1 per cent of the total landholdings in the Baltic states.[23] The economic power of the Baltic German nobles in Estonia and Latvia and that of the polonised nobles in Lithuania was broken, and the major socio-economic antagonism which communists could exploit was eliminated.[24] The appearance of the Lithuanian and Latgalian countryside also changed radically: village organisation along the open-field system (similar to the Russian *mir*) disappeared as individual homesteads were established.

The years of independence witnessed the remarkable growth and success of an impressive network of consumers' societies, dairy cooperatives and credit cooperatives, which compensated for the fact that small family farms were not the most efficient means of production. The new states had been established by men who represented the peasants and their basic goal was to end the dominance of the large land-owners. Agriculture was not regarded as simply one sector of the economy: farmers were considered to be the backbone of the nation. State protection of agricultural producers was particularly notable under the authoritarian regimes of Päts and Ulmanis, for whom farming had a mythical and sentimental importance. Export was concentrated into central cooperative unions under state supervision.

The long years of war left physical devastation in their wake. Only Belgium suffered greater destruction than Latvia in World War I.[25] During the war, factories were evacuated to Russia from where they were not later returned. The rapid industrialisation of the Baltic provinces prior to 1914 had been geared to the Russian imperial market. In the early 1920s there was hope that the Baltic states could serve as an economic bridge between Russia and Europe, but by the mid-1920s these hopes had evaporated. Soviet policy frustrated the desire of the Balts to resume export to their primary market in Russia. Latvia, the most industrialised of the Baltic states, was the hardest hit. The Baltic states were thus forced to reorientate their exports from Russia to Western Europe, where their chief markets were Germany and Great Britain. These exports no longer consisted of industrial goods; they were largely agricultural products such as bacon and butter. Flax and timber also remained important. The new focus was on developing an efficient, modern agriculture on the Danish model. The Baltic states remained rural societies: 77 per cent of the population in Lithuania and 60 per cent in Estonia were engaged in the agricultural sector.[26] Latvia suffered a remarkable reversal in its industrialisation and urbanisation trajectory because of the devastation visited upon it during the war: the percentage of the population working in the agricultural sector actually increased from 59 to 66 per cent.[27]

The worldwide economic depression of the early 1930s was a significant factor in the advent of authoritarian regimes in Estonia and Latvia. Great Britain's decision to abandon the gold standard in 1931 had a sharply negative effect on the Estonian and Latvian currencies and on the value of exports. This resulted in a rise in unemployment, a drop in the states' revenues, and a growth in farmers' indebtedness. After the depression of the early 1930s the Baltic authoritarian regimes began, as elsewhere in Europe, to support more state intervention in the economy, particularly investment in industry. There were some notable advances in innovation: Walter Zapp (1905–2003) invented the Minox subminiature camera, which went into production in Rīga in 1938 and later became a favourite tool of Cold War spies.

With the achievement of independent statehood, Lithuanian, Latvian and Estonian cultures were, for the first time, given state support. Their native languages became the official means of communication for the purposes of government and education. The ability to express oneself freely in one's native language brought about rapid developments in art, music and literature. Amateur theatre groups evolved into professional organisations, performing newly written works by local playwrights as well as the international classical repertoire. National museums, art academies and musical conservatories were established. National culture and the arts reached a new level of maturity, exemplified by the works of Lithuanian writer Vincas Krėvė-Mickevičius (1882–1954), Estonian novelist Anton Hansen Tammsaare (1878–1940) and Latvian landscape painter Vilhelms Purvītis (1872–1945). Ballet and opera flourished, particularly in Rīga where top Russian and German artists worked. The 1920s were also pioneering years for radio broadcasting and cinema.

The network of schools at all levels was expanded dramatically. At the end of World War I, the only functioning university in the Baltic states was the *Landesuniversität zu Dorpat*, which became the Estonian-language University of Tartu in 1919. The Riga Polytechnical Institute was transformed into the University of Latvia in the same year. The situation was most difficult in Lithuania because Wilno University remained under Polish jurisdiction and so a completely new university had to be founded at Kaunas in 1922. It was a remarkable achievement for these overwhelmingly peasant nations to establish institutions of higher education in their own native languages which, at the time, were lacking scientific terminology. The thirst for higher education was great – by the 1930s Latvia and Estonia had among the highest number of students per capita in Europe enrolled at university.[28]

In creating their own distinct national cultures, the Estonians and Latvians aimed to reduce the dominance of German influence, and the Lithuanians tried to diminish Polish influence. They did this by deliberately reorienting themselves to Western European cultures, particularly French and English. The building up of national cultural identities also inspired large numbers of Estonians and Latvians to change their German-sounding surnames to native ones. As elsewhere in Europe, nationalising states encouraged the standardisation of national languages and the moulding of peasants into Estonians, Latvians and Lithuanians. The use of peripheral languages or dialects – that of the Võros and Setos in Estonia, the Latgalians and Livs in Latvia, and the Lithuanians who had lived for centuries under Prussian rule in the Klaipėda area – was discouraged.

One of the first challenges for the new republics was to reintegrate the hundreds of thousands of residents who had been displaced by the series of conflicts. The peace treaties with Soviet Russia provided for those Estonians, Latvians and Lithuanians whose abode was in Russia voluntarily to resettle in their ancestral homeland. Additionally, there was also an influx of Russian refugees fleeing the violence and terror of the civil war in their homeland.

Estonia was the most homogeneous of the three states: the titular ethnic group comprised 88.2 per cent of the total population of 1,130,000 in Estonia (according to the 1934 census), 83.9 per cent of the 2,030,000 in Lithuania (1923 census)[29] and 75.5 per cent of the 1,950,000 in Latvia (1935 census).[30]

Although the Baltic Germans in Estonia and Latvia were the ethnic group whose status declined most sharply, they nevertheless remained

**Table 1**  Major national minorities (percentage) in the inter-war Baltic states[31]

| Ethnic group | Estonia (1934) | Latvia (1935) | Lithuania (1923) |
|---|---|---|---|
| Russians | 8.5 | 10.6 | 2.7 |
| Germans | 1.5 | 3.2 | 1.4 |
| Jews | 0.4 | 4.8 | 7.6 |
| Poles | 0.1 | 2.5 | 3.2 |

the wealthiest segment of the population. Many of those who could not adjust to the abrupt change from being the privileged ruling elite to simply a 'minority' – a term they found insulting – emigrated to Germany. The Baltic Germans were the most highly organised national minority in Estonia and Latvia – their political party always managed to obtain the maximum possible parliamentary representation corresponding to their proportion of the population. Baltic Germans were also active on a pan-European level: Paul Schiemann (1876–1944) and Ewald Ammende (1892–1936) were key figures in establishing and leading the Nationalities' Congress in Geneva.[32]

Conversely, Russians – the largest minority in Estonia and Latvia – were the least active politically. Unlike the wealthy, urban and highly educated German community, the bulk of the Russians were poor peasants living in the eastern borderlands, although there was also a notable community of Russian civil war refugees, particularly in Rīga. This latter group contributed to the success of the Rīga Russian-language paper *Segodnya* (Today) which was the most professional media enterprise in the Baltic states and enjoyed a wide readership elsewhere in Europe.[33]

Jews were the largest minority in Lithuania (7.6 per cent of the population), but the highest concentration of Jews, 44,000, lived in Rīga – almost half of the 95,000 Jews in Latvia. In contrast, the Jewish community in Estonia was tiny, just over 4000 people. The Jewish communities were not homogeneous, but were split along religious and political lines, with the major groups being the Zionists, the religiously Orthodox, and the politically active Socialists. At the same time, there was serious disagreement in the community over whether Yiddish (favoured by secular Jews) or Hebrew (favoured by religious Jews and Zionists) should be used in schooling. Several Latvian and Lithuanian Zionists later became leading figures in the founding of the state of Israel. A vibrant Jewish intellectual life continued also in Polish-ruled Vilnius, the shining example being the Yiddish Scientific Institute (YIVO) established in 1925.

Initially, Lithuanian policy towards national minorities was quite liberal, partly in the vain hope that they would strengthen Lithuania's claim to Vilnius. The Jews were granted cultural autonomy, their highest organ being the National Council, and until 1924 the government even included a minister for Jewish affairs (as well as one for Belarusian affairs). Although the Jewish National Council was dissolved in 1924, Jewish religious and cultural rights continued to be respected.[34]

One of the greatest achievements in inter-war Europe for the protection of national minorities was the 1925 Estonian cultural autonomy law, recognised at the time as one of the most progressive in the world. Its key innovation was the idea that autonomy should based on the individual, rather than on territory, as in previous European practice.[35] The Estonian cultural autonomy law, drafted mainly by Baltic German parliamentary deputy Werner Hasselblatt (1890–1958), catered to the specific needs of the Baltic Germans and the Jews, who chiefly resided in the towns and intermingled with the majority population.[36] The law allowed national minorities to establish cultural councils with the power to collect taxes from their members. Every citizen could determine his or her own ethnic identity and voluntarily register with the cultural council whose primary function was to administer schooling in the mother tongue. The other significant national minorities in Estonia – the Russians and the Swedes (the latter formed 0.7 per cent of the population) – lived mainly in compact rural areas and could therefore govern their own affairs simply through control of elected district councils where they formed a majority of the population. Although Latvia never enacted a cultural autonomy law, in practice it allowed educational autonomy similar to that in Estonia. Again, it was the Baltic Germans who advanced the idea and realised it most fully. The Baltic Germans even managed to run a private university in Rīga, the Herder Institute.

The onset of the authoritarian regime in Lithuania resulted in policies which were less liberal toward the national minorities. The Nationalist regime's passionate rhetoric against the Polish seizure of Vilnius exacerbated the situation of the Polish minority in Lithuania. The advent of authoritarian regimes in Estonia and Latvia did not bring any radical departures in terms of policy towards the minorities, although it strengthened existing trends towards affirmative action in favour of the formerly underrepresented majority. The national minorities were alarmed by rising nationalism, but they knew that Smetona, Päts, and Ulmanis were personally more favourably inclined towards them than almost any other leading Lithuanian, Estonian and Latvian politician and were grateful that they thwarted the rise of the extreme right. The minority most distressed by the changes implicit in the growth of national cultures were the Baltic Germans. They resented the changing of names of towns and streets, and the fact that, in Latvia, proper names had to be written in the Latvian style. The loss of privileges, such as the Baltic German congregation losing its possession of Rīga Cathedral, also rankled. In the 1930s, Nazism emanating from the Third Reich proved increasingly attractive for Baltic Germans and the Germans in Lithuania's Klaipėda district, especially for the younger generation. Nevertheless, there were also positive developments: a Chair of Jewish Studies was established at Tartu University in 1934, the only one of its kind in Eastern Europe. Some Jews escaping persecution in the Third Reich found refuge in the Baltic states.

The treatment of minorities in the Baltic states was in stark contrast to the fate of Estonian and Latvian communities in Soviet Russia who were the target of ethnic cleansing during the Great Terror. Although the precise figure will probably never be known, at least 35,000 ethnic Estonians and Latvians were killed in the 1938 secret police operation against 'enemy nations'.[37] Old Bolsheviks who had reached the top echelons of power in the USSR, such as Latvian Jānis Rudzutaks (1887–1938), the deputy chairman of the Council of People's Commissars (deputy prime minister) and Politburo member, and Jānis Bērziņš (1889–1938), the chief of Soviet military intelligence (the GRU), were executed during Soviet dictator Joseph Stalin's purges of 1937–8.


IN SEARCH OF SECURITY

The newly independent Baltic states sought to secure their place in the international system. They had high hopes of the newly created League of Nations, with its collective security guarantee of taking action against any aggression towards its member states. The new 'border states' between Soviet Russia and Germany immediately sought ways to enhance their security. While many grand schemes for smaller or larger regional blocs were mooted, an alliance of the former subjects of the Romanov Empire from Helsinki to Warsaw appeared feasible. However, the Vilnius dispute undermined all efforts to establish an effective Baltic league by making it impossible to include both Lithuania and Poland in the same alliance. Lithuania's northern neighbours preferred Poland, with its vastly superior military power, as their partner. In 1922, Finnish, Estonian, Latvian and Polish foreign ministers reached an agreement on an alliance, only to founder on the opposition of the Finnish parliament. The Finns did not want to risk being dragged into war by their southern neighbours and began instead to pursue a Scandinavian orientation.[38] Only the minimum version – a defence alliance between just Estonia and Latvia – was eventually concluded in 1923. A supplementary proposed customs union never materialised.

Of the three Baltic states, Lithuania's predicament was the least enviable. The question of Vilnius, which was named as the capital in the constitution, determined Lithuania's foreign policy. The League of Nations appointed former Belgian foreign minister Paul Hymans to mediate the Vilnius dispute, but there was simply no way to reconcile the sides. Hymans' plan for a Polish–Lithuanian federation with Swiss-style cantons was unacceptable to the Lithuanians. The Poles had might and important allies on their side and by 1923 the League had given up hope of reaching a settlement and accepted the status quo. Lithuania remained alone in rejecting Polish sovereignty over Vilnius; only the USSR recognised the Lithuanian claim. Lithuania maintained the rhetoric but was powerless to undertake any action. When the Lithuanian premier, Voldemaras, raised the issue at a session of the League of Nations in Geneva in 1927, the Polish leader, Marshal Piłsudski, reputedly told him bluntly: 'There's only one thing I want to know: do you want war or peace?'[39] The border between Lithuania and Poland was one of the flashpoints of inter-war Europe where tensions remained high.[40] Transportation and communications did not function across the border, and border guards on either side were shot at in various incidents over the years.

Lithuania was initially more successful with its other territorial claim: the Memel (Klaipėda) region, the northernmost tip of East Prussia which had belonged to Germany but which had after the Great War been placed under a League of Nations mandate administered by France. In 1923 the Lithuanians followed the Polish example on Vilnius, and staged a military takeover of the Memel region. The great powers yielded to Lithuania's *fait accompli* after the latter's acceptance of a statute drafted by the League guaranteeing the rights of Memel's majority German population. Lithuania gained an economically vital seaport, but failed to win the loyalty of the local population.

Lithuania relied on Germany and the Soviet Union to balance Poland. However, after the rise of Adolf Hitler to power in Germany in 1933, Lithuania found itself hard-pressed to exercise control over the Klaipėda region. After Poland signed non-aggression treaties with both Germany and USSR in 1934, Lithuania found itself isolated and therefore revised

**Map 6** The Baltic states between the world wars

its previously negative attitude towards Baltic cooperation. At this point, the USSR was more amenable to the idea of Baltic cooperation since it had a 'gentleman's agreement' with Lithuania that the latter would inform the USSR of discussions of 'mutual interest' within the Baltic Entente.[41] Finally, in 1934, the Treaty of Cooperation and Friendship between Lithuania, Latvia and Estonia – the Baltic Entente – was signed. Agreement was reached only because the 'special cases' of Vilnius and Klaipėda were excluded. The main result was diplomatic and cultural cooperation: for example, half-yearly conferences of foreign ministers. In retrospect, historians have been highly critical of the failure of the Baltic states to create an effective alliance. However, Germany, Poland and particularly the Soviet Union did everything possible to prevent the establishment of the Baltic Entente and subsequently continued to undermine its functioning.

Baltic co-operation was hampered by differing perceptions of threat: the Estonians saw Soviet Russia as the only potential enemy; the Latvians were equally worried about the USSR and Germany; for the Lithuanians, the USSR was its sole supporter against Poland, the country which the Latvians and Estonians viewed as a vital ally. Lithuania was the only Baltic state which did not share a border with the USSR and also the only one with a border with Germany. The Soviet Union viewed Baltic cooperation as a threat and used the conflict between Lithuania and Poland over Vilnius to impede it. Moscow used Lithuania to counteract the influence of Poland in the region. Lithuania was the first country to sign a mutual assistance treaty with the USSR in 1926. The Soviet leadership even supported Smetona's coup d'état in 1926 because the Lithuanian Nationalists pursued the most uncompromising anti-Polish policy.[42] For their part, Smetona and the Nationalists had accepted Soviet funding because they believed that only Moscow could help Lithuania regain Vilnius.

The security of the Baltic states deteriorated drastically in the second half of the 1930s. The expansionist policies of Nazi Germany and Fascist Italy undermined the League of Nations upon whose collective security guarantee the Baltic states had placed their hopes. The Anglo-German naval agreement of 1935 effectively left the Baltic Sea under German control and extinguished any hope of British assistance in a future crisis. Poland sought to reduce the ring of enemies around her. After a border incident in March 1938 when a Polish guard was killed, the Polish government presented an ultimatum to Lithuania to establish diplomatic relations. The Lithuanian government was forced to accept a Polish diplomatic representative in Kaunas, thus indirectly recognising Kaunas rather than Vilnius as the capital. This humiliation was soon followed by another: on 20 March 1939 the German foreign minister, Joachim von Ribbentrop, threatened military action against Lithuania if it did not immediate return the Klaipėda region to Germany. Kaunas quickly acquiesced since Hitler had demonstrated Germany's deadly intent in occupying Czechoslovakia five days earlier.[43]

As anxiety over a potential war in Europe escalated at the end of the 1930s, the Balts, following the Scandinavian example, sought refuge in declarations of neutrality (Estonia and Latvia in December 1938 and Lithuania in January 1939). Although they had signed non-aggression treaties with the USSR (Lithuania in 1926; Estonia and Latvia in 1932) and with Germany in the spring of 1939, their declarations of neutrality would not deter these powerful neighbours.

# 6

## Between Anvil and Hammer (1939–1953)

The rise of Stalin in the USSR and Hitler in Germany resulted in the destruction of Baltic independence. The 1940s were a tragic decade for the Baltic states. They suffered catastrophic population losses, during both war and peace, under three successive foreign occupation regimes: that of the Soviet Union in 1940–1, Nazi Germany during 1941–4 and the USSR again from 1944. Although the Baltic countries were non-belligerents in World War II, Estonian, Latvian and Lithuanian men had to fight and die in the military uniforms of their two enemies. The heaviest losses were borne by the civilian population, who were targeted on ideological grounds: the Soviet regime deported 'class enemies' to prison camps in Russia; the Nazis exterminated the Jews on the basis of race. After the war ended, armed resistance to the Soviet regime continued in the forests, but was dealt a fatal blow with the mass deportations of 1949, part of the campaign to collectivise farming.

SOVIET ANNEXATION

As storm clouds gathered over Europe and rumours of impending war grew in 1939, Soviet leader Joseph Stalin negotiated with the British and French on the one hand and Nazi Germany on the other. Stalin had the luxury of deciding which of the 'capitalist imperialist' powers could offer the USSR the better deal. One of the principal sticking-points in the negotiations with the British and French was Stalin's demand to allow the Red Army to traverse the territory of neighbouring neutral countries: the Baltic states. Hitler had fewer reservations since he was in a hurry to invade Poland and wanted at all costs to avoid a two-front war as in World War I. On 23 August 1939 the world was shocked to learn that the two ideological arch-enemies had concluded a non-aggression treaty, often referred to as the Molotov–Ribbentrop Pact after the foreign ministers who signed the agreement. The treaty included a secret protocol dividing Eastern Europe into spheres of influence: Finland, Estonia, Latvia, eastern Poland and Romanian Bessarabia (Moldova) fell under the Soviet sphere, while western and central Poland and initially also Lithuania were allotted to Germany.

After World War II, the Soviet Union justified the treaty with Nazi Germany and its subsequent annexation of the Baltic states as necessary to buy time to prepare for a German attack by moving its defences forward. However, the USSR acted as a loyal ally to Nazi Germany for almost two years, supplying it with vital resources, and the offensive nature of Soviet military plans suggest that Stalin had expected Germany and the Western capitalist powers to exhaust each other, as in World War I. Afterwards, the Red Army would have been poised to spread 'Socialist revolution' westwards across the fatally weakened continent.[1]

Germany attacked Poland on 1 September 1939, triggering World War II. Hitler prompted the Lithuanians to use the opportunity to seize Vilnius from Poland, but they did not succumb to the temptation. Instead, Lithuania accepted an influx of 30,000 Polish refugees. The USSR invaded Poland on 17 September and immediately occupied Vilnius. After having successfully cooperated in destroying Poland, the USSR and Nazi Germany revised their pact on 28 September by trading Lithuania for a larger share of Poland.[2] Thus all three Baltic states came into the Soviet sphere and Stalin had fewer Poles to worry about. Stalin had wasted no time in securing his part of the bargain. He first set his sights on Estonia. Moscow created the pretext of a Polish submarine which had eluded the Nazi onslaught and found refuge in neutral Tallinn harbour. The Estonian authorities had interned the vessel, but it escaped and eventually joined the British navy. The Kremlin claimed that Estonia was unable to control its territorial waters and on 24 September demanded the immediate stationing of Soviet army, navy, and air force bases at strategic locations across Estonia. The Estonian delegation in Moscow was given only a few days to comply. The ultimatum was backed by an intimidating show of Soviet military force, and the Red Army was ordered to be prepared to invade Estonia on 29 September. The Estonian government caved in to Soviet pressure on 28 September, having secured a promise of non-interference in Estonia's internal affairs.

An almost identical ultimatum to station Red Army troops on her territory was issued to Latvia the following week. Molotov bluntly told the Latvian foreign minister, Vilhelms Munters (1898–1967), that, like Peter the Great, the USSR needed ice-free ports on the Baltic Sea.[3] Latvia bowed to Soviet demands on 5 October. The Lithuanian situation differed as Moscow used a carrot as well as a stick. As the USSR now occupied the eastern portion of Poland, Stalin offered Lithuania the return of Vilnius.[4] The agreement with Lithuania was signed on 10 October. The USSR also demanded territorial concessions from Finland, but she refused to be bullied. The Red Army invaded Finland in November and the Finns resisted heroically in the Winter War until March 1940 when they sued for peace. Finland was forced to cede more territory than Moscow had originally demanded, but retained her independence. Many Balts later bitterly regretted that their leaders had not acted as resolutely as the Finns. At the time, however, Baltic leaders clung to the naïve illusion that, by not offering any resistance to the Red Army, their nations could somehow avoid the devastation of war.[5] As the Nazi and Soviet fleets controlled the Baltic Sea, there was no hope for aid from abroad. Mobilising a common front of the three Baltic states was not considered to be a realistic option.

On 18 October, the same day as the Red Army entered Estonia, the first ship to transport Baltic Germans, who were answering Hitler's call to 'return home' to the German *Reich*, departed from Tallinn harbour. The resettlement of 14,000 Germans from Estonia and 52,000 from Latvia was hurriedly accomplished by spring 1940, although most were actually resettled on conquered Polish territory.[6] A second, smaller round of resettlement took place in early 1941 after which only a few hundred, mainly elderly, people remained.[7] Thus ended the history of the proud community which had been the ruling elite for seven hundred years. At the same time in early 1941, 52,000 Germans from Lithuania, mainly farmers inhabiting areas adjacent to East Prussia, were repatriated.

Until the spring of 1940, the Soviet bases' agreement regime functioned correctly (leaving aside the fact that the Soviets used airbases in neutral Estonia to bomb Finland; the Estonians did not dare to protest), although Moscow continually made new demands to expand the bases and bring in supplementary personnel. The Balts strenuously avoided any actions that Moscow could possibly consider provocative. After Hitler's dramatic military successes in Western Europe in spring 1940, however, it was only a question of time before the USSR increased pressure on them. As the world's attention was riveted on the German army entering

Paris, Stalin acted. As in 1939, Moscow isolated one state, this time in reverse order, with Lithuania first on 14 June and Latvia and Estonia two days later. Stalin's ultimata demanded an immediate increase in the number of Red Army troops in the Baltic states and the formation of 'friendly' governments. Three Soviet armies were prepared to move against the Baltic states and a total air, land and sea blockade of the Baltic states was imposed.[8] The ultimata had been preceded by the absurd accusation that the Lithuanians had kidnapped Soviet soldiers who had gone missing from their bases. Soviet newspapers accused the Balts of sympathy towards the British and hostility to their ally Nazi Germany, and alleged that the Balts were secretly forming a military alliance aimed against the Soviet Union.[9] Pressure was purposefully escalated: a passenger plane en route from Tallinn to Helsinki was shot down by Soviet fighters and a Latvian border guard post was attacked. This time, the Balts were given not days but only hours to decide their fate. In 1940 there could be no question of serious military resistance because the Soviet troops already stationed in bases across the Baltic states outnumbered the regular Baltic armies.

Only the Lithuanian president, Smetona, favoured resistance, but his government and military commanders did not support his position. Smetona fled the country after deputising his prime minister, Antanas Merkys (1887–1955). The leadership of the three Baltic states meekly acquiesced to Soviet demands without issuing any protest. In fact, they went even further than required by restricting movement at borders to ensure that nationals would not flee, misinforming their own embassies abroad about the true nature of the situation, and not making preparations for governments-in-exile. The Red Army's entry itself took place in an orderly manner as the Baltic governments did their utmost to prevent any incidents and maintain a façade of normality. The military occupation of the Baltic states was completed within a few days (by 21 June). Magnus Ilmjärv has aptly characterised this as 'silent submission'.[10]

There is perhaps some truth in the assertion that regime type explains the difference in behaviour between the Baltic states and Finland in 1939–40. In the Baltic authoritarian regimes only a small circle of individuals made decisions, whereas in Finland the views of the democratically elected parliament could not be ignored. In any case, the authoritarian regimes did enable a smooth transition to Soviet rule by keeping their own people uninformed or intentionally misinformed of the gravity of the threat to their independence. The Germans advised Baltic governments to agree to the Soviet demands, but intimated that they viewed Soviet control as temporary. Baltic leaders hoped that they could break free of the Soviet grip when Germany eventually turned her arms against the USSR. They calculated that by fulfilling all Soviet demands and avoiding any potential provocations in the meantime, they might be able to hold their nations and institutions intact.[11]

As soon as the Red Army moved in, street demonstrations were organised by communist activists, supported by Soviet armoured vehicles, to pressure the governments to resign. These events would later be characterised by the Soviet regime as 'socialist revolutions'. To orchestrate the formation of pro-Soviet governments, senior Communist Party officials were immediately dispatched from Russia to the Baltic capitals: Leningrad party boss and Soviet Politburo member Andrei Zhdanov (1896–1948) to Tallinn; Andrei Vyshinsky (1883–1954), who gained international notoriety presiding over Stalin's show trials in the 1930s, to Rīga; the Soviet deputy commissar for foreign affairs, Vladimir Dekanozov (1898–1953), to Kaunas. These three men were Stalin's proconsuls, the real rulers of the Baltic states, during the next two months. They followed a plan roughly similar to that first devised by Zhdanov for implementation in Eastern Poland. Their first task was to determine the composition of the new Estonian, Latvian and Lithuanian cabinets. The new pro-Soviet governments initially contained only a few communists, not only in order to create a false impression but also simply because there was a dearth of Communist Party members in the Baltic states. The new governments were headed by left-wing intellectuals: the Estonian physician and poet Johannes Vares (1890–1946), Latvian bacteriology professor Augusts Kirhenšteins (1872–1963) and Lithuanian journalist Justas Paleckis (1899–1980). The new regime also reassured the anxious public by persuading some highly regarded progressive figures such as Tartu University history professor Hans Kruus (1891–1976) and Kaunas University literature professor Vincas Krėvė-Mickevičius (1882–1954) to join the governments.

The Kremlin lacked the personnel or cadres to administer its new realm. At the end of 1939, there were 500 Communist Party members in Latvia and fewer than 150 in Estonia. The Lithuanian Communist Party was the largest, with over a third of its 1400 members being Jewish.[12] The leading Baltic Communists had remained in Soviet Russia after failing to obtain power in the wars of independence, but almost all of them were executed in Stalin's purges of 1937–8. Ironically, the few original Baltic Bolsheviks who survived were those who spent the inter-war years in 'bourgeois' prisons in their home countries. After June 1940, opportunists swelled the ranks of the Baltic Communist Parties. Viewing Lithuanians, Latvians and Estonians as 'counter-revolutionary' nations, Stalin deliberately empowered the Russian and Jewish minorities.[13] Nevertheless, Moscow still had to send thousands of Communist Party cadres from the USSR in order to control the new domains.

The next act in the synchronised Soviet script was 'dechoiced' general elections which took place simultaneously in Estonia, Latvia, and Lithuania on 14–15 July, even though they had been announced only ten days earlier. The Communist Parties drafted the officially approved electoral slates, titled the Estonian, Latvian and Lithuanian Unions of Working People all others who attempted to register as candidates were eliminated from the ballot. The ballot papers contained only one name, and although voting was mandatory, participation figures had to be falsified to show total support – some districts reported a turnout of 100 per cent. At their first session on 21 July, the new People's Assemblies unanimously voted in favour of joining the USSR, although that possibility had not even been mentioned during electoral campaigns. As Presidents Päts and Ulmanis were no longer needed to sign decrees authorising the dismantlement of the state's institutions, they were deported to the USSR, where they later died in captivity. Smetona's flight allowed the Soviets to act more directly in Lithuania: arrests and deportation to the USSR of Lithuanian political leaders had already started before the elections. The new legislatures sent delegations to Moscow to present their 'applications' to join the USSR. The USSR Supreme Soviet granted their 'requests' and during the first week of August, Lithuania, Latvia and Estonia, one after another, became the fourteenth, fifteenth and sixteenth Soviet Socialist Republics respectively.

After incorporation into the USSR, the Baltic marionette legislatures speedily and without any debate adopted new constitutions modelled on the Soviet system and renamed themselves the 'Supreme Soviets'. The USSR Politburo approved the drafts of the Estonian, Latvian, and Lithuanian constitutions on 22 August.[14] The Baltic governments were re-formed on the Soviet model as Councils of People's Commissars. The fellow-travellers and technical experts of the June governments were now replaced by an executive consisting of Communist Party members approved by Moscow. The initial three prime ministers were shifted to the ceremonial post of Chairman of the Presidium of the republican Supreme Soviet and trusted communists were appointed in their stead: Mečys Gedvilas (1901–81) in Lithuania, Vilis Lācis (1904–66) in Latvia, and Johannes Lauristin (1899–1941) in Estonia. After Stalin's plenipotentiaries had accomplished their task and departed, real power did not revert to the governments but to the First Secretary of the Communist Party: Antanas Sniečkus (1903–74) in Lithuania, Jānis Kalnbērziņš (1893–1986) in Latvia, and Karl Säre (1903–43?) in Estonia. However, the Baltic Communist Parties themselves were now formally subordinated to the All-Union Communist Party.

Sovietisation had already begun before the annexation and proceeded rapidly: in July 1940 banks and large industrial enterprises were nationalised. Private homes larger than 170 m$^2$ (or 220 m$^2$ in the big cities) were nationalised. The maximum amount of land which could be retained by an individual farmer was restricted to 30 hectares. Confiscated land was redistributed in plots no larger than 10 hectares to landless peasants. These plots, however, were too small to be economically viable and served only to stoke up resentment and class conflict in the countryside, helping to pave the way for later collectivisation.

The wages of workers and civil servants were raised, but the standard of living plummeted precipitously, particularly after November when absurdly low exchange rates with the Soviet rouble were set for the Baltic currencies, effectively destroying the people's savings. Goods which were formerly readily available disappeared from shop shelves. Four months later, the *kroon*, *lats* and *litas* were withdrawn from circulation entirely.

The national armies, after a purging of senior officers, were incorporated into the Red Army as the 22nd Estonian, 24th Latvian and 29th Lithuanian territorial rifle corps. A Soviet Baltic Military District with its headquarters in Rīga was formed in 1940. All sorts of voluntary organisations such as the YMCA, Salvation Army and Girl Guides were forcibly disbanded. In most respects, the former civil society was destroyed. The press, radio, literature and the arts were heavily censored and inundated with the Stalinist cult of personality, ceaselessly praising Stalin as the 'great teacher', 'brilliant genius of humanity', and so forth.

The predominant characteristic of the Stalinist system was terror. Its main instrument was the NKVD (Peoples' Commissariat of Internal Affairs) which included the regime's dreaded secret police with its vast powers of surveillance, arrest and detention. While initial arrests and deportations targeted political leaders, senior civil servants, police and military officers, entrepreneurs, clergy and Russian émigrés, the terror spread to include all walks of life – just about anyone could be accused of being an 'enemy of the people'. Terror reached a climax in the early hours of 14 June 1941 when simultaneous mass deportations were carried out in all three countries. Those on the NKVD list were woken in the middle of the night and given a couple of hours to pack a suitcase. The families were then taken to the railway station where the men were separated from the women and children. The transit to Siberia lasted weeks. The freight cars were crowded, there was little food or water and many did not survive the long journey. 10,000 people from Estonia, 15,000 from Latvia and 18,000 from Lithuania were deported in this operation.[15] Most of the men were sentenced to 25 years' imprisonment for 'counterrevolutionary activity' according to the notorious all-encompassing Article 58 of the Soviet Penal Code, which also applied retroactively to all those who had fought for liberty and opposed the Bolsheviks in 1918. Few survived more than a year or two in the inhumane conditions of the Soviet Gulag (forced labour camps).

## NAZI *OSTLAND*

On 22 June 1941 Hitler launched a surprise attack against the USSR. German troops overran Lithuania in a matter of days, Latvia in a couple of weeks, and Estonia by September. The German invasion gave hope for relief from Soviet terror and the restoration of statehood. Baltic men formed guerrilla bands, mostly based on the pre-war civil guard and those who fled to the woods in the wake of the Soviet deportations. Fighting was most intense between Estonian partisans and Soviet 'destruction battalions' since the German advance stalled for several weeks in southern Estonia. The evacuation of Soviet personnel from Tallinn in August by the Soviet Baltic Fleet resulted in heavy loss of life (more than fifteen thousand people – one of the largest death tolls in naval history) as the convoy, attacked from the air and shelled by coastal artillery batteries, ploughed directly through a minefield laid by Finnish and German navies in the Gulf of Finland near Juminda.

As a result of the activities of the Lithuanian Activists' Front (LAF), headed by Colonel Kazys Škirpa (1895–1979), the Lithuanian ambassador who had remained in Berlin in 1940, the Lithuanians were best prepared for regime change. The LAF organised underground cells and prepared for liberation from the USSR. On 23 June, the day after the beginning of the German invasion, the LAF announced the establishment of a provisional government which would restore the institutions of the pre-war republic. The resistance organised by the LAF against the Soviet regime could be characterised as a mass national uprising. When the

German army marched into Kaunas on 25 June, they found the city already under the control of the Lithuania Provisional Government. Škirpa was slated to head the government but was detained in Berlin by the Germans. In his stead, Professor Juozas Ambrazevičius (1903–74), the minister of education, took the reins and proceeded to restore the pre-war Lithuanian administration. The Germans were caught by surprise by the establishment of the Lithuanian Provisional Government, but they nevertheless initially tolerated it. The provisional government had to cooperate with the Germans to function, but was unwilling to collaborate as simply a puppet administration and disbanded after six weeks. The fate of the Lithuanian provisional government dissuaded Latvians and Estonians from attempting to restore their independence in 1941.

In the Nazi new order, the Baltic states, together with most of Belarus, constituted *Reichskomissariat Ostland*, ruled from Rīga by *Reichskomissar* Hinrich Lohse (1896–1964), previously the Nazi Party boss (*Gauleiter*) of Schleswig-Holstein. *Ostland* came under the jurisdiction of the Ministry for the Occupied Eastern Areas, headed by Alfred Rosenberg. Within *Ostland*, each Baltic state constituted a general district ruled by its own Nazi *Generalkomissar*. Parallel but subordinate to their own civil administration the Germans created a native self-administration (*landeseigene Verwaltung*), headed by a directorate (council in Lithuania). The Estonian, Latvian and Lithuanian directorates were headed by Dr Hjalmar Mäe (1901–78), General Oskars Dankers (1883–1965) and General Petras Kubiliūnas (1894–1946) respectively. The Germans failed to enlist esteemed personalities to serve as their quislings. Mäe and Kubiliūnas had both been imprisoned in the 1930s for involvement in right-wing plots to overthrow the government; during the Soviet occupation Dankers and Mäe had both managed to resettle to Berlin and ingratiate themselves there. These were men whom the Germans felt they could trust to do their bidding.

Initial goodwill towards the Germans as 'liberators' quickly dissipated as the Baltic states were treated as occupied Soviet territory and the Third Reich retained the property nationalised by the USSR. The main aim of German policy was maximally to exploit the resources of the Baltic nations for the benefit of their war effort. Although having no intention of respecting native culture in the long term, in the eyes of most of the population the Germans nevertheless compared favourably to the communists because they allowed the national symbols to be used, religious instruction to be reinstated and many of the local organisations and institutions dissolved by the Soviet regime to be re-established. At least Nazi repression and violence was predictable, whereas Soviet terror appeared random – individuals could suddenly find themselves classed as 'enemies of the people'.

The Baltic experience of World War II differed from that of the rest of Europe because the Baltic peoples endured three brutal occupations by the two totalitarian powers. They had little opportunity to make morally untainted choices between two evils. The term 'collaborator', implying 'traitor', is, therefore, inaccurate for those individuals who cooperated with the Nazis in the Baltic countries, since the state to whom they owed allegiance had already been destroyed by the USSR.[16]

There was practically no armed resistance to the Germans, with the exception of partisans trained by Soviet forces to commit sabotage behind German lines. However, these found little support among the people and had only limited success in the Lithuanian–Belarusian border areas. The national opposition desisted from undermining the German war effort as it would have hastened the return of the dreaded Red Army. It viewed the USSR as 'enemy number one', whereas Germany was seen as the immediately less dangerous 'enemy number two'.[17]

Surviving leading figures from the independence era who represented various former political parties, such as the Latvian social democratic leader Pauls Kalniņš (1872–1945) and the last Estonian prime minister, Jüri Uluots (1890–1945), formed underground national opposition groups which maintained contact with Baltic diplomats in exile in the West via Stockholm and relayed information about the Nazi occupation to the world. By 1944 they had managed to overcome their ideological differences and formed united, central organisations: the Supreme Committee for the Liberation of Lithuania, the Central Council of Latvia and the Estonian National Committee. These were underground organisations which operated conspiratorially and were constantly hindered by the German security police, who arrested many of their leaders in 1944.

The Nazis had grandiose fantasies for the racial reordering of Eastern European populations. Hitler sought to create *Lebensraum* (living space) for German colonists and force the 'racially inferior' peoples eastwards. The Nazis regarded the Estonians and Latvians as the most 'racially worthy' among Eastern Europeans because of their perceived 'Nordic' racial characteristics, partly derived from centuries of blood intermingled with that of the Baltic Germans. *Generalplan Ost* foresaw that 50 per cent of Estonians and 25 per cent of Latvians were deemed racially valuable enough to be assimilated with Germanic colonists. The rest would be resettled eastward on Russian territory. The perspective for the Lithuanian nation, not having the 'benefit' of blood intermingled with that of the Baltic Germans, was even less palatable.

The new occupier replaced class war with race war. For the Nazis, the first priority ideologically was the annihilation of the Jews. The Holocaust in *Ostland* can be divided into three phases: 1941 – the execution of the majority of the local Jews by *SS Einsatzgruppe A* (*SS* Operational Group A) and native collaborators; 1942 to spring 1943 – the exploitation of Jewish labour in ghettos; summer 1943 to August 1944 – the liquidation of the ghettos.[18]

Immediately on the heels of the military invasion, *Einsatzgruppe A* commanded by SS General Walter Stahlecker (1900–42) organised the murder of most of the Baltic Jews during the summer and autumn of 1941. Stahlecker immediately sought to instigate pogroms in order to give the appearance of spontaneity and local initiative, but had only very limited success in Lithuania and none in Latvia and Estonia.[19] The Nazis ordered the Jews to be confined to ghettos, from where they were taken in groups to secluded locations to be shot and buried in large, open pits. The largest single such 'action' was conducted by SS General Friedrich Jeckeln (1895–1946) who was dispatched to Rīga in November 1941 by *Reichsführer-SS* Heinrich Himmler (1900–45) to hasten the pace of the killings. On 30 November and 8 December, 25,000 Jews from the Rīga ghetto were marched to the sandy pine forest at Rumbula and executed.[20] By the end of 1941, most of the Baltic Jews had been killed. The first to be completely eliminated were the Estonian Jews: the Nazis declared Estonia *Judenfrei* (free of Jews) in December 1941 after having executed 950 Jews. Nevertheless, three-quarters of the tiny Estonian Jewish community survived by evacuating with the Red Army. The much more numerous Latvian and Lithuanian Jews had less time to escape the German advance in June 1941 and thus most were trapped.

After the initial massacres, the second phase, 1942 to spring 1943, was comparatively stable. The surviving Jews were confined to ghettos in Vilnius, Kaunas, Šiauliai, Rīga, Liepāja and Daugavpils, where the Germans exploited their labour. During this period the Nazis transported tens of thousands of Jews, primarily from Germany but also from Austria, Czechoslovakia and France, to *Ostland*. Many were executed immediately upon arrival, but most were sent to work in the ghettos or to camps supplying labour to Estonian oil-shale mines. The final phase of the Holocaust occurred after the Warsaw ghetto uprising. In June 1943 Himmler ordered the liquidation of the ghettos in *Ostland* and the placement of Jews under SS authority. The inmates of the Rīga ghetto were resettled to the nearby Kaiserwald (Mežaparks) concentration camp, and the Kaunas and Šiauliai ghettos were compressed and turned into camps. The Vilnius ghetto was liquidated in September: its able-bodied inmates were transferred to camps in Latvia and Estonia, and those unfit for work – the elderly and children – were sent to be killed in Auschwitz. As the Red Army reached the Baltic in the summer of 1944, the Nazis evacuated the surviving Jews to concentration camps in the Reich, mainly Stutthof and Dachau, although some, such as the 2000 mainly Lithuanian Jews at the Klooga camp in Estonia, were hastily massacred on the spot. Altogether, about 95 per cent of Lithuania's Jews, almost 200,000 people, were killed between 1941 and 1945.[21] Likewise, of the 70,000 Jews who remained in German-occupied Latvia, only a couple of thousand survived.[22]

As elsewhere in Nazi-occupied Europe, it would have been difficult for the Germans to carry out the 'final solution of the Jewish question' without some local collaboration. The most notorious perpetrator was a Latvian security police (*Sicherheitsdienst*) commando led by Viktors Arājs (1910–88) which murdered 25,000 Jews in Latvia and Belarus.[23] It would, however, be misleading to ascribe participation in genocide to 'ancient hatreds', since Jews had enjoyed a relatively good life in the three independent republics, and almost three thousand Lithuanian families rescued Jews during the Nazi German occupation.[24] The causal explanation is linked to the preceding year of brutal Soviet rule when Jews for the first time rose to positions of power, which created resentment because many Estonians, Latvians and Lithuanians perceived them as having been complicit in the destruction of their statehood.[25] Communist terror ripped apart the social fabric of Baltic societies and desensitised them to violence. Nazi propaganda deliberately conflated communists and Jews into a single enemy ('Judeo-Bolsheviks'). While many Jews had been empowered by the Soviet regime, Jewish businessmen and religious and community leaders were among the victims of Soviet terror.

The Nazis also exterminated the Roma, but their numbers were much smaller: 2000 in Latvia and about 500 in Lithuania and Estonia. In addition to the Jews and Roma, 18,000 Latvian, 7000 Estonian and 5000 Lithuanian civilians, some of whom were Russian or Polish, were killed during the Nazi occupation. Most of these were accused of collaboration with the Soviet regime. A group of victims who have received little attention are the Soviet POWs who died of starvation or disease or were killed in the inhuman conditions of German POW camps hastily erected in *Ostland*. The largest number of Soviet POWs, 170,000, perished on

Lithuanian soil.[26] The Germans ignored international conventions and acted according to their racial ideology, which deemed the Slavs to be an inferior race.

## FIGHTING IN FOREIGN UNIFORM

Alhough the Baltic states were neutral in World War II, their citizens were forced to fight in the uniforms of the two totalitarian powers bent on the destruction of their nations. It was not uncommon for Baltic men to experience service in both the Red Army and Waffen-SS. The pre-war national armies which had been transformed into Red Army territorial corps were sent to training camps at the end of May 1941. There many of the officers were arrested and sent to prison camps above the Arctic Circle, primarily Norilsk, where most were shot. After the Nazi invasion, the remains of the former Estonian and Latvian national armies fought defensive battles in north-western Russia, suffering substantial losses. Subsequently they were sent to labour battalions in the Soviet rear, where a large number perished in appalling conditions during the winter of 1941. This fate was also shared by many Balts mobilised into the retreating Red Army in the summer of 1941, the largest number (33,000) of whom were Estonians, since the rapid advance of the Germans prevented the Soviets from carrying out conscription in Lithuania and Latvia.[27] After their brutal treatment in the Red Army, many Balts used the first opportunity when sent to the front line in the summer of 1942 to desert to the German side in order to return home.

Motivated by a desire for revenge against the Soviet regime and to liberate family members deported by the communists, several thousand Baltic men volunteered for German military service. Various police and auxiliary battalions were formed from Baltic volunteers who were mainly employed in guarding facilities and fighting Soviet partisans in the areas adjacent to *Ostland*. Some of these police battalions were directly involved in the execution of Jews in Belarus and Ukraine. The collaborationist self-administration sought greater autonomy for their countries (on the model of Slovakia) in exchange for promising to provide troops for the German war effort. Leading figures in the Estonian and Latvian directorates, Oskar Angelus (1892–1979) and Alfrēds Valdmanis (1908–70) respectively, prepared memoranda outlining such plans, but were opposed by *Reichskommissar* Lohse.[28] Seeking to bolster local support for the German war effort, Rosenberg made a modest proposal in this direction to Hitler in 1943 but was rebuffed. However, as the fortunes of war turned against the Third Reich on the Eastern Front in 1943, the Germans made increasing efforts to recruit Balts. In contrast to the police battalions manned mainly by volunteers, the Germans began to conscript Estonians, Latvians and Lithuanians for Waffen-SS legions. Since Eastern Europeans were not allowed to serve in the Wehrmacht (regular army), Baltic conscripts were assigned to Waffen-SS units and deemed 'volunteers' because mobilisation in an occupied territory contravened the Hague Convention. The Lithuanians and the Poles were the only nations of Nazi-occupied Europe not to provide a division for the Waffen-SS. An effective boycott campaign by Lithuanian patriotic underground organisations led the Germans to abandon recruitment for the Waffen-SS in 1943. Another form of protest was registered by 3500 Estonians who managed to avoid German service but still fought against the USSR by clandestinely crossing the Gulf of Finland and enlisting in the Finnish military. Failing to net as many men for cannon-fodder as they had hoped, the Germans exploited Baltic manpower in other forms. Over 125,000 Balts, the majority of them Lithuanians, were conscripted for labour service in Germany in the war industries.

The situation changed dramatically as the Red Army neared the borders of the Baltic states in early 1944. Balts who had earlier been reluctant to serve the Third Reich now grimly responded to the call to arms in order to defend their homeland. In February 1944, almost 40,000 Estonians were enlisted. During the war, 110,000 Latvian men were mobilised into German military units, half of them into the Latvian Legion (the 15th and 19th Waffen-SS divisions).[29]

As attacks by Soviet partisans along Lithuania's eastern border intensified in early 1944 as the Red Army approached, the Germans announced the formation of a Lithuanian territorial defence force headed by the respected Lithuanian general, Povilas Plechavičius (1890–1973) (who had earlier refused to go along with the Waffen-SS recruitment campaign). Unlike earlier failed attempts to recruit Lithuanians, this time more than twenty thousand men enlisted because the Germans promised that the men were to be used only on Lithuanian territory and that they would be commanded by Lithuanian officers. The Germans immediately had second thoughts about the unit, which they rightly suspected of preparing to become the nucleus of a Lithuanian national army, and attempted, with little success, to redirect the men to serve in units under German command. When they demanded that the Lithuanians swear an oath to Hitler, the Lithuanians deserted en masse. In May, Plechavičius was arrested and several members of his staff were executed. Most of the men fled to the forests with weapons in hand later to re-emerge as the nucleus of the armed resistance to the Soviet regime.

The Red Army's thrust into Estonia on the Narva front was halted at the Tannenberg line (Sinimäed) by German and Estonian troops in July 1944. The Red Army suffered over a hundred thousand casualties while repeatedly trying unsuccessfully to smash through the German defences in the bloodiest single battle on Baltic territory.[30] However, German Army Group North, including Baltic combat units within it, did not have the resources or manpower to stop the advance of the Red Army further south. Vilnius had already been overrun in July and the Red Army sought to cut off Army Group North in Estonia by thrusting towards Rīga. The Germans abandoned Estonia in September, just as Finland was concluding a separate armistice with the USSR. Rīga fell in October.

As the Germans retreated and the Red Army poured into Baltic territory, Baltic patriots sought to re-establish independent governments. Many naively believed that a scenario similar to that of 1918 could reoccur: independence could be recovered if Baltic troops succeeded in hindering the Soviet advance until Nazi Germany capitulated to the Western Allies. The basis for this hope was the Atlantic Charter, which rejected territorial aggrandisement and supported the principle of national self-determination. This vision of the post-war world agreed upon by the USA and Britain in 1941 was incorporated in the Declaration by United Nations of 1 January 1942 to which the USSR was also party. However, the Balts were unaware that at the meeting of 'the Big Three' in Tehran in 1943, the US president, Franklin D. Roosevelt, and the British prime minister, Winston Churchill, indicated that they would not oppose Stalin's desire to reimpose control over the Baltic states.

In September 1944, as the Germans abandoned Tallinn, the last pre-war prime minister, Uluots, whom the Estonian National Committee and diplomats in exile recognised as acting president, named an Estonian government headed by Otto Tief (1889–1976). However, most of the members of this government were arrested by Soviet forces within days, although Uluots managed to escape to Sweden and thus embodied the legal continuity of the independent republic. The underground Central Council of Latvia envisaged the German-uniformed home guard regiment led by General Jānis Kurelis (1882–1954) as the nucleus of a Latvian army which would defend Courland against Soviet military after Germany's capitulation. However, the council's plan was quashed in November 1944 by the Nazis, who executed eight Latvian officers and sent thirteen hundred Latvian patriots to German concentration camps.[31] In the final days of the war in May 1945, a futile attempt was made to form an independent Latvian government in German-held Liepāja to continue fighting against the Red Army. In Lithuania – mostly overrun by the Red Army by August 1944 – no attempt was made to set up a provisional government. The negative experience of 1941 dissuaded another attempt.[32]

Upon re-establishing control, the Soviet authorities immediately conscripted tens of thousands of Baltic youths to replenish the ranks of the Estonian, Latvian and Lithuanian Red Army corps. The largest number, 82,000, were mobilised in Lithuania. Thousands of young men avoided conscription by fleeing to the forests and joining the national partisans. The remnants of almost thirty German divisions, together with one Latvian division, fought on in the encircled Courland pocket right up to the end of the war in May 1945. Tragically, in the final months of the war, the Latvian and Estonian Red Army corps were also deployed in Courland, sometimes fighting against their brethren.

While there was little love for the Germans, the imminent return of the Red Army gave rise to intense fear. Baltic citizens who had lost family members, relatives and friends to the Red Terror had ample reason to fear for their own lives and were eager to escape. No German propaganda was necessary to warn people of the new horrors which awaited them under renewed Soviet rule. Because of lack of transport, and the rapidly moving front line, escape was difficult. The German authorities only sanctioned movement to Germany, where the refugees were put to work in the war industry. Nevertheless, substantial numbers of Estonians and Latvians were able to flee to Sweden, in overcrowded fishing boats, although an unknown number perished in stormy seas. Those who had no access to boats chose evacuation to Germany: overland from Lithuania; by sea from Estonia and Latvia. Several German ships transporting Estonian and Latvian refugees were sunk by Soviet planes or submarines.

While refugees came from all walks of life, the intellectual elite was disproportionately represented. A large number of scientists, artists, writers, musicians, teachers and clergymen left their homelands for an uncertain future in order to avoid probable arrest. Proportionally fewer peasants fled – many could not bear to abandon their livestock. However, the main determinant was access to means of transportation. Those who lived near the coast, therefore, were overrepresented among the refugees. Altogether more than 140,000 Latvians, 75,000 Estonians and 65,000 Lithuanians fled their homeland.[33]

Most Baltic military units retreated with the Germans and fought defensive actions in Germany in the final months of the war, including several thousand juvenile Baltic boys forcibly conscripted in 1944 to serve as Luftwaffe (air force) auxiliaries in Germany, mainly loading munitions for flak guns. After Germany capitulated, the refugees strove desperately to end up in the American or British occupation zones in Germany. The USSR sought to repatriate these refugees as Soviet citizens. However, unlike Ukrainians for example, the Balts were eventually saved from this fate by the Western policy of non-recognition of the Soviet annexation. Most refugees spent four or five years in displaced persons camps in Germany before resettling somewhere further removed from the perceived Soviet threat, chiefly the USA, Canada and Australia.

The face of the eastern Baltic littoral changed dramatically once again, in terms of both borders and populations, with the end of the Second World War. The boundaries of Poland were shifted westwards at the expense of Germany and to the benefit of the USSR. On the ashes of Königsberg, Stalin created a completely new entity in 1946: the Russian oblast of Kaliningrad, which formed a wedge between Lithuania and Poland along the Baltic Sea. The German inhabitants of East Prussia fled or were driven out and an entirely new Slavic population was brought in to repopulate the area. In the North, Finland managed to preserve its sovereignty and democracy, but lost Karelia and was made partly dependent on the Soviet Union. Estonia, Latvia and Lithuania were the only countries eliminated from the map of Europe, becoming constituent republics of the USSR. Furthermore, Stalin transferred the Petseri (Pechory) and trans-Narva regions (5 per cent of Estonia's territory) and the Abrene region (2 per cent of Latvia's territory) to the Russian SFSR. Lithuania recovered Klaipėda from Germany and Vilnius from Poland (although most of the territory south and east of Vilnius that Soviet Russia had recognised as Lithuanian in the 1920 peace treaty now became part of the Belarusian SSR).

Few other countries (Poland, the USSR and Yugoslavia) suffered greater population losses than the Baltic states. Latvia lost close to one-third of its population and Estonia almost as much.[34] Lithuania had fewer losses but would suffer the greatest losses in the post-war years. The war destroyed four historic ethnic-minority communities: the Baltic Germans, the Jews, the Roma and the Estonian Swedes.[35] In 1945 the Baltic countries were ethnically more homogenous than at any point in their modern history.

The population was partially replaced in the post-war years by new-comers, who originated mainly from Russian areas adjacent to Estonia and Latvia and who were directed voluntarily or non-voluntarily to participate in the reconstruction effort after the devastation of the war. German POWs were also used for reconstruction work. The Baltic republics were attractive since their standard of living and their level of development were significantly higher than those of Russia and the other republics of the USSR. The immediate post-war years witnessed a crime wave which was amplified by the numerous Russian carpetbaggers who took advantage of the situation.[36]

Baltic cities were devastated by the war. Narva, Paldiski, Šiauliai, Klaipėda, Daugavpils and Jelgava suffered the worst physical damage. Typically, the cities were rebuilt in the standard style of a Soviet modern urban landscape; they did not have their historically valuable architecture restored. Narva was an extreme example of this, particularly since its population was also almost entirely new – Russians from across the border, as former residents were not allowed to return. Of the Baltic cities, Vilnius underwent the greatest transformation: it saw a change of regime five times during the war: Polish to Soviet to Lithuanian to Soviet to Nazi and back to Soviet. Most of its original inhabitants perished in the Holocaust or were relocated after the war. Between 1945 and 1947 Vilnius was Lithuanianised as 170,000 Poles were 'repatriated' from Lithuania to Poland. Ironically, the communists accomplished what pre-war Lithuanian nationalists could only have dreamt of.[37]

## RESISTANCE, REPRESSION AND COLLECTIVISATION

Armed conflict did not cease in the Baltic states with the end of World War II. Fighting against the Soviet occupation forces continued in the forests and swamps. Armed resistance was greatest in Lithuania. Whereas in Estonia and Latvia the 'forest brothers' were organised in small autonomous bands, the Lithuanian resistance managed in 1949 to establish a national central command, the Council of the Lithuanian Freedom Fighters, which was led by the Lithuanian pre-war army captain Jonas Žemaitis (1909–54). In Lithuania, an estimated 50,000 men and women participated in the fight against the Soviet regime, 20,000 of whom were killed; 13,000 were killed on the Soviet side.[38] In comparison, the scope and intensity of the conflict was not as great in Estonia and

Latvia, where the number of forest brethren killed in each country was approximately 2,000.

One of the reasons why Lithuanian resistance was significantly stronger was simply because there were more young Lithuanian men available. Compared to Estonians and Latvians, very few Lithuanians had been mobilised to serve in the Soviet and German armed forces during the war. Only in Lithuania had there been any notable organised resistance during the Nazi occupation, and it was relatively easy for the partisans to reorient themselves to fighting the other occupier. Furthermore, the tight-knit Catholic rural communities of Lithuania provided a greater support network for the guerrillas.

Soviet security forces purposely injected elements of civil war into the guerrilla struggle by forming 'destruction battalions' from weakly disciplined and poorly motivated local recruits.[39] Soviet operatives managed to infiltrate the resistance by posing as forest brethren, thus enabling them to betray partisan bunkers and their local supporters. Fake forest brethren occasionally also committed atrocities to turn local communities against the partisans. Great Britain recruited and trained agents from among Baltic refugees in order to establish communication with the resistance. However, almost all of those who were landed in their homeland were captured immediately since the operation was betrayed at its outset by Soviet infiltration of the British counter-intelligence service, MI6.[40]

The resistance persevered in the hope that the Cold War which had developed between the erstwhile allies of the West and the Soviet Union would flare into a hot war, resulting in the liberation of the Baltic states. This illusion was finally extinguished after the USA stood by while the Red Army crushed the Hungarian uprising in 1956. The Hungarian uprising was also a watershed moment for the Baltic peoples' relationship with the Soviet regime. They began to accommodate themselves to the permanence of the Soviet regime and no longer viewed it as one in a series of temporary military occupations. After Stalin's death in 1953 most remaining resistance fighters accepted the amnesties offered by the Soviet authorities. Žemaitis was captured in 1953 and taken to Moscow, where he was tortured and personally interrogated by the Soviet security chief, Lavrenty Beria (1899–1953), before being executed. Nevertheless, a few forest brethren continued living beyond the reach of the authorities – the last known Lithuanian resister died as late as 1986.[41]

Upon their return in 1944, the Soviet security organs immediately arrested and deported those whom they deemed opponents and German collaborators. Despite this massive new wave of political arrests, the Soviet authorities were temporarily somewhat tolerant of local norms and customs in the Baltic republics during the immediate post-war years of 1944–7 because it took time to build up the party and security apparatus and suppress the partisans.[42] However, the years 1947–53 saw renewed repression as the goal of the Soviet regime was not simply military occupation but permanent incorporation of all aspects of Baltic societies within Soviet institutions. Terror was the chosen method to enforce compliance with the new order. The Stalinist regime's paranoia was boundless, targeting not only 'bourgeois nationalism' but also 'formalism' and 'cosmopolitanism': a group of Latvian intellectuals who met informally to discuss contemporary French literature, for example, were imprisoned in 1951.[43] The Communist Party maintained tight control over ideology in all aspects of life in the USSR. In the final years of the Stalin era, the 'cult of personality' was a constant presence; praising the genius of Stalin, the great leader and teacher, was a public duty. Art, literature and theatre were heavily censored, with 'socialist realism' being the party's preferred mode of expression. Paeans to heroic collective-farm tractor drivers and factory workers were ubiquitous. Books on the proscribed list were destroyed on a massive scale: in Latvia by 1950, for example, 12 million books and 750,000 periodicals had been removed from circulation.[44] For the Baltic nations, there were constant reminders of their 'eternal friendship' with their 'big brother' the Russian nation. History texts were rewritten to emphasise the 'progressive' role of Russia in the pasts of Estonia, Latvia and Lithuania. Monuments and memorials from the independence era were demolished and new statues and plaques honouring communist figures and the Red Army were erected.

Throughout the Soviet era, ideological indoctrination was relentless, particularily in education. Young people were expected to participate in communist organisations, children in the Pioneers and youths in the Komsomol. To combat religion and to propagate atheism, the Soviet authorities introduced the subject of 'scientific communism' into school curricula. The Soviet regime permitted only registered churches to function and this was under strict state supervision. A number of churches were taken from their congregations and turned into museums, concert halls or simply warehouses. Since seminaries and schools of theology were closed, the major challenge for the churches was to train new clergy. They were already in a desperate situation since many had fled into exile in 1944 and the remaining clergy faced physical repression during the Stalin era. Of the Lithuanian Catholic bishops who did not escape into exile, only one was not deported.[45] The last systematic deportation was of Jehovah's Witnesses in 1951.

In the immediate post-war years (1944–7), the Central Committee of All-Union Communist Party kept tight control over local decision-making by establishing special bureaus for the three republics, each led by a Russian comrade dispatched from Moscow to 'assist' the Estonian, Latvian and Lithuanian Communist Party leaderships. The Soviet regime initially lacked sufficient personnel or cadres to administer its new realm. Although new party members were recruited rapidly during the first occupation in 1940–41, they had incurred many losses during the war. As of 1 January 1945, of the 3536 Communist Party members in Lithuania, 1127 were Lithuanians. Similarly, only 1263 of the 3592 in Latvia and 961 of the 2409 in Estonia were native-born.[46] Moreover, half of these were on the rolls of the repressive apparatus, the NKVD and NKGB, or the military. Within two years (1945–7) the size of the Communist Party membership increased five-fold. However, this was mainly the result not of co-opting locals but of the migration of party members from the USSR and from among the ranks of the demobilised Red Army. The Estonian and Latvian Communist Parties were built up with ethnic Estonians and Latvians whose parents or grandparents had emigrated eastwards in the late nineteenth or early twentieth century. This external human resource for party cadres was largely absent in the Lithuanian case since most Lithuanian emigration had been westwards. These ethnic Estonians and Latvians were trusted because of their Soviet education and were assumed to be loyal to Moscow because they had no local power base.

Native communists were never entirely free from the suspicion of ideological impurity. At the height of paranoid Stalinism, the Estonian Communist Party first secretary, Nikolai Karotamm (1901–69), was accused of shielding 'bourgeois nationalists' within the party's ranks at the eighth plenary session of the Central Committee of the Estonian Communist Party in March 1950. Karotamm was exiled to an academic post in Moscow and hundreds of others were expelled from the party. The purge also had a devastating impact on Estonian culture life since approximately one-third of all Estonian artists, writers, actors, musicians and university faculty were banned from employment in their profession.[47] Karotamm, nevertheless, was more fortunate than one of his accusers, the deputy chairman of the Council of Ministers, Hendrik Allik (1901–89), who was sentenced to 25 years' imprisonment in December 1950. Ironically, Allik had already received a 25-year prison term for his part in the failed communist insurrection in Tallinn in 1924.[48] Karotamm's main accuser, Ivan (later Johannes) Käbin (1905–99), the propaganda secretary of the party's Central Committee, who had been raised in Soviet Russia and came to Estonia after the war, became the new first secretary. A native-born Estonian would not lead the party again until 1988.

The Baltic republics were rapidly integrated into the highly centralised Soviet planned economy.[49] While large and medium-sized commercial enterprises in the Baltic republics had been nationalised in 1940, the remaining small businesses were eradicated by 1947. Private ownership of any means of production was forbidden. All production in the Soviet command economy was determined according to a Five-Year Plan produced by *Gosplan*, the State Planning Committee, in Moscow. The Communist Party 'dictatorship of the proletariat' was based on the state ownership of all means of production, both industrial and agricultural.

The final measure in irreversibly sovietising Baltic society was the destruction of family farms through the establishment of collective farms. The first steps had already been taken during the earlier Soviet occupation when farmers were stripped of landholdings greater than 30 hectares and small 10 hectare plots were created for previously landless peasants. This land reform was rescinded during the German occupation but was immediately reintroduced by the Soviet authorities after the war. From the Soviet viewpoint, this measure was also useful in smoothing the way for collectivisation later because it created new tensions and stoked up class conflict in the countryside between those whose land was taken away and those who received it. The first collective farms were established in 1947. Simultaneously, drastic tax increases were imposed on farmers in order to render private farming unviable and to force peasants to join the new collective farms. Nevertheless, very few farmers were willing voluntarily to surrender their livestock and property to the state. As in Russia and Ukraine in the early 1930s, Stalin's instrument of choice was terror.[50]

Operation *Priboi* (Surf) was meticulously planned in Moscow and carried out without any warning in all three Baltic republics simultaneously during the night of 24–25 March 1949. It was officially aimed at 'kulaks', 'bandits' and 'nationalists' and their families. The Russian term *kulak* originally referred to better-off peasants, but in Soviet parlance it meant anyone whose farm managed to provide more than a bare subsistence for its owner. After the 1940 Soviet land reform, there were hardly any farmers who could be considered as wealthy. In fact, these terms were sufficiently elastic that almost anyone out of favour with the local Communist Party bosses could end up being branded a *kulak*. Stalin aimed physically to 'liquidate' the kulaks as a class. The central authorities provided a quota of 30,000 families to be 'resettled' from the Baltic republics. All in all, 95,000 people (21,000 Estonians, 42,000 Latvians and 32,000 Lithuanians),[51] almost three-quarters of whom were women and children, received a night-time knock on their door and were given an hour to pack their belongings. They were placed in cattle cars for a journey of several weeks in cold, cramped, inhumane conditions before reaching their final destinations in Irkutsk, Omsk, Tomsk and other oblasts of Siberia; it was a huge logistical operation, involving 76 trains to transport the deportees.[52]

After the deportations, the remaining farmers hurried 'voluntarily' to join the new collective farms. Although the deportations initially resulted in more men fleeing to the forests, collectivisation succeeded in eliminating the bases of support for the resistance. By 1952 almost all farmers had joined the collective farms. Compared to the earlier 1941 mass deportation, more of the deportees survived and were able to return (although not necessarily to their homes) after the amnesties of the mid-1950s. Unlike 1941, most were not placed in prison camps but had to suffer resettlement in the harsh conditions of Siberia.

Although the March 1949 deportations represented the greatest of the crimes against humanity perpetrated by the Soviet regime in the Baltic countries, they were not the only such operation. The post-war deportation of those resisting collectivisation was most massive in Lithuania, with the first wave having already occurred in May 1948 when 11,400 families (40,000 people) were deported. After Operation *Priboi* there was a third massive deportation in October 1951 of 4000 families (16,000 people). Between 1944 and 1953 there were 34 deportations of various magnitudes in Lithuania. Altogether, 128,000 people were deported from Lithuania (5 per cent of the population) during the post-war period.[53]

# 7

# Soviet Rule (1953–1991)

After the death of Stalin, terror subsided, and Estonians, Latvians and Lithuanians gradually accommodated themselves to the Soviet regime. Baltic Communist Party leaders manoeuvred, with various degrees of success, within the strict dictates of Moscow, while Estonian, Latvian and Lithuanian intellectuals sought to defend their cultures in the face of rapid demographic change and Russification. Baltic societies were transformed from mainly agricultural to predominantly urban societies. Estonians, Latvians and Lithuanians seized the opportunity created by Soviet leader Mikhail Gorbachev's reforms in the late 1980s to end the Communist Party's monopoly of power through the Singing Revolution. Weathering extreme pressure from Moscow, the Balts worked together through peaceful means to restore their independence and gain international recognition in 1991.

## THAW

Overt terror was no longer a necessary political tool for the Soviet regime after the death of Stalin in 1953, since Estonian, Latvian and Lithuanian societies had been psychologically pummelled into submission and a permanent state of fear. Imprisonment on political grounds continued until the 1980s, but the number of arrests was on a much diminished scale: tens, rather than thousands, of individuals annually in each Baltic republic.[1] Amnesties were declared for various categories of political prisoners in the gulag. The surviving deportees began to return home in the mid-1950s, although many were not allowed to return to their former place of residence. Many had trouble reintegrating into society and were often viewed with suspicion. The new Soviet leader, Nikita Khrushchev (1894–1971), denounced Stalin's Great Purge at the Twentieth Congress of the Communist Party in 1956, signalling a relaxation of centralised authoritarian control, often referred to as the Thaw. Local authorities in the Baltic Soviet Socialist Republics gingerly began to test the limits of autonomy and cultural figures probed the boundaries of censorship. Nevertheless, the USSR remained a single-party state where no political activity outside of the Communist Party was tolerated. The party and the government were parallel institutions with the former being decisive. The Leninist system of administration can be conceptualised as consisting of two power pyramids, the party and the government, with the latter contained inside the former.[2] At the apex of the outer, larger pyramid stood the first secretary of the Communist Party who was far more powerful than the head of government (the chairman of the Council of Ministers) or the titular head of the republic (the chairman of the Presidium of the Supreme Soviet). To ensure the Kremlin's tight control over the local communists, the second secretary of the party was usually a Russian appointed by Moscow. The Estonian, Latvian and Lithuanian Communist Parties were themselves not free-standing entities, but simply branches of the Communist Party of the Soviet Union (CPSU).

Upon Stalin's death, the Lithuanian Communist Party leadership quietly initiated a nativisation campaign, replacing party officials brought in from Russia with younger Lithuanians. In 1952 less than a third of the members of the Lithuanian Communist Party were ethnically Lithuanian; by 1965 almost two-thirds were Lithuanian.[3] However, the limits of the Thaw became apparent most starkly in Latvia, where a group of younger, energetic, idealistic, native Communist Party members came to the fore led by Vilis Krūmiņš (1919–2000), the new second secretary (exceptionally a native Latvian in this position), and Eduards Berklāvs (1914–2004), the new deputy chairman of the Council of Ministers. They sincerely believed that building communism in Latvia would succeed if those sent to assist from Russia learned to communicate in the Latvian language. This idea proved to be too radical for the old guard and they were purged from the party. Although it is commonly assumed that the purge of the Latvian 'national communists' was the result of Khrushchev's dissatisfaction during his visit to Rīga in June 1959, the purge was actually initiated by Arvīds Pelše (1899–1983), head of the Latvian Communist Party's Propaganda and Agitation Department, and supported by the local Soviet military leadership.[4] It was a power struggle between the old-guard, Stalinist wing of the party and the younger, more nationally minded members. As in the earlier Estonian purge in 1950, personal ambitions played an important role: the main accuser of the leadership, Pelše, became the new party boss. Hundreds of Latvian national communists were demoted or expelled from the party. Berklāvs, the main scapegoat, was exiled to Russia. However, unlike the violent purges of the Stalinist era, there were no executions or long prison sentences.

Lithuania was the only Baltic republic to avoid a purge of its Communist Party leadership. Antanas Sniečkus was the most durable figure among Baltic Communist Party bosses and was one of the longest-serving leaders in the entire Soviet bloc. He survived as Lithuanian Communist Party leader (first secretary) from 1936 until his death in 1974, adroitly managing to adapt himself to the changing policies and personalities in the Kremlin.

The post-Stalinist thaw also brought about efforts to rationalise and decentralise economic production. The most important step in that direction was the establishment in 1957 of Regional Economic Councils (*sovnarkhozy*), which transferred much of the operational decision-making to the republics, although they still had to adhere strictly to the guidelines of the Five-Year Plan produced by the State Planning Committee in Moscow. This reform helped the Baltic republics to equal their pre-war level of production and standard of living in the 1960s, almost two decades after the end of the war.[5] However, in 1965 the Regional Economic Councils were liquidated in a reform which ostensibly aimed to increase the independence of enterprises but actually resulted in their being more dependent on the all-union ministries. In practice, this meant that enterprises responded primarily to the demands of their sector or branch in the all-union industry, and there was no longer any connection with economic developments in the home republic.

The immediate results of collectivisation had been disastrous for the economy: agricultural production fell precipitously in the early 1950s. The situation improved in 1958 when the collective farms began to pay money wages and were allowed to purchase their own tractors and farming machinery. Previously these had only been available on loan from state-owned machine tractor stations, which had now been dissolved. However, the continuing inefficiency of the collective farms is illustrated by the fact that the farmers' own small garden plots – constituting a fraction of the arable land – produced a substantial part of the national fruit and vegetable crop. These allotments were not only important for their survival but also enabled farmers to carve out a small autonomous space for themselves within the Soviet system.[6]

The Thaw enabled cultural production cautiously to free itself of the straitjacket of turgid 'socialist realism'. The 1960s witnessed a cultural flowering of a new generation of writers and artists who pushed the boundaries of Soviet censorship and broke taboos. Within the USSR, the Baltic republics gained the reputation of being the 'Soviet West'. Certainly, from the perspective of the rest of the Soviet Union, the *Pribaltika* looked and felt more European, with a more liberal atmosphere and greater contact with Western trends. Tallinn and Vilnius were hotspots of the jazz music scene in the USSR. Many authors hitherto banned in the USSR, such as Franz Kafka and Albert Camus, were first published in one of the Baltic republics, as were uncensored versions of some Russian classics.[7] Some Russian intellectuals even sought internal refuge in the Baltic republics. The pioneering Russian semiotician Yuri Lotman (1922–93), whose career had been blocked in Leningrad because of his Jewish heritage, received a professorship at the University of Tartu. Alexander Solzhenitsyn (1918–2008) wrote much of his famous *Gulag Archipelago* manuscript during his stays at the summer house of his former cellmate in Estonia in the 1960s. Another future Russian Nobel Prize laureate, poet Joseph Brodsky (1940–96), who would later be expelled from the USSR, found Vilnius to be the most congenial place to express his creativity in the 1960s. Jūrmala, Palanga and Narva-Jõesuu were popular summer beach resorts among the intelligentsia from Moscow and Leningrad.

An important breakthrough in the move away from isolation was the opening of a passenger ferry service from Helsinki to Tallinn in 1965. This remained the only direct transport link – air, sea or rail – from the Baltic republics to outside of the Soviet bloc until the end of the 1980s. Proximity to Finland also gave the Estonians access to objective information about the outside world and a glimpse of consumer society via Finnish television broadcasts.[8] The Lithuanians also had more varied sources of information than average Soviet citizens because of their closeness to Poland. Furthermore, many Baltic families had some contact, at least in the form of correspondence, with relatives in the refugee communities in the West and were aware that free, uncensored Baltic culture existed outside the boundaries of the USSR.

Vibrant exile communities had sprung up in such cities as Stockholm, Toronto, Chicago, Sydney and New York. Until the Thaw, not only the quality but also the quantity of Estonian-, Latvian- and Lithuanian-language publications produced by the refugees abroad was greater than that in their homelands. The political struggle for the exile community focused on maintaining the non-recognition policy of the annexation of the Baltic states initiated by the USA in 1940 and followed by most Western countries. The Soviet authorities waged a continual ideological propaganda battle against the exiles. One of their more effective smears was to label émigré Balts as Nazi collaborators.[9]

## STAGNATION

Although Khrushchev was removed from power in 1964 by a triumvirate led by Leonid Brezhnev (1906–82), hopes for the continuation of liberalisation lingered for a few more years. Remaining illusions were shattered with the Soviet invasion of Czechoslovakia in 1968, which crushed the attempt by the reformist Communist Party leadership in Prague to create 'socialism with a human face'. Brezhnev served as Soviet leader until his death in 1982, even though during the last few years of his life his mental and physical capacities were limited. The Brezhnev era would later be labelled as a period of 'stagnation'. He was succeeded by Yuri Andropov (1914–84) and then Konstantin Chernenko (1911–85), both of whom quickly expired while in office. By 1985 the leadership of the CPSU appeared to be a gerontocracy desperately in need of fresh blood.

The conservative stagnation in the Kremlin was also reflected in the Communist Party leadership of the Baltic republics. The Estonian Communist Party was headed for almost three decades by Käbin, and the period in office from 1966 to 1984 of the Latvian first secretary Augusts Voss (1919–94) paralleled that of Brezhnev, but even they could not match the remarkable longevity of Sniečkus as the Lithuanian Communist Party chief. Equally as long-serving as the party leaders during this period were the chairmen of the council of ministers (heads of government): Valter Klauson (1914–88) in Estonia from 1961 to 1984, Jurijs Rubenis (1925–2004) in Latvia from 1970 to 1988 and Juozas Maniušis (1910–87) in Lithuania from 1967 to 1981, none of whom were native-born. The Latvian leadership had the best connections with the leadership in Moscow. Voss's predecessor Pelše was promoted to the CPSU Politburo, the only Balt to rise to the highest political level in the USSR apart from the early Latvian Bolsheviks and the leaders of the pro-Moscow wing of the Party in the three republics in 1990.[10]

The late 1970s and early 1980s saw renewed repression, which corresponded with a change in leadership in the Baltic republics. When Sniečkus died in 1974 he was replaced by Petras Griškevičius (1924–87) who occupied the position until his own death in 1987. Käbin was bumped upstairs to the ceremonial post of chairman of the presidium of the Supreme Soviet in 1978 and replaced by Karl Vaino (b. 1923), a Russified Estonian who had no local power base and was, therefore, absolutely loyal to Moscow. Voss was succeeded in 1984 by Boriss Pugo (1937–1991), who had headed the Latvian branch of the Committee for State Security (KGB). These leaders loyally followed the conservative Kremlin line and intensified the repression of dissidents in the early 1980s. They are also associated with a renewed campaign of linguistic Russification beginning in the late 1970s and typified by Vaino's speech at the 26th CPSU Congress in 1981, where he stated, 'For everything that we have achieved, we owe a debt of gratitude to our elder brother, the great Russian nation.'[11]

After Stalin's death, individuals rarely joined the Communist Party for ideological reasons or for survival, but primarily for the advancement of their careers. Most individuals who were offered a promotion to a senior management position in their field of professional employment were expected to join the party. Few declined to do so. Party membership also gave some material benefits, such as priority in the queue for obtaining valued consumer goods such as telephones. The most distinctive privilege enjoyed by party members was foreign travel. The profile of the party membership in the 1960s and 1970s changed, therefore, to that of an organisation dominated by university graduates rather than representing the earlier ideal of a working class. This gradual shift increased professional competence within the party and increased the proportion of native-born Balts in the party, but weakened its ideological commitment.[12] Party membership among the republic's titular ethnic group was always highest in Lithuania. During the last 25 years of Soviet rule, more than two-thirds of the members of the Communist Party were ethnic Lithuanians, whereas the corresponding proportion in Estonia was approximately half, and in Latvia less than half.[13]

In the late 1960s a new type of non-violent opposition to the Soviet system arose in the form of 'dissidents'. These courageous individuals demanded that the authorities honour the rights laid down by the Soviet constitution. They were encouraged by the Final Act of the Conference on Security and Cooperation in Europe signed in Helsinki in 1975. Since the signatories, including the USSR, undertook to respect human rights, Soviet dissidents were able to refer to this international obligation in setting up 'Helsinki monitoring' groups. Broadly speaking, the dissidents could be categorised by their focus on universal human rights, religious freedom or national identity, although such categorisation is somewhat artificial since all of these were obviously interlinked within the Soviet context, and in practice it was simply a question of emphasis. In Lithuania, where the struggle to defend the right to practise religion was strongest, this was clearly connected with aspirations of national freedom.

The Catholic Church and its priests played an important role in Lithuanian opposition to the Soviet regime. The longest-running underground publication in the entire USSR was the *Chronicle of the Catholic Church in Lithuania* (1972–89).[14] Amazingly, the KGB never discovered the identity of the priests editing the chronicle. Lithuanian dissent was given a significant moral boost by the election of the Polish cardinal Karol Wojtyła as Pope John Paul II in 1978 and the rise of the opposition Solidarity labour movement in Poland the following year. In the late 1960s and 1970s Lithuanian believers organised several petitions to the Soviet authorities, the largest being the gathering of 148,000 signatures for a Klaipėda church to be returned to religious use.[15] As an universal organisation, the Catholic Church in Lithuania was more difficult for the KGB to deal with than the dominant Lutheran Church in Estonia and Latvia which was prepared to a certain extent to collaborate with the Soviet authorities.[16] A similar pliancy characterised the Russian Orthodox Church in the Baltic republics, a leading figure of which was Aleksei Ridiger (1929–2008), who was born in Tallinn and descended from a Baltic German family. Ridiger served as the metropolitan of Estonia from 1968–86 and was elected Alexius II, Patriarch of the Russian Orthodox Church in Moscow in 1990. The only truly anti-Soviet elements who could not be cowed were small groups of evangelical Christians and the Russian Old Believers.

Apart from the Catholic activists in Lithuania, the active dissidents were never more than a handful of individuals and their impact inside their countries was relatively limited. However, they had a more significant external impact by signalling to the world that there existed alternative voices to the official Soviet one. They were able to smuggle out to the West memoranda detailing Soviet repressions. Their most significant achievement was the Baltic Appeal to the United Nations in 1979, signed by 37 Lithuanian, 4 Latvian and 4 Estonian dissidents, on the 40th anniversary of the Nazi–Soviet pact, demanding that its secret protocols be published and its consequences be declared void. Baltic dissidents also developed contacts with dissident circles in Leningrad and Moscow. However, unlike famous Russian dissidents, such as nuclear physicist Andrei Sakharov (who supported the Baltic Appeal), the Baltic dissidents were mainly ordinary men and women. Many had not had the opportunity to acquire a higher education since they had been in and out of Soviet prison camps since their youth. The dissidents were most active during the 1970s. However, the party leadership had little tolerance of dissent and by the early 1980s almost all the Baltic dissidents were again in Soviet prison camps.

In addition to organised activity, there were sporadic eruptions. The most dramatic act of protest was the self-immolation of 19-year-old student Romas Kalanta in central Kaunas in 1972. His funeral became a mass protest against the Soviet regime. Occasionally, rock music concerts also served as vehicles for protests. The largest spontaneous public manifestation in Estonia was a youth riot sparked by the cancellation of a punk rock concert, scheduled to follow a football match in Tallinn 1980. The heavy-handed response of the authorities to this event provoked the most noteworthy public criticism of the Estonian Communist Party leadership and its policy of Russification, the 'Letter of Forty'. Unlike the effort of the marginalised dissidents, the letter was signed by many of Estonia's most respected intellectuals, most of whom were also party members themselves. A letter by 17 Latvian Communists, detailing Russification, was published in the West in 1972.[17]

Dissent against the Soviet regime was also demonstrated by attempts to leave or defect from the Soviet Union. In 1970 Lithuanian sailor Simas Kudirka jumped ship in US waters, becoming a *cause célèbre* when the US coastguard returned him to the Soviet authorities who sentenced him to a ten-year prison term.[18] As a rule, in order to ensure that a traveller returned home, the authorities did not permit family members to travel abroad together. When Estonian Valdo Randpere and his wife sought asylum in Sweden in 1984, the Soviet authorities would not permit reunification with their 13-month-old daughter.

The most dramatic change for Latvia and Estonia during the Soviet era was demographic. Both republics saw a massive influx from the East during the post-war years. While Estonia was over 90 per cent ethnically Estonian at the end of the war, by 1989 the percentage of Estonians in the population had dropped to 62 per cent. During the same time period, the percentage of ethnic Latvians in Latvia dropped from over three-quarters of the population to barely half. The disheartening prospect of becoming a minority in their own homeland appeared on the horizon.

Most of the newcomers were Russians directed for work assignments, but people came from all regions of the USSR. In the 1950s the influx

**Table 2**   Titular ethnic groups as a percentage of the population[19]

| Soviet Republic | 1945 | 1959 | 1970 | 1989 |
|---|---|---|---|---|
| Estonia | 94 | 75 | 68 | 62 |
| Latvia | 80 | 62 | 57 | 52 |
| Lithuania | 78 | 79 | 79 | 80 |

temporarily waned as many returned to Russia and the surviving deportees came home. The subsequent waves of settlers in the 1960s and 1970s were often industrial workers assigned for employment in large new industrial plants or in the military industrial complex. The locals particularly resented the fact that the newcomers were often given priority in the queue for sparse housing. The new residential districts consisted mainly of prefabricated apartment blocks which were identical to those elsewhere in the USSR, be it Armenia or Uzbekistan. Since this workforce was highly mobile, relocating from one region of the USSR to another as more attractive opportunities appeared, most did not bother to learn the local language and integrate into the local community and they therefore lived separate lives.[20] In addition, the massive Soviet military presence was an alien body. The larger cities of the Baltic republics, particularly Rīga, the headquarters of the Soviet Baltic Military District, were popular locations for Soviet military officers to retire to.

Demographic change in Lithuania was far more limited than in Estonia and Latvia. Lithuania avoided the fate of its northern neighbours for four reasons: the country remained more agricultural in character and was not targeted for rapid industrialisation; the guerrilla warfare during the first decade of Soviet rule discouraged the arrival of colonists; the native leadership of the Lithuanian Communist Party was able to exert some influence over the movement of migrants; the Lithuanian fertility rate remained higher and family size larger.

During the Soviet era, all three republics shifted from a predominantly agricultural economy to one that was largely industrial and urban. In comparison with the rest of the USSR, there was a greater proportion of light industry, which was mainly determined by the pre-war structure of the economy. Enterprises which were well-known across the USSR were the State Electronics Factory (VEF) in Rīga – the flagship of inter-war Latvia's electronics industry – producing radios and telephones, the Rīga Autobus Factory manufacturing 'Latvija' microbuses, and the Lithuanian Snaigė producing refrigerators. For the USSR, industrial output was the ultimate measure of success. Coffee-table books celebrating the achievements of the Baltic SSRs proudly featured billowing smokestacks. Concerns for environmental pollution did not have any place in this mindset. Oil shale reserves in Estonia were extensively exploited, with annual production peaking at 31 million tons in 1980. The oil shale was burned in the world's two largest oil-shale based thermoelectric stations near Narva.[21] The Ignalina nuclear power plant in Lithuania started operating in 1983 and was designed to be the world's largest (6000 megawatt) at the time, supplying power to neighbouring Belarus and Latvia, but only two of the planned four reactor blocks were ever completed. In response to such developments, the Baltic republics were the first in the USSR to introduce legislation on nature protection in the 1950s, and conservation societies created by local activists in the 1960s gained huge memberships. The Soviet authorities often looked at conservation projects askance, considering them as a disguised form of nationalism, which, to some extent, they were. The first national park in the USSR was a local initiative established in 1972 at Lahemaa on the Estonian northern coast to preserve the area from further industrial encroachment.[22] Although initially viewed with suspicion in Moscow, the Estonian promoters of the park were able to secure approval by buttressing their arguments with quotes from Lenin.

Despite the emphasis on industrial production, agriculture remained an important sector of the Baltic republics' economies. In the 1960s and 1970s, the Baltic republics became the leading dairy and pig-farming area of the USSR. Most of this production supplied the Russian market, primarily Leningrad. This period also saw the conversion of many collective farms into relatively more efficiently managed state farms (*sovkhozes*). By the 1980s, the salaries of collective and state farm workers surpassed average urban wages.[23] The Kirov collective fishery farm in Viimsi near Tallinn was reputedly the wealthiest in the USSR, engaging in various auxiliary economic production activities and providing its members with a high standard of living.[24] The more successful and dedicated farm managers built cultural centres and supported recreational activities for the local community. The Soviet authorities intended to provide collective farmers with modern conveniences, such as central heating, which led to the construction of large apartment blocks in small rural villages which had been converted to collective farm centres – a ludicrous rationalisation of the rural landscape.

The rigidly centralised control of the Soviet economy resulted in shortages and deficits in consumer goods, as well as products of shoddy quality. For the Soviet consumer, this meant long queues and the use of bribery or 'gifts' to obtain scarce goods and services. For major purchases, such as a car, one first needed a purchase permit and then had to suffer a waiting period, often several years. A similarly long waiting period had to be endured to obtain a rental apartment or telephone. In an economy of scarcity, a network of contacts was the key to success. Those who had control over access to some goods or services, such as restaurant doormen, enjoyed a privileged status. Soviet life was full of absurd contradictions. Genuine Western consumer products not available in the local market, such as nylons, jeans, quality coffee, pop records and chewing gum, were highly prized by Soviet consumers. Plastic shopping bags bearing the logo of a Western company became status symbols in the 1970s.[25]

Alcoholism became a major problem, contributing to poor work discipline, low productivity and serious social and health problems, resulting in low life expectancies, especially for men. Alcohol was inexpensive and was the socially acceptable way to relax. Along with increased alcoholism, the Soviet era saw a loosening of social norms, with high numbers of abortions, a decrease in the number of marriages, and an increase in the number of divorces and common-law unions. After Stalin's death, Soviet legislation allowed easy access to abortion (the main method of birth control), and both marriage and divorce were easily available, since there was no longer any religious aspect to these social covenants and rituals.

Although the Soviet slogan was the 'Baltic Sea – sea of peace', in fact it was a highly militarised region, being part of the USSR's front line during the Cold War. The territory of the Baltic republics was littered with bases for ballistic missiles, aircraft, warships and Soviet military personnel. For example, about 1 per cent of Lithuania's territory was under direct Soviet military control and more than 5 per cent of the territory was used by it in various ways.[26] The military not only dislocated the local residents, it damaged the environment. Not untypical was the long-range bomber aircraft base at Tartu where crews dumped fuel on to the ground in order to claim the requisite flying hours. As a border zone, much of the coastal area was off-limits: it was an area which had to be guarded not only from external infiltration but also, and more importantly, from citizens attempting to escape to the West. These restrictions disrupted the traditional maritime way of life of coastal Estonians and Latvians, who were also squeezed out of the merchant marine by Russians.

An onerous burden for young men was the obligatory two-year military service, which as a rule meant being sent outside one's republic.

This also meant occasionally fighting and dying in the USSR's foreign wars, such as that in Afghanistan in the 1980s. Thousands of young men from the Baltic republics were among those drafted for the clean-up of the nuclear disaster at Chernobyl in 1986 without being provided sufficient protection from radiation.

Although the Soviet constitution in theory guaranteed national self-determination for the republics, the guiding principle of Soviet cultural policy as defined by Stalin was the development of cultures 'national in form and socialist in content' which would ultimately be merged into 'one General Culture'. The Soviet concept of the *sliyanie* (fusion) of nationalities with Russian as the language of 'inter-national communi-cation' was expressed explicitly by Andropov in 1982: 'Our final goal is obvious. It is, in Lenin's words, not only the convergence of nations, but their merging.'[27] The end product would be the *homo sovieticus* – a person without any specific national roots or identity, who would work in whatever part of the USSR that the authorities assigned him or her to, exemplified by the chorus of a Russian pop song of the Brezhnev era, 'My address is no house or street, my address is the Soviet Union.'

A vital part of the shaping of a new identity was the ideological indoc-trination of children and youths in the Communist Party's Pioneer and Komsomol organisations' respectively. Political lectures expounding the Party's position on current affairs were regularly organised at the work-place. The replacement of official holidays with new ones was also part of this process. Important Soviet holidays requiring mandatory participation in the commemorations and parades were 1 May, International Workers' Day; 9 May, Victory Day, the end of the Great Patriotic War (World War II); and 7 November, the Great October Revolution. In the USSR, Christmas was not a holiday and the regime attempted to displace it with the celebration of the New Year. In Latvia, the atheism campaign even involved the banning of the traditional Midsummer's Eve festivities, not only during the Stalinist era but also again during the 1960s after the purge of 'nationalists' in the Communist Party.[28]

In practice, the sovietisation of the Baltic republics entailed linguis-tic Russification, as the Latvian Communist Party first secretary, Voss, made clear in a 1982 speech: 'Everywhere people very much strive for mastering the Russian language, and this striving manifests itself more and more widely. Therefore the party organisations and Soviet bodies constantly have to see to it that all conditions are created to sat-isfy the wish, which in our country is caused by the objective logic of the building of communism.'[29] The Balts, however, clung tenaciously to their cultural traditions. The open-air summer festivals of song and folk dance in Estonia, Latvia and Lithuania, which were held every five years and involved massed choirs of up to 20,000 singers and audiences of sometimes more than 100,000 people, were the most prominent manifestation. Although the content of the programmes was carefully vetted by the authorities, some songs escaped the censors' notice. An example of the balancing act between the official ideology and one's conscience (or reading between the lines) was Veljo Tormis's 'Lenin's words' which featured at the 1975 Estonian song festival and whose lyrics were about the right of peoples to self-determination. The song festivals often culminated in a powerful emotional outpouring as the massed choirs and the audience spontaneously sang unofficial patriotic encores together. As the totalitarian system maintained control over the population by the atomisation of society, these occasions provided rare moments confirming national identity and solidarity.

The 'creative intelligentsia', organised in creative unions (writers' and artists' associations), was relatively well supported by the state, provided that their artistic output remained within accepted boundaries. Writers and artists were held in high esteem by society and many were well known, even to the man on the street. Since there was limited public entertainment, people were voracious readers and provided the writers with a huge readership. Theatre attendance was popular and plays were considered important. Writers and artists who collaborated with the regime lived well. Nevertheless, there were several poets and novelists who pushed the boundaries of Soviet acceptance, and were highly respected and regarded as the conscience of their nation. Poetry became the most influential art form because it could express ideas which would otherwise have been censored.[30] Collections of poetry were published in great quantities, unimaginable in a free-market system, and often sold out quickly. Among the most influential and popular poets were Estonians Hando Runnel (b. 1938) and Juhan Viiding (1948–95), Latvians Ojārs Vācietis (1933–83) and Imants Ziedonis (b. 1933) and Lithuanians Vytautas Bložė (b. 1930) and Sigitas Geda (1943–2008). One way to resist Soviet homogenisation was to write about characters in earlier Baltic history. Works in this genre by Estonian novelist Jaan Kross (1920–2007) and Lithuanian dramatist Justinas Marcinkevičius (b. 1930) were hugely popular. Another popular method was the use and reinterpretation of old folk motifs and ethnographic traditions. Prominent practitioners of this approach were Estonian composer Veljo Tormis (b. 1930) and Lithuanian poet Marcelijus Martinaitis (b. 1936). Latvian culture revived later than Estonian and Lithuanian culture because the political purge of the national communists in 1959 stymied development for several years.[31]

Some Baltic cultural figures, such as Latvian pop composer Raimonds Pauls (b. 1936), Estonian baritone Georg Ots (1920–75) and Lithuanian film director Vytautas Žalakevičius (1930–96), acquired fame across the USSR. On the other hand, many Baltic actors were typecast as German Nazis in Russian war films. Being denied free access to other European cultures, the Balts began interacting more intensively with each other. For example, triannual Baltic art exhibits in Tallinn, Rīga and Vilnius were opportunities to experiment and to push the boundaries of official tolerance.[32] A Baltic regional identity compromising Estonia, Latvia, and Lithuania solidified during the Soviet period when there were very active cultural, scientific and athletic exchanges.

The lack of artistic freedom resulted in some of the most talented Balts, such as Estonian composer Arvo Pärt (b. 1935), Latvian violinist Gidon Kremer (b. 1947) and Lithuanian poet Tomas Venclova (b. 1937) leaving the USSR during the 1970s and early 1980s. More dramatically, some defected, such as the Kirov ballet dancer Mikhail Baryshnikov (b. 1948) who was a native of Rīga. The only group allowed legally to leave the USSR (with some restrictions) were the Jews, who were permitted to emigrate to Israel, beginning in the 1960s.

Travel abroad to the West was the most prized reward for the loyal Soviet citizen, usually available only to prominent artists, world-class athletes and Communist Party members. Unexpectedly for the Soviet authorities, the strictly controlled contacts with the West proved to be a two-way street. For example, beginning in the 1970s when the Soviet authorities allowed trusted senior academics to participate in Baltic studies conferences in Stockholm, the ideological impact of their papers on the Western audience was negligible, whereas the contacts which were established facilitated the exposure of the Soviet Baltic academic establishment to Western literature. Ordinary citizens could not hope for more than an opportunity to travel in escorted groups within Eastern Europe and to bring back consumer goods unavailable at home.

THE SINGING REVOLUTION

By 1985 it appeared that Soviet rule was firmly entrenched in the Baltic states. However, the appointment that year of Mikhail Gorbachev as the general secretary of the CPSU provided the opportunity for dramatic change. The USSR had devoted huge resources to an arms race with the USA during the ideological Cold War between the two superpowers but had neglected the production of consumer goods. Gorbachev realised that the arms race was not sustainable, particularly after US President Ronald Reagan launched the 'Star Wars' initiative in 1983. Stagnation and the dearth of consumer goods such as meat in the shops had become a common phenomenon. Gorbachev sought to make the USSR more efficient in order to compete with the West. In an attempt to achieve these goals, in 1986 he introduced the policies of *glasnost* (openness) and *perestroika* (restructuring).

Unwittingly, Gorbachev unleashed forces that he could not control. Balts eagerly grasped the opportunity provided by *glasnost* to fill in the 'blank spots' of history. At first they proceeded cautiously, recalling that Khrushchev's Thaw was soon followed by renewed repression. They began commemorating the victims of Stalin's mass deportations. Dissidents organised 'calendar demonstrations' which marked officially unacknowledged historical events. Latvian human-rights activists, under the banner of Helsinki-86, organised the first of these in Rīga on 14 June 1987 to commemorate the victims of the 1941 mass deportations. The first anti-regime demonstrations occurring simultaneously in all three republics were organised by dissidents on 23 August 1987, the anniversary of the Molotov-Ribbentrop Pact. Several of the organisers of these meetings were sent into exile abroad but the willingness of the authorities to use force was crumbling: the last use of force to break up political demonstrations was on 28 September 1988 in Vilnius.[33] The last remaining Baltic political prisoners were released from the gulag during 1988.

The first mass protests, in 1986 and 1987, were about environmental issues: the proposed building of a hydroelectric dam on the Daugava river, the expansion of open-pit phosphate mining in north-eastern Estonia, and the construction of a third reactor at the Ignalina nuclear power plant in Lithuania. At that time, it would not have been possible to organise large-scale demonstrations about political issues. These ostensibly apolitical environmental issues, therefore, provided the first opportunity for the expression of public discontent. The Chernobyl nuclear power plant disaster in Soviet Ukraine in 1986 gave a strong impetus to public discussion of ecological concerns. Baltic activists were also deeply concerned about the demographic effect of the proposed large-scale projects, since they would bring about a substantial influx of labour from the rest of the USSR, further tilting the negative demographic trend against the Latvians and Estonians. The environment provided the first opening for alternative public mobilisation and organisation. In the forefront was the Latvian Environmental Protection Club (*Vides Aizsardzības Klubs*). In Estonia, a similar role was played by the Estonian Heritage Society (*Eesti Muinsuskaitse Selts*), which started innocently by tidying up old cemeteries, but soon began restoring memorials from the war of independence.

Although the Estonian, Latvian and Lithuanian Communist Party leaderships were reluctant, society eagerly seized the opportunity presented by Gorbachev's call for *perestroika*. One of the first benefits of *glasnost* for the people was the lessening of restrictions on travel abroad. As earlier, the Baltic states were seen as a laboratory for economic experimentation. Some of the first Soviet joint ventures with foreign companies were located in Estonia. In response to the all-union ministries' disregard for local conditions and opinions, four Estonian intellectuals published the Self-Managing Estonia proposal (IME) on 26 September 1987.[34] This initiative was met with disapproval in Moscow.

The drive for democratic reform became overtly political in April 1988 at the plenary meeting of Estonian Creative Unions. Speakers criticised the republic's party and government leadership, and some outspoken delegates even dared to question Estonia's belonging in the USSR. The creative intelligentsia, particular writers who had achieved great moral authority, played the leading role in broaching previously forbidden subjects and emboldening people to speak freely.

The first challenge to the Communist Party's monopoly of power came with the establishment of the 'Estonian Popular Front in Support of *Perestroika*' announced on a live television talk show on 13 April 1988 by its founding leader, economic planner and Communist Party member Edgar Savisaar (b. 1950). This initiative received Gorbachev's blessing: he saw it as a means of applying pressure on the republican Communist Party leaderships who were dragging their feet in implementing his reforms. The Popular Front rapidly gained tens of thousands of members and supporters across the republic and its example was quickly emulated in Latvia and Lithuania.

In spite of slogans of democratisation, in May the Estonian Communist Party leadership handpicked the delegates for the 19th Party Conference in Moscow as usual. In response, the Estonian Popular Front organised political protests. Unsanctioned all-night gatherings took place in June at the grounds of the Tallinn song festival, where the people demanded the replacement of the old-guard Estonian Communist Party leadership and waved the banned national colours. Gorbachev rejected the plea of the beleaguered Karl Vaino to bring tanks onto the streets and instead appointed Vaino Väljas (b. 1931), the first native-born Estonian Communist Party leader since 1950. Väljas immediately signalled his willingness to work together with the Popular Front, and participated in the culmination of the Singing Revolution[35] – a mammoth rally organised by the Popular Front in September at the grounds of the song festival, where 250,000 people, one-quarter of all Estonians, sang in unison. The only word to describe the intense feelings of this time is euphoria. Anatol Lieven memorably described the song festivals as 'Rousseau's General Will set to music'.[36]

Latvians and Lithuanians experienced their own 'new awakening', although this was not initially accompanied by political change. The long, hot summer of 1988 was full of feverish patriotic activity and new unheard-of democratic initiatives. The banned national flags appeared everywhere. Huge rallies attended by tens of thousands were held in Rīga and Vilnius. A rally in Vilnius on 23 August brought out more than two hundred thousand Lithuanians. The Latvian and Lithuanian Communist Party leaderships managed to resist the winds of change for a few more months. The Lithuanian Communist Party leadership ordered the forcible dispersal of a demonstration organised by the dissidents of the Lithuanian Freedom League on 28 September, but this only served to demonstrate how out of step it was with times. In October, the old-guard Brezhnevite party and governmental leaders in Latvia and Lithuania were replaced by Gorbachev allies sympathetic to the nascent Popular Fronts. Algirdas Brazauskas (b. 1932), the physically robust and politically nimble party secretary responsible for industry, was promoted to the top job in Lithuania. He won immediate popularity by announcing the return of Vilnius Cathedral to the Catholic Church. In Latvia, the old guard was more entrenched, and the favourite of the Communist Party reformers, Anatolijs Gorbunovs (b. 1942), was made not first secretary but chairman of the Presidium of the Supreme Soviet, while his predecessor in that post, the lacklustre Jānis Vagris (b. 1930), was given the executive job.

The three Popular Front movements held their formal founding congresses in October where they also pledged to work together. Their platforms called for democratisation and economic self-management, while stressing that their demands were based on the principles of Gorbachev's *perestroika*. Although they also had concerns such as making the titular language the official language, the Popular Fronts construed themselves in a broader context than just as national movements. The Latvian Popular Front elected journalist Dainis Īvāns (b. 1955), a leading campaigner against the construction of the hydroelectric dam, as its leader, and the Lithuanian Movement for *Perestroika*, known simply as *Sąjūdis* (Movement), elected musicologist Vytautas Landsbergis (b. 1932) to fulfil the same role. The founders of the Popular Fronts were mainly intellectuals, scientists and writers, but the movements rapidly burgeoned to include a vast cross-section of society, a membership of hundreds of thousands, the largest political movements ever in the Baltic countries. Subsequently, the Baltic Popular Fronts provided role models for 'non-formal' organisations and democratisation throughout the USSR.[37]

At about the same time, organisations were created which were even more radical. Dissidents founded the Estonian National Independence Party on 20 August 1988, the first political party besides the Communist Party to be allowed to function in the USSR. The Latvian National Independence Movement was founded by the former communist Berklāvs and his supporters on 20 June 1988, and the Lithuanian Freedom League, which had previously been active underground in the 1970s, was now able to operate openly. Launched by dissidents, and initially viewed as marginal and dangerously radical, the discourse of these principled and uncompromising organisations was eventually adopted by the Popular Fronts.

Seeking to strengthen his position vis-à-vis his conservative opponents in the CPSU, Gorbachev initiated constitutional changes to create a presidential system. His package of constitutional amendments, however, alarmed the Baltic republics since it also dropped any mention of the right of secession from the Union. The Estonian Supreme Soviet reacted to this potential usurpation of power on 16 November 1988 by making its 'Declaration about Sovereignty', stating that republican laws had precedence over federal ones. The Kremlin's fierce criticism did not succeed in forcing the Estonians to back down, but did ensure that the Lithuanian and Latvian Supreme Soviets did not follow suit until six months later. Similar sovereignty declarations by other republics followed soon thereafter. These declarations seriously undermined the USSR, particularly when the Russian SFSR led by Boris Yeltsin (1931–2007) declared its sovereignty in June 1990.

In the first multicandidate elections held in the USSR in March 1989 – the elections to the USSR Congress of People's Deputies – candidates supported by the Popular Fronts won overwhelmingly in all three republics. These deputies were to play an important role in explaining Baltic aspirations and forming alliances with Russian democrats. Furthermore, the activities of the Balts provided an inspiration for reformists and nationalists from other republics. During the sessions of the congress in Moscow, Estonian, Latvian and Lithuanian deputies worked closely together to push for economic autonomy and the acknowledgement of the existence and condemnation of the secret protocols of the Molotov-Ribbentrop Pact.[38]

In May 1989 the Baltic Assembly met in Tallinn for the first time on the initiative of Popular Front deputies, and a Baltic council was initiated later as a format for Estonian, Latvian and Lithuanian cooperation on the ministerial level. These bodies held regular meetings to coordinate activities and adopt resolutions explaining Baltic positions to the outside world. The Baltic Assembly organised a 600-kilometre human chain ('the Baltic Way') from Tallinn to Vilnius via Rīga: nearly two million people joined hands on 23 August 1989, the fiftieth anniversary of the Molotov-Ribbentrop Pact. This unprecedented demonstration put the Balts' aspirations on the front pages of international newspapers and demonstrated the strength of Baltic cooperation and unity of purpose.

The collapse of the communist regimes in the USSR's Eastern European satellites during the autumn of 1989, particularly the fall of the Berlin Wall in November, emboldened the Balts by demonstrating that their dreams were not utopian. In the common narrative of the collapse of communism, the achievement of liberty in the Warsaw Pact countries opened the way for the captive nations of the USSR. However, it should be noted that the breakthrough in the Baltic republics had occurred already one year earlier. The Singing Revolution in 1988 had already brought a degree of freedom, although not yet democracy and independence.


TOWARDS INDEPENDENCE

By the end of 1989, the internal debate within the Baltic national movements between proponents of greater autonomy or outright independence had been resolved in favour of the latter. The republican Communist Party leaderships struggled to keep up with the pace set by the popular movements, but became increasingly irrelevant. In a desperate attempt to maintain some popular support, the Lithuanian Communist Party declared its independence from the Communist Party of the Soviet Union in December 1989. Realising the mortal danger that this move posed for the USSR, Gorbachev flew to Vilnius, but could not budge Brazauskas. Gorbachev's ultimate failure stemmed from the fact that he never appreciated the strength and genuineness of national sentiment in the USSR. Subsequently, the three Baltic Communist Parties split mainly along ethnic lines into old guard and pro-independence organisations. Only in Latvia were hardline communists, led by Alfrēds Rubiks (b. 1935), able to maintain control of the party organisation.

An unprecedented grass-roots movement – Citizens' Committees – emerged in Estonia in April 1989. The idea formulated by Trivimi Velliste (b. 1947), the leader of the Estonian Heritage Society, was to register the citizens of the pre-1940 republic and their descendants (including exiles) and to restore independent statehood on the basis of the popular will of the citizenry without any reference to Soviet institutions. By February 1990, most Estonians – 800,000 people – had registered themselves as citizens. The movement culminated in elections organised by the Citizens' Committees where 90 per cent of registered citizens voted on 24 February 1990 for an assembly called the Congress of Estonia.[39] The voluntary organisation of elections despite the opposition of the Soviet authorities was a remarkable achievement. Participation in the process was a psychological and moral breakthrough.

The congress elected an executive body known as the Committee of Estonia which was headed by dissident Tunne Kelam (b. 1936), one of the leaders of the Estonian National Independence Party. The committee did not attempt to exercise power but chose to remain purely a moral authority. In a certain sense, there was a historical parallel to the revolutionary situation in 1917 when both the provisional government and the Soviets claimed to be the ultimate authority. The national movement split between restorationists, who stressed the principle of legal continuity and viewed Soviet institutions as illegitimate, and the Popular Front, who sought to undermine the system from within by taking control of the Soviet institutions. The former did not trust the ex-communists leading the Popular Front, whereas the fundamentalists' approach appeared unrealistic to most. Although this led to rivalry and recriminations within the independence movements, in the end both approaches made an important contribution and their competition actually helped advance the Baltic cause. The fundamentalists forced the pace and ensured that the leadership of the Popular Front did not make any fatal compromises with the Kremlin, while the Popular Front could claim to be 'moderate' interlocutors with Moscow reformers.[40]

Citizens' Committees were also formed in Latvia, but they did not gain the same amount of influence as the Estonian initiative. Nevertheless, as in Estonia, there was tension between the uncompromising and pragmatic wings of the national movement. No Citizens' Congress emerged in Lithuania because the national movement was united under the *Sajūdis* umbrella. The restitutionist model had less appeal in Lithuania as a result of the fact that, unlike Estonia and Latvia, Lithuania had actually gained territory as a consequence of Soviet annexation and remained ethnically relatively homogenous.

The drive to independence became institutionalised when the Popular Fronts won majorities in all three Baltic republics in the first free Supreme Soviet elections held in February–April 1990. First Kazimiera Prunskienė (b. 1943) in Lithuania and then Savisaar in Estonia and Ivars Godmanis (b. 1951) in Latvia formed popular front-led governments. Most of the new government ministers were reform-communist technocrats. The chairmen of the presidiums of the Supreme Soviets (equivalent to heads of state) in Latvia and Estonia remained the high-ranking national-minded communists, Gorbunovs and Arnold Rüütel (b. 1928) respectively. The Lithuanians made a more radical break by electing *Sajūdis* leader Landsbergis to the post. One of the first acts of the newly elected bodies was to discard 'Soviet Socialist' from their titles and restoring the symbols of the pre-war republics.

The renamed Lithuanian Supreme Council pressed ahead faster than the others and declared Lithuania's independence on 11 March 1990. The Kremlin predictably denounced this act as unconstitutional. The Estonians (on 30 March) and the Latvians (on 4 May) moved more cautiously by only declaring an intentionally ambiguous 'transition period to independence'. Moscow sought to bring Lithuania to heel with an economic blockade in April. After three months of hardship, a diplomatic resolution proposed by French and German leaders allowed both sides to save face: Gorbachev terminated the blockade and the Lithuanians 'suspended' their independence declaration.

In all three republics there were Communist Party hardliners who opposed democratisation and Gorbachev's reforms. Together with reactionaries in Moscow, they set up 'International Fronts' generally known as the Interfront (in Lithuania *Yedinstvo* (Unity)), as opposed to the Popular Fronts or national movements. The Interfronts' typical supporters were Russian-speakers (in Lithuania also ethnic Poles) employed in the Soviet military-industrial complex who were alarmed by the new language laws which made the titular language the official language of the republic. They sought to maintain the dominant position of Russian as the 'inter-national' language (hence the name 'International Front'). The Interfronts first attempted to flex their muscles with strike actions in 1989, but these were stymied by Estonians, Latvians, and Lithuanians voluntarily stepping into the breach. Conflict was narrowly averted in May 1990 when Interfront mobs unsuccessfully attempted to storm the Supreme Council buildings in Rīga and Tallinn.

Baltic cooperation in this period could be compared to a team cycling race where one cyclist (nation) does the hard work for a few laps while the others follow close behind. The initial Latvian phase was briefest, starting with the environmental protests in 1986 and 'calendar' demonstrations in 1987; the Singing Revolution was led by the Estonians from the self-management proposal in September 1987 through to autumn 1989; the Lithuanians led the drive to independence beginning from late 1989 when the Lithuanian Communist Party split off from the CPSU. This sequence was largely determined by the demographic situation in each republic.[41] Latvians acted first because they felt most acutely the existential threat of becoming a minority in their own country, but they could not push very far without provoking a strong counterforce among the Russian-speaking residents. The Estonian situation was more favourable, but they also could not risk putting all of their cards on the table at once. The Lithuanians awoke last but, being the most homogeneous and strongly united, were able to lead the final push to independence and overcome the sharpest confrontations.

Seeking to consolidate his power, Gorbachev vacillated between siding with the liberals or with the conservatives in the Soviet establishment. In the autumn of 1990 he aligned himself closer to the latter. The old guard sought to bring the Balts back into line by imposing direct presidential rule on the rebellious republics. The hardliners clearly hoped to act while the world's attention was diverted to the looming Gulf War. In December 1990 a series of a dozen low-yield bombs detonated outside various Soviet military installations and Communist Party buildings in Latvia. Moscow quickly put the blame on 'extreme nationalists'. The explosions resulted in no casualties, but the simultaneous formation by Soviet hardliners of a Latvian National Salvation Committee and the bringing in of additional Soviet military units, ostensibly to hunt draft-dodgers, indicated that the ground was being prepared for the restoration of Soviet order by direct 'presidential rule'. However, when the Lithuanian government unexpectedly collapsed as a result of economic difficulties on 7 January 1991, the conspirators shifted their focus to Lithuania, mistakenly believing that the moment had come to capitalise on the perceived disunity in Lithuanian ranks.[42] On the night of 12 January 1991 a shadowy Lithuanian National Salvation Committee declared that it was assuming power. Soviet military units were brought into the republic with instructions to seize control of strategic sites. Lithuanians heroically formed a human shield around the Supreme Council building, and 14 unarmed people died defending the television tower. The vivid and unforgettable image of that night, which was seen around the world, was of Lithuanians attempting to push a Soviet tank off the body of one of their fellows.

In addition to the courageous non-violent resistance and unwelcome Western media coverage, the hardliners were thwarted by the surprise visit of Boris Yeltsin, chairman of the Supreme Soviet of the Russian SFSR on 13 January to Tallinn, where he signed declarations establishing bilateral relations with the three Baltic republics. Yeltsin understood that the fate of democratisation in Russia hung in the balance and he called upon Russian troops not to act against the people. However, the danger had not yet passed. Barricades were hastily erected to defend public buildings in Rīga and Tallinn as Soviet Interior Ministry special units (OMON) escalated tension and the Latvian National Salvation Committee demanded the replacement of the government. On 20 January, OMON units ransacked the Latvian ministry of the interior in Rīga, killing five civilians in the process. Gorbachev's subsequent claim of ignorance of the violent crackdown and his blaming the events on local extremists was clearly disingenuous.[43]

The resort to violence by the Kremlin only strengthened the resolve of the Balts in their aim of self-determination. Gorbachev's remaining strategy was to make separation as difficult as possible. To this end, he proposed a new union treaty to transform the USSR into a looser federation of republics. The Baltic governments boycotted Gorbachev's All-Union referendum scheduled for 17 March 1991 and pre-empted it with their own referenda on independence. On 9 February Lithuanians voted 91 per cent in favour of independence. On 3 March 78 per cent approved Estonian independence, and even in Latvia, with its large Russian-speaking minority, 74 per cent of residents supported independence on 3 March.

The situation in spring 1991 resembled a stalemate. The Balts sought fruitlessly to engage the Kremlin in negotiations about independence. The Baltic governments exercised almost all the functions of a state but did not control their own territory, even though they established their own unarmed border guard services. Thus one of the crucial criteria for international recognition was lacking. The Kremlin continued to label democratically elected Baltic leaders as 'extremists' and attempted to destabilise the republics in order to discredit their drive for independence.

One of the most direct instruments for doing so were the OMON units which perpetrated multiple attacks in the first half of 1991. OMON units hunted Red Army draft-dodgers and seized telecommunications facilities, printing presses, and buildings claimed for the pro-Moscow Communist Party. The most brutal incident was the cold-blooded execution of seven Lithuanian border guards on 31 July 1991. Part of this strategy was to intimidate the Balts, but the main goal was to provoke them into some kind of violent response. International sympathy for the Balts depended on their peaceful and democratic behaviour. If violence could be provoked, then the Soviet authorities could implement direct presidential rule in the name of maintaining order. Remarkably, the Balts succeeded in keeping their cool during months of extreme pressure.

During this time, the Estonian, Latvian, and Lithuanian Popular Front governments pursued international recognition. Although there were some high-level meetings with Western governments, these were mostly unofficial, in order to maintain international stability. While there was sympathy for the Baltic cause, the international community's priority was to support Gorbachev's reforms and end the Cold War. There was a tacit agreement that nothing should be done which might conceivably undermine or weaken Gorbachev's position. Although most Western states adhered to the principle of non-recognition of the annexation of the Baltic states, as formulated by the USA in 1940, the message to the Balts was to be patient and not to rock the boat too much.[44]

Although Gorbachev's Union Treaty was rejected by the Balts, it also went too far for the Communist Party hardliners who organised a putsch in Moscow on 19 August 1991, the day before the scheduled signing of the treaty. They placed Gorbachev under house arrest in his Crimean summer residence. A State Emergency Committee (consisting mainly of members of Gorbachev's own government and including interior minister Boriss Pugo, formerly Latvian Party boss) took control, claiming implausibly that Gorbachev was too ill to carry out his duties. The commander of the Soviet Baltic Military District, General Fyodor Kuzmin, announced the implementation of martial law to the Baltic governments, who refused to comply and condemned the coup. Soviet troop columns and OMON units were dispatched to the Baltic cities by the conspirators. They managed to take control of some key buildings such as the television studios in Kaunas and the central telephone exchange in Rīga, but were thwarted at other strategic sites, notably the television tower in Tallinn. As in January, the Balts quickly erected barricades and people rushed out to protect important government buildings. Estonians, Latvians and Lithuanians acted resolutely and in unison.

The putsch removed remaining doubts about the prudence of going forward with full independence. On 20 August Lithuania reaffirmed its independence and the Estonian Supreme Council voted to restore Estonian independence immediately, with Latvia following suit the next day. The decisive events occurred in Moscow where the conspirators did not count on the heroic defence of the Russian Supreme Soviet by Yeltsin. By 22 August the coup attempt collapsed and the troops returned to their barracks. Gorbachev returned to office but the power was now in Yeltsin's hands.

Nordic and East European countries and the Russian SFSR led the wave of international recognition for Baltic independence which followed in the final week of August and culminated with the USSR's grudging acceptance of the fact on 6 September. On 17 September the Baltic states were admitted to the United Nations. Three months later, Yeltsin dissolved the Soviet Union. Although the achievement of Baltic independence is usually attributed to the collapse of the USSR, the opposite is closer to the truth. The Baltic popular movements hastened the pace of democratisation within the USSR and undermined the foundations of the Soviet Empire.

# 8

# Return to the West
# (1991–2009)

After the euphoria of the restoration of their independence, the Balts had to overcome many new challenges. They faced several years of a desperate economic situation which was the inevitable outcome of the transition from a command economy to a market economy. They also confronted the difficult tasks of state-building and dealing with the legacies of the Soviet era, including coming to terms with a radically altered demographic situation. The Baltic states set ambitious goals for themselves: a reorientation of their trade towards the West, integration into the European community, and attainment of the standards and conditions necessary for membership of the European Union and NATO.

BUILDING DEMOCRACY

As in their earlier period of independence, the three Baltic states chose similar frameworks for their new political systems. This was understandable because they were again reacting against their common previous regime and restoring their pre-war institutions. Just as in the 1920s, one of the main models for constitutional design that they followed was that of Germany. The Estonian constitution, drafted by a special constituent assembly, was again the first to be completed and approved in a national referendum in June 1992. The Lithuanian Supreme Council drafted a constitution which was also approved in a national referendum in October 1992. Latvia emphasised continuity with the pre-war republic in July 1993 by bringing back into force the 1922 constitution and simply making modernising amendments to it.[1]

According to these constitutions, the head of state in all three republics is the president, whose powers are mainly symbolic. The Estonian and Lithuanian presidents are elected for a five-year term and the Latvian president for a four-year term,[2] and they can serve a maximum of two terms. The election of the Latvian president is by an absolute majority in the parliament. Estonia requires a two-thirds majority in the parliament, which in practice has been difficult to obtain. All presidential elections in Estonia, with the exception of the first, have, therefore, been decided in a specially convened electoral college composed of the members of parliament plus delegates from local governments. In a departure from the other two constitutional models, Lithuania followed the French style of directly elected presidency, featuring a run-off between the two front-runners. Although the Lithuanian system is often referred to as semi-presidential, the powers of the presidency differ little from those in Estonia and Latvia. However, the Lithuanian president's moral authority is clearly enhanced by the fact that his or her mandate is derived directly from the people.

All three countries have unicameral parliaments, the 101-seat Estonian *Riigikogu*, the 100-seat Latvian *Saeima*, and the 141-seat Lithuanian *Seimas*, which are elected for four years[3] and have a 5 per cent threshold[4] for political parties to gain representation. Unlike Estonia and Latvia, which opted for a parliamentary electoral system based on proportional representation and party lists, Lithuania chose a mixed system, similar to that in Germany, with half of the parliamentary deputies being elected in a first-past-the-post fashion[5] and the other half by party list. The use of direct democratic means – referenda – has become a feature of only the Latvian political system, although 300,000 Lithuania citizens can also initiate referenda. Latvian citizens have on several occasions availed themselves of this instrument, since a referendum can be initiated by the collection of the signatures of 10 per cent of the electorate.

Estonia made the cleanest break with the Soviet past in its founding elections in September 1992 with the victory of Pro Patria (*Isamaa*), led by the youthful historian Mart Laar. The new government had few links with the past: several ministers, including Laar, were under 35 years of age, and three were émigrés. Laar's government immediately embarked on radical free-market reforms, liberalisation of the economy and privatisation. The election of the polyglot Lennart Meri as president emphasised the rupture. Meri, a writer and ethnographic film-maker, known for his erudition and whimsical humour, had established the Estonian Foreign Ministry in 1990.

In contrast, Lithuania stunned the world by being the first post-Soviet country to return the former communists (renamed as the Democratic Labour Party) to power in the October 1992 elections and their leader Algirdas Brazauskas as president of the republic in February 1993. The ex-communists' victory could be ascribed to the plummeting economy and dissatisfaction with Landsbergis' confrontational style, but also to the fact that, unlike the Communist Parties in Estonia and Latvia, the Lithuanian Party had deeper roots in local society. The Estonian and Latvian Communist Parties were strongly identified with foreign occupation and ethnic Russian dominance. Furthermore, Brazauskas, as the final first secretary of the Communist Party, had played a leading role in Lithuania's break from the USSR.

Latvia took the longest to establish its new institutions. It chose a middle path of continuity, with the victory of Latvia's Way, a centre-right party which grew out of the Popular Front, in the founding election of 1993. A government was formed under Valdis Birkavs of Latvia's Way. Guntis Ulmanis, a moderate figure, whose main asset was his surname which symbolised continuity with the pre-war state, was elected president by the *Saeima*.[6]

After living five decades in a one-party state, Estonians, Latvians and Lithuanians were eager, but not well prepared, to participate fully in a free and open civil society. The connection between the new political parties and society was weak. Since the political parties were not based on any particular interest groups in society, the parties were formed mainly around personalities rather than socio-economic cleavages. This resulted in a volatile political party system, with frequent changes in party allegiances by the elected representatives, particularly in Estonia and Latvia during the 1990s. The second and third post-independence elections in all three Baltic states rejected the incumbent governments. Nevertheless, broad outlines of policy – free market reforms and integration with Western Europe – remained consistent.

The 1995 *Riigikogu* elections in Estonia were won by former premier Tiit Vähi's Coalition Party (*Koonderakond*), which touted its managerial experience. Vähi formed a coalition government, first with the Centre Party, headed by another former prime minister, Savisaar, and then with the liberal Reform Party, led by Siim Kallas, the former governor of the Central Bank. The Coalition Party managed to survive in office until the 1999 general election, but in the final two years it was a minority government led by former broadcaster Mart Siimann. The 1999 election gave a second opportunity for Laar and his Pro Patria Union, who formed a centre-right coalition government together with the Reform Party and the social democrats.[7] The Laar government completed infrastructural privatisation, but was weakened by the outcome of the 2001 presidential election, in which the failure of the governing parties to agree upon a joint candidate to succeed Meri led to the unexpected victory of a relic from the past, Arnold Rüütel. Rüütel had been Meri's main rival in the previous two elections, and in many respects was his opposite. Rüütel had served as the last chairman of the Presidium of the Supreme Soviet, but had gained popularity for his pro-independence position during the Singing Revolution and enjoyed strong support from the countryside. After this setback, the government began to crumble, and it resigned in January 2002.

A new governing coalition was formed by the pro-business Reform Party and the Centre Party, the champion of the discontented. The new government was headed by the Reform Party's Kallas, previously finance minister in Laar's government, although the Centre Party held the majority of cabinet portfolios. This coalition of ideological opposites proved to be surprisingly effective. Estonian domestic politics since 1990 is best understood not by viewing it on a left–right scale, but by positioning around the wily Savisaar – consistently both the most admired and most vilified politician – and his Centre Party, the largest party but one which the other parties have sought to exclude from power.

The political landscape in post-Soviet Latvia has been chaotic and the political party system has not yet consolidated. Until 2006, every general election held since the restoration of independence was won by a new party which had not even existed at the time of the previous election. The 1995 general election was won with a mere 15 per cent of the vote by a new populist left-wing party, the Democratic Party *Saimnieks* ('The Master'), followed closely by a new populist right-wing party, the Popular Movement for Latvia, led by Joachim Siegerist (Zigerists), a controversial German-Latvian politician. Siegerist's party was kept out of office by a six-party coalition headed by Andris Šķēle, a prominent entrepreneur without political affiliation. After being forced out of office in 1997, Šķēle launched his own political party, the People's Party, which won the 1998 elections but had to allow Vilis Krištopans of Latvia's Way to head the new government.

After Ulmanis' second term ended in July 1999, the election of the new president by the *Saeima* was a cliff-hanger. The favoured candidate was the famous pop composer Raimonds Pauls but, after seven rounds

**Map 7**  The Baltic states today

of deadlock, the parliament voted for a compromise candidate, Vaira Vīķe-Freiberga, a psychology professor from Montreal. She became the first female head of state in Eastern Europe. Her perfect command of English and French enabled her to make a mark internationally and her Thatcheresque mannerisms won her the label of 'Iron Lady' of the Baltic states. While Estonian President Meri was the shining star, media favourite and international spokesman of the Baltic states in the 1990s, Vīķe-Freiberga played that role with poise and self-assurance at the beginning of the twenty-first century.

Vīķe-Freiberga reappointed Šķēle as prime minister in July 1999. However, his governing coalition disintegrated in less than a year as a result of disagreements over privatisation. Subsequently, Andris Bērziņš of Latvia's Way formed a new cabinet based on the same four coalition parties, which managed to stay in office until the *Saeima*'s term expired in October 2002.

Compared to Estonia and Latvia in the 1990s, the political party system in Lithuania appeared to be more consolidated but also more polarised, with two large parties representing the left and right and alternately in power. The pendulum swung back to the right in the second general election in 1996, when the Homeland Union–Lithuanian Conservatives, the successor party to *Sajūdis* and led by Landsbergis, won an absolute majority. No prime minister in the Baltic states has yet been able to serve the full term of one parliament. The longest-serving in the 1990s were Adolfas Šleževičius (1993–6) and Gediminas Vagnorius (1996–9). At the end of his first term as president in 1998, Brazauskas announced his retirement from politics. As his arch-rival Landsbergis fared poorly in the first round of the 1998 presidential election, it appeared that there was an opening for a new generation in Lithuanian politics, but Brazauskas' favoured successor, Artūras Paulauskas, lost in the second round to Valdas Adamkus, a retired US Environmental Protection Agency senior official, who had fled Lithuania as a teenager at the end of the war. As president, Adamkus did much to enhance Lithuania's bid for EU and NATO membership. Brazauskas' retirement proved to be premature, as in October 2000, leading a left-wing coalition, he trounced the right in the general election. After a brief spell of a minority government headed by the mercurial centrist Rolandas Paksas, Brazauskas became prime minister in 2001 at the head of a majority coalition, and would remain in office for nearly five years.

## POLITICS IN THE TWENTY-FIRST CENTURY

The first years of the new millennium witnessed a wave of new and successful insurgent populist parties in all three states.[8] Although both the governing Centre and Reform Parties did well in the March 2003 Estonian *Riigikogu* elections, a new, populist centre-right party, Res Publica, which championed law and order, transparency and the fight against corruption, came out on top. Its leader, former state auditor Juhan Parts, led a new government which included the Reform Party. The Parts cabinet was exceptionally young and inexperienced, even by Estonian standards. Its popularity soon nosedived as a result of the government's failure to satisfy overinflated expectations. It managed to remain in office for two years until March 2005. The Reform Party's leader, the former mayor of Tartu Andrus Ansip – having taken over from Kallas, who had become a vice-president of the European Commission – became the new prime minister, and Savisaar's Centre Party replaced Res Publica in the government.

The Centre–Reform ruling coalition was split over the 2006 presidential election. President Rüütel was denied a second term by the narrow victory of Toomas Hendrik Ilves in the electoral college. Ilves, who grew up in New Jersey, had distinguished himself as the foreign minister who led Estonia into the European Union. With Ilves' election, all three Baltic states simultaneously had heads of state who had spent most of their adult lives in North America. Nevertheless, although several Baltic émigrés occupied positions of high visibility in public life, the number of those who actually returned to take up permanent residence in their homeland was in the hundreds rather than the thousands.

In the 2007 *Riigikogu* elections, the two main governing parties both increased their share of the vote, but the Reform Party managed to best the Centre Party. For the first time, a governing party won the parliamentary elections. Prime Minister Ansip, however, decided to drop his coalition partner and form a new government together with an ideologically closer partner, the Pro Patria and Res Publica Union, and also, initially, the smaller Social Democrats. Ansip became the longest continually serving prime minister in the Baltic states.

In Latvia, the new populist wave was initiated by the respected governor of the Central Bank, Einārs Repše, who resigned in 2001 in order to form his own political party, New Era. Campaigning on an anti-corruption platform, New Era triumphed in the 2002 elections, receiving almost one-quarter of the votes cast and becoming the largest party in the *Saeima*. Repše's drive for transparency and accountability led to a row with his coalition partner, Latvia's First Party, another new populist party formed by entrepreneur Ainārs Šlesers. This resulted in the collapse of the government in February 2004. Indulis Emsis of the Greens and Farmers' Union formed a new, minority, centre-left government – notable as the first government in the world headed by a Green prime minister.[9] However, his administration lasted only until December 2004 when Aigars Kalvītis of the People's Party formed a new centre-right coalition.

In the 2006 *Saeima* elections, the governing party, which claimed the credit for the rapid economic growth, was re-elected for the first time. Prime Minister Kalvītis' new government, however, soon faced a series of allegations of political corruption. Commentators had noted that three wealthy 'oligarchs', Šķēle, Šlesers and Aivars Lembergs (the long-time mayor of Ventspils, the port city which prospered from the Russian oil transit trade), enjoyed a large measure of influence over political parties in the government. Political and business interests appeared to be closely interconnected and Latvia had one of the least transparent systems in the EU for financing political campaigns. President Vīķe-Freiberga left office at the end of her second term in July 2007, warning that the Kalvītis government was doing the bidding of the 'oligarchs' in introducing legislation which curbed the independence of investigative bodies. She was succeeded by the politically inexperienced orthopaedic surgeon Valdis Zatlers, whose election by the *Saeima* was greeted with concerns that he was a pliant figurehead for the ruling parties. The government's hasty dismissal of the anti-corruption bureau chief occasioned a large demonstration in November 2007 (dubbed the 'umbrella revolution') which forced Kalvītis to resign. Nevertheless, the same coalition continued to govern, led by the political veteran Ivars Godmanis.

In despair at having no way of influencing the government until the next elections, more than 200,000 citizens gave their signatures in support of a constitutional amendment which allowed one-tenth of the electorate to initiate a referendum to dissolve the *Saeima*. In August 2008, 97 per cent voted in favour of the constitutional amendment in a national referendum, but the turnout fell short of the required one-half of the electorate. Anger at the government and distrust of the political parties continued to mount, particularly after Godmanis was forced to curtail public spending as the economic boom turned to bust. In March 2009 Godmanis resigned and was replaced by Valdis Dombrovskis from the New Era Party, whose main priority was to make draconian cuts in the state budget and restructure the economy in order to fulfil the requirements of the loan from the International Monetary Fund (IMF).

In Lithuania, the shifts in power between the two large parties of the left and right was rocked by the rise of the new populist challengers in the beginning of the twenty-first century. In the presidential election of 2003, the disaffected – the losers in the transition period – rallied behind the populist mayor of Vilnius, stunt pilot Rolandas Paksas, who unexpectedly defeated Adamkus. Suspicions immediately arose regarding the sources of funding for Paksas' campaign. The *Seimas* impeached President Paksas in April 2004 after he unconstitutionally awarded citizenship to his main financial backer, Yuri Borisov, a Russian arms dealer. Adamkus was returned to the presidency in July 2004.

Astonishingly, after having fallen for one fraudulent populist, Lithuanians immediately turned to another: Viktor Uspaskich, an ethnic Russian who made his fortune in the food-processing business. His populist Labour Party won the 2004 *Seimas* election. However, President Adamkus made it clear that he would not allow the Labour Party to lead the government. The Labour Party therefore became a coalition partner in a government once again headed by Brazauskas, who symbolised continuity. The Labour Party crumbled when a double-accounting scheme for making payments to the party's MPs was uncovered in 2006, and Uspaskich temporarily sought refuge from criminal charges in Russia. The scandal prompted Brazauskas finally to retire in 2006. His longtime right-hand man, Gediminas Kirkilas, became leader of the Social Democrats and led the government until the general election in October 2008.

Renewing the traditional pattern of alternation between left and right, the conservative Homeland Union won the election, while the Social Democrats recorded their most dismal result. The old populists, Paksas and Uspaskich, were trumped by the newly formed National Resurrection Party, the vehicle of the popular television entertainer Arūnas Valinskas, who became chairman of the *Seimas*. His party became the junior partner in the new ruling coalition led by the Homeland Union's Andrius Kubilius. In the midst of the sharp economic downturn in 2009, Lithuanians elected Dalia Grybauskaitė, the European commissioner for budgetary planning, as their new president.

## ECONOMIC REFORMS

After the euphoria of achieving recognition of their independence, the Baltic states faced several years of a desperate economic situation and the transition from a command economy to a market economy. Their economies were still closely connected to that of the former Soviet Union, which was rapidly descending into hyperinflation and chaos. In June 1992, while the IMF and the World Bank were advising the Baltic states to remain in the rouble zone since the great majority of their trade was with the former Soviet Union, the interim Estonian government, headed by Vähi, took the courageous step of being the first ex-Soviet country to introduce its own currency, the *kroon*. The reform succeeded in curbing runaway inflation, bringing goods which had not been seen for years back on to shop shelves and putting an end to the black market. Being pegged to the German mark through a currency board system, the *kroon* provided Estonia with the necessary financial stability to plough ahead with radical free-market reforms and laid the basis for economic recovery. Unlike Estonia, Latvia and Lithuania both introduced temporary currencies parallel to the rouble, the Latvian *rubelis* and the Lithuanian *talonas*, before establishing their own currencies, the *lats* (pegged to a basket of major international currencies) and the *litas* (pegged to the US dollar) in 1993.[10]

Estonia launched the most rapid and radical free-market reforms. The economic philosophy of the first government headed by Mart Laar was inspired by Milton Friedman and Margaret Thatcher and was coined 'shock therapy'. Laar's bold approach won plaudits from the IMF but angered farmers and pensioners, whose situation deteriorated markedly. Latvia followed Estonia's path with some delay, while Lithuania in the first half of the 1990s attempted to pursue a more evolutionary approach, which some have ascribed to Lithuanian society's more collectivist instincts as opposed to Estonian individualism.[11]

The economies reached the bottom in 1993: the economy contracted by 16.2 per cent in Lithuania, 14.9 per cent in Latvia, and 9.0 per cent in Estonia. Inflation was 90 per cent in Estonia, 109 per cent in Latvia and 410 per cent in Lithuania. By 1996 recovery was well on its way: the economy grew by 3.3 per cent in Latvia, 4.0 per cent in Estonia, and 4.7 per cent in Lithuania, and inflation was brought down to 23 per cent in Estonia, 18 per cent in Latvia, and 25 per cent in Lithuania.[12]

Inefficient manufacturing enterprises, often relatively small units, could not compete successfully and were closed, resulting in substantial unemployment, particularly outside the major cities. Industrial production which was geared for the Soviet market, particularly for military use, was rendered redundant. The economic reforms of the early 1990s brought with them substantial social costs, including a drop in the already-low life-expectancy rate, particularly of men. The rapid transition to a private market economy left various groups, notably pensioners, at a disadvantage. The new republics could not afford to pay ample pensions, yet the cost of living rose perceptibly as a result of market forces. After the straitjacket of communism, the new liberal regime seemed chaotic. Public order deteriorated and crime surged, particularly organised crime, popularly referred to as 'the mafia'. During the 1990s, intimidation of business rivals by violent means was not unusual. Corruption, a characteristic of the Soviet system, continued unabated.

A foundation for the creation of a market economy was the privatisation of property. Differing schemes were utilised by the three states. Housing and enterprises were most commonly purchased using privatisation vouchers which were issued according to individuals' employment record. Privatisation also involved returning land and buildings which had been forcibly nationalised by the Soviet regime to the original owners or their descendants. Restitution of property was an extremely difficult, complex and socially divisive process. Many disputes continued well into the second decade of independence.

Grossly overstaffed Soviet-era state and collective farms could not compete in a market economy and were dissolved. In order to function efficiently, many farms required modernisation – this in turn required capital investment. In a number of cases, attempts were made to run former state farms as cooperatives, but few of these succeeded. With the restitution of property to the original owners, or their heirs, much of the farmland was parcelled into smaller units, comparable to pre-war family farms. An outcome of these transitional processes was that there were many underemployed, as well as some unemployed, people in the countryside.

Like pensioners, these people were the casualties of the economic transition, and they lacked the initiative and capital to do much about it.[13] Gradually, some enterprising farmers began to assemble larger, more economically viable tracts of farmland. They were able to do this because much of the land which had been returned to the original owners lay fallow, unused, since many owners lacked either the interest or the ability to exploit the land. These parcels of farmland were either sold to, or rented by, the entrepreneurs, who were willing to undertake farming as a modern agribusiness. The transition to a market economy dragged on longer in Lithuania because, unlike in Estonia, the government did not immediately end subsidies for farmers. There were also differences in productivity, as reflected in the percentage of the population employed in the agricultural sector, with the highest percentage, and lowest productivity, in Lithuania. The privatisation of large infrastructures which was carried out in the late 1990s and early 2000s occasioned political controversy and scandals. There were some shining successes, such as the privatisation of the state telecommunications companies, but also notable failures, such as the privatisation of Estonian Rail and the sale for strategic reasons of the Lithuanian Mažeikiai oil refinery to a US firm, which then sold it unexpectedly to a Russian company.

In the latter half of the 1990s, the Baltic states became among Europe's most attractive destinations for foreign direct investment.[14] Estonia led the way by unilaterally introducing free trade and introducing radical initiatives in taxation: it was the first European country to introduce a flat rate of income tax (set initially at 26 per cent) in 1994 and to abolish the tax on reinvested corporate profits in 1999. Latvia and Lithuania soon followed suit by introducing the flat rate of tax, as did several other, mainly Eastern European, countries.

After the economic recovery of the mid-1990s, the Baltic states were hit hard by the Asian and Russian financial crises in 1998. The Baltic stock-market bubble burst and many Baltic companies whose main export market was Russia went bankrupt. Fortunately, the setback was only temporary and had the salutary effect of weaning Baltic companies from the eastern market and forcing them to reorient to the EU.

The tempo of economic growth soared in the first decade of the twenty-first century. The Baltic states were the fastest-growing region in the EU, and the 10–12 per cent growth in gross domestic product achieved in 2005–6 placed the Baltic states among the world's best economic performers. An area where Estonia led the way was the spread of information and communications technologies (ICT): the popular software application *Skype*, for example, which allowed voice calls via the internet, was developed in Estonia. Enthusiasm for ICT was also promoted by the public sector which championed 'paperless government'. In 2007, Estonia became the first country in the world to use electronic voting via the internet in a national election.

At the same time, the first years of EU membership saw an outflow of tens of thousands of individuals of working age who sought higher wages, as in the case of Estonian bus drivers and medical doctors to neighbouring

Finland, and Latvian and Lithuanian construction workers to Ireland and the UK, two EU members which did not restrict the entry of labour from the new member states.

The weakness in the remarkable economic success of the Baltic states in the mid-2000s was that the dynamic growth was fuelled not so much by producers but more by domestic consumption, particularly the housing construction boom driven by cheap credit provided by the Nordic banks which dominated the banking sector. A large trade deficit had always been a worrisome indicator of the real state of the Baltic economies. The crunch came in 2008, when growth stalled while inflation increased. The situation was compounded by the global financial crisis which started in September 2008. The Baltic states were plunged into double-digit negative growth in 2009 and had drastically to slash state spending. Latvia found itself in the greatest difficulties and was forced to take a loan from the International Monetary Fund in order to remain solvent and avoid the devaluation of its currency.[15] The terms of the loan required sweeping reductions in expenditure, the raising of taxes and the rationalisation of the public sector.

## SOCIETAL TRANSITION

The most dramatic Soviet legacy was the drastically altered demographic situation of Estonia and Latvia which had endured a massive influx of mainly Russian immigrants since World War II. Reconciling the interests and rights of the indigenous nations and Soviet-era settlers proved to be a complex and emotional conundrum, which also elicited much international attention (becoming the most studied and written-about aspect of Baltic life). The dominant ethnic group in the former empire suddenly found itself as a marginalised minority within the new nation-states. Tens of thousands of Russians and people of other nationalities from the former Soviet Union departed immediately after Baltic independence, but not nearly as many as some Latvian and Estonian nationalists had hoped. Most considered the Baltic states to be their homeland and enjoyed a noticeably higher standard of living than in other parts of the former Soviet Union. For many, there was no one awaiting their return.

Since Estonia and Latvia were restored on the basis of the principle of legal continuity, all those who were citizens prior to the Soviet takeover in 1940 and their descendants were recognised as citizens; all others had to apply for naturalisation. In practice, this meant that a large part of the ethnic Russian population was left disenfranchised. According to the citizenship laws introduced in Estonia in 1993 and in Latvia in 1994, the key requirement for naturalisation was a language exam. The Russian minority in Estonia and Latvia was split into three groups: citizens, stateless persons and those who opted for Russian citizenship, primarily because it allowed visa-free travel to Russia. The Latvian citizenship law attracted severe international criticism for stipulating a quota system whereby only a fixed number of individuals from a certain age group could apply for naturalisation in a given year. Responding to international pressure, Latvia abolished the quota system in a referendum held in 1998.[16] Clearly, the most important impetus for the liberalisation of the citizenship law was the prospect of EU membership.

The other instrument through which Baltic nationalists tried to reassert their dominance over the monolingual Russian settler community was the language law. Although having lived in the country for decades, many ethnic Russians had little knowledge of the Estonian or Latvian language and little desire to learn. As during the Soviet era, separate Russian-, Estonian- and Latvian-language schools continued to exist. In 1999 the Latvian parliament passed legislation which required not only all public institutions but also certain categories of companies in the private sector to conduct their business in Latvian. This law received international condemnation and the newly elected president, Vīķe-Freiberga, vetoed the legislation.

EU conditionality influenced the Estonian and Latvian governments' policies towards their Russian minority.[17] By the end of the 1990s a shift in thinking had occurred, brought about partly by a more realistic assessment of the actual situation but chiefly by the need to meet EU membership requirements. Whereas in the first years after the re-establishment of independence many Estonians and Latvians hoped that many of the Soviet-era settlers would simply return home to Russia, by the end of the millennium the Estonian and Latvian governments had begun to realise that time alone would not solve the problem and that a more proactive approach was needed. Consequently, Estonia and Latvia adopted State Integration Programmes in 2000 with the declared aim of integrating Russian-speakers into society.

The implementation of the state integration programmes faced apathy and opposition. In 2004, Latvian Russians, including school children, demonstrated against changes to school curricula whereby 60 per cent of classes in Russian-language schools would be taught in Latvian. Estonia adopted a more cautious approach by introducing the first

Estonian-language subjects into Russian-language schools only in 2007. Within the EU, the rights of third-country permanent residents were brought into line with those of citizens in 2007. Paradoxically, although the EU has pushed for the faster naturalisation of non-citizens, the extension of the EU's Schengen regime in 2007 to include the Baltic states (allowing permanent residents with third-country (Russian) passports and those with Estonian and Latvian Aliens' passports to travel as freely within the EU as citizens) reduced the incentive for naturalisation. The integration of Estonian society suffered a setback in 2007 when the government's relocation of a Red Army monument in Tallinn caused a riot by Russophone youths. The statue was resented as a marker of occupation by most Estonians but cherished as a memorial for fallen Soviet troops by most Russophones. A breakthrough for the empowerment of the Russian minority in Latvia occurred in 2009 when 33-year-old Russian television journalist Nils Ušakovs, the leader of the Harmony Centre Party, was elected mayor of Rīga.

Lithuania remained a much more homogenous society which did not face the same problems as its northern neighbours and thus could afford to grant citizenship automatically to all residents. In the early 1990s there was still some mutual mistrust in relation to the Polish minority who had largely sided with the *Yedinstvo* hardline communists against independence. Most of the Poles inhabited the countryside around Vilnius – the area which had been the subject of dispute between Poland and Lithuania in the inter-war era. There were fears that Poland could reopen the issue, but the Lithuanian and Polish governments signed a treaty in 1994 which respected the border and the rights of minorities, and the problem quickly faded.

After the collapse of the USSR, Balts who had joined the Communist Party were branded by many as 'collaborators' with the 'occupation regime'. On the other hand, party members themselves tended to justify their actions as having been purely pragmatic, often claiming that they joined the party to help their nation from within the Soviet system. Typically, they claimed that had they not occupied the position they did, then it would have been someone worse – a Russian with no sympathies towards the native culture. The Soviet era entailed moral and ethical compromises and it is therefore not possible to view it purely in terms which are black and white, only various shades of grey. By and large, a societal compromise emerged whereby only those who had worked for the repressive organs (the KGB) faced lustration. The past of a public figure was occasionally compromised when the media revealed his or her role as a KGB informer. Most of the high-ranking communists in Estonia and Latvia did not continue in politics; they generally went into business (and often were quite successful because they were well connected) and thus did not present a political problem. An exception was Rubiks, the last leader of the Latvian Communist Party, who was briefly imprisoned for supporting the 1991 putsch, but was elected to the European Parliament in 2009. It was more of an issue in Lithuania since the successor to the Communist Party continued to govern. One reason why there were no 'witch-hunts' of former communists was the fact that Baltic societies are small societies where most people know each other through various social networks and where the limited pool of human resources would have been diminished by political retribution.[18]

Concomitantly with the political changes, the Baltic states experienced a religious revival in the early 1990s. When church attendance and religious rites were no longer proscribed by the State, christenings, confirmation classes and church weddings became fashionable. The Catholic Church in Lithuania and the Lutheran Church in Estonia and Latvia regained a public role, but Estonia and Latvia nevertheless remained two of the most irreligious nations in the world. Unlike the mainstream churches, the evangelical congregations enjoyed rapid growth, with many new churches built with the financial support of evangelical congregations such as Jehovah's Witnesses, Pentecostals and Methodists from the USA or Western Europe. Mormon missionaries, not to mention Hare Krishnas, were a common sight. On the one hand, this could be explained as a reaction to the repressive Soviet policies; on the other hand, it could be seen as a search for eternal values in societies undergoing rapid change, uncertainty and painful transition.

The new freedom broke down many formerly taboo subjects and liberated modes of behaviour. Soviet society had in many respects been deeply conservative, and Estonian, Latvian and Lithuanian societies were forced to make up decades of social development in a few short years in order to follow the norms of their progressive Nordic neighbours on issues such as gender equality and the public display of homosexuality. The Russian minorities were notably more traditional in their values than Estonians and Latvians.

The 1990s was a contradictory period for culture and the arts and sciences. While they gained their freedom from Marxist dogma and censorship and were able to rejoin the international community, they lost most of the state subsidies that they had enjoyed under the Soviet regime. Museums, theatre troupes, orchestras and other cultural organisations had

difficulty remaining financially afloat. An important role in the development of a civil society was played by international funding bodies, such
as those associated with the US-Hungarian philanthropist George Soros,
whose foundations played a vital role in promoting an 'open society' and
in developing non-governmental civic organisations.

Building a civil society proved to be no easy task: while the Soviet
regime had destroyed personal initiative and accountability, the newly
found freedom unleashed an entrepreneurial spirit which emphasised
personal gain at the expense of social responsibilities. Status was now
defined by the ownership of wealth, particularly status symbols such as
expensive cars. A formerly egalitarian society rapidly became a stratified society. Within a few years, an economy of rationing and scarcity of
consumer goods was transformed into a consumer society valuing instant
gratification, as exemplified by large shopping malls. The cheaper prices
and lower taxes in the Baltic states, when compared to Western European
countries, attracted foreigners, notably Finnish tourists who brought cart-
loads of alcoholic beverages in Tallinn, and young, rowdy British men for
whom Rīga was a favourite destination for stag party weekends. Probably the aspect of freedom which was most appreciated by citizens was
the ability to travel. The world was now open to Estonians, Latvians
and Lithuanians, although it was several years before Western countries
removed visa requirements. The opportunity to study abroad was particularily important for broadening horizons and bringing new ideas to
Baltic societies.


RETURN TO EUROPE


After achieving independence, Estonia, Latvia and Lithuania sought to
distance themselves as rapidly as possible from the Soviet legacy. Their
primary foreign-policy objective was to integrate quickly into European and international institutions. Two important milestones were the
admission of Estonia and Lithuania into the Council of Europe in 1993
(Latvia's entry was delayed by two years as a result of concern about the
status of the Russian-speaking minority) and Estonian and Latvian membership of the World Trade Organisation in 1999 (Lithuania in 2001).

In the first half of the 1990s, while they were still outside of European
structures, Estonian, Latvian and Lithuanian cooperation played an
important role. The formal institutions of cooperation, the interparlia-
mentary Baltic Assembly and the Baltic Council of Ministers, which had

been established earlier in 1990 as forums for coordinating strategy in their struggle for independence, were developed further along the lines of Nordic cooperation. A Baltic free-trade area, established in 1994, was mainly for political reasons rather than for economic benefit, because the economies of the three countries compete with, rather than complement, each other, producing similar goods for the same markets.[19] Estonian–Latvian–Lithuania tripartite cooperation was strongly encouraged by Western countries as a means of demonstrating their maturity and readiness for eventual membership of the European Union and NATO.[20]

Cooperation with neighbours in their region, first and foremost the Nordic countries, particularly Finland, Sweden and Denmark, also played a crucial role in the successful transition of the Baltic states to a free-market economy and democracy. Expanding the zone of stability and prosperity in their region was also clearly recognised as being in the Nordic states' own interest. From 1992 an institutional framework for cooperation was provided by the Council of Baltic Sea States, comprised of 11 members. The Nordic countries were the most significant investors in the region and supported the interests of the Baltic states in international organisations. By the end of the 1990s, a 5+3 format of the five Nordic countries plus the three Baltic states had become common for multilateral cooperation. Regional interaction was not only at an official level but also flourished at the grass-roots level: churches, schools, professional associations, sport clubs, cultural societies and various other components of civil society eagerly established a dense network of people-to-people contacts across the Baltic Sea. A special relationship blossomed between Estonia and Finland, not only because of the short distance between their capitals and Finland's status as Estonia's largest trading partner but also because of their linguistic kinship and close cultural ties. Similarly, Lithuania has enjoyed a close relationship with Poland. Particularly in its drive for NATO membership, Lithuania stressed its Central European character, as opposed to its Baltic identity. Likewise, Estonia, in trying to distinguish itself as the frontrunner for EU membership, sought to rebrand itself as a more attractive 'Nordic' country.[21]

After the withdrawal of Russian troops in 1994, the Balts could concentrate their energies on obtaining EU and NATO membership – the former to ensure economic prosperity and the latter to guarantee their security. Estonia, Latvia and Lithuania submitted formal applications for EU membership in 1995, shortly after two of their closest neighbours and most important trade partners – Sweden and Finland – became EU members. In the same year an association agreement with the EU was secured.

Owing to its more rapid economic reforms, Estonia was the only Baltic state among the five Central and Eastern European countries invited to commence EU membership negotiations in 1998. While this differentiation produced concerns about the future of Baltic solidarity, Estonia's success proved to be a great stimulus for Latvia and Lithuania. When the EU began negotiations with them two years later, they worked hard to catch up with Estonia in a race to close the negotiating chapters. The strategy of the Baltic states in the EU membership negotiations was to fulfil all the necessary criteria and to implement fully the EU's *acquis communautaire* (the body of EU legislation, treaties and case law) as quickly as possible, without presenting any awkward problems. They were in the most unfavourable starting position of the candidate countries, being the poorest and the only ones from the former Soviet Union. As Estonian President Meri perceptively stressed, the Baltic states needed to seize the window of opportunity – if they lagged behind, time would not work in their favour. Obtaining membership hinged on fulfilling the 'objective criteria' and doing the 'homework' set by the EU. In this, the Balts proved to be eager pupils; EU conditionality created the necessary domestic consensus for rapid reforms. In December 2002, accession negotiations were successfully completed at an EU summit meeting in Copenhagen.

Paradoxically, of the Central and East European candidate countries, opinion polls consistently showed the Estonians and Latvians to be the most sceptical about the benefits of EU membership, although the principal political parties were unanimous in their support for membership. As in many EU member states, there was a clear divergence between the political elite and the general public. The most popular argument of the opponents of EU membership was that, having recently escaped from an involuntary union, the Balts did not need to enter another union, where they would again have to surrender part of their sovereignty. The prospect of a higher standard of living, however, proved a stronger argument. In the national referenda held in 2003, 90 per cent of Lithuanians voted in favour of EU membership, but only two-thirds of Estonians and Latvians approved accession. Together with Poland, Hungary, the Czech Republic, Slovakia, Slovenia, Malta and Cyprus, the Baltic states formally joined the EU on 1 May 2004.

The entire accession process – from application to membership – took almost nine years. The new members had to 'harmonise' their legislation with the over 80,000 pages of the EU's *acquis communautaire*. The EU's conditionality forced them to undertake painful reforms, such as overhauling the legal system and imposing stringent physiosanitary regulations and costly environmental standards. One of the most difficult requirements for these small countries was the administrative capacity actually to implement the necessary EU standards. For Lithuania, the single most problematic issue was the EU's demand – as a result of safety concerns regarding the Soviet design of its reactors – that the Ignalina nuclear power plant be closed.

For Estonia and Latvia, the treatment of the Russian-speaking minority was the most sensitive political issue. Since the EU lacked competency on minority issues, it mainly deferred to the evaluations made by other international organisations, specifically the Council of Europe and the Organisation for Security and Cooperation in Europe (OSCE), the latter charged with monitoring the treatment of the Russian-speaking minority and making recommendations to help avoid potential conflict. As ethnic conflict erupted in the Balkans in the 1990s, many international observers feared that something similar could occur in the Baltic states. In 1993, Estonia and Latvia invited the OSCE[22] to establish missions for the purpose of providing the international community with objective and reliable information about the treatment of the Russian minority and to promote dialogue. One of the final recommendations made by the OSCE high commissioner for national minorities, Max van der Stoel, was the abolition of the language requirements for elected deputies, which was followed only with great reluctance by the Estonian and Latvian governments – a clear example of conditionality in the EU accession process.[23] After the Estonian and Latvian governments undertook to implement the OSCE's recommendations, the OSCE missions in Tallinn and Rīga were closed at the end of 2001. This stamp of approval by the international community cleared the way for Baltic accession to the EU and NATO.

Once inside the EU, the issues that the Baltic states prioritised during their first years of EU membership were increased competitiveness and the free movement of services, the promotion of an information society and the strengthening of the EU's Neighbourhood Policy, with particular regard to Ukraine, Moldova and the southern Caucasus. Having successfully completed the EU accession process, the Baltic states were well situated to transfer their knowledge and experience to other post-Soviet states.[24] EU enlargement also reinforced the trend towards closer cooperation among the Baltic and Nordic countries. Their interdependence was further elaborated when the EU adopted its Baltic Sea Strategy in 2009.

Initially, the Baltic states zealously guarded their newly won sovereignty, however, they quickly came around to the idea of supporting the deepening of European integration: the three parliaments ratified the EU's Constitutional Treaty, and later, in 2008, its revised version, the Lisbon Treaty, without much debate. Among the final steps in their full integration into the European Union was their accession to the Schengen regime in December 2007, which eliminated border controls within the EU. It also meant dismantling the border control points which had been erected among themselves in 1991. Lithuania and Estonia were expected to be among the first new EU member states to join the EU single currency in 2007, but were forced to postpone their hopes of doing this since their rapid economic growth raised inflation above the eurozone criterion. After the financial crisis in 2008, budget deficits became the new problem, but joining the eurozone still remained an important priority for Baltic governments, with Estonia set to adopt the euro in 2011.

Parallel to European integration was the process of the accession to NATO. The lesson from the first period of independence was that neutrality was not a viable option. The unhappy experience of 1939 taught the Balts not to rely on neutrality, although many in the international community recommended that they follow the example of neutral Finland, which enjoyed a good relationship with Russia. The Balts were afraid of being left in a 'grey zone' between the West and Russia. Membership of NATO was widely considered to be the only possible guarantee of Baltic security following independence. The Baltic states eagerly joined NATO's new Partnership for Peace programme in 1994, although there was apprehension that it was offered as a substitute for actual membership. The USA created a Baltic Charter in 1998 to reassure the Balts that they would not be forgotten, even though they were not included in NATO's 1999 Central European enlargement. The main argument against Baltic NATO membership was that, because of their geographic position, they would impossible to defend. The three Baltic states struggled hard to overcome Western apprehension that their membership would prompt a negative Russian reaction. While NATO sought to avoid antagonising Russia, there was nevertheless a steady stream of threatening remarks made by Russian politicians and officials. In addition to implementing the necessary military reforms, the Baltic states had to counter the widely held belief that the former boundaries of the USSR constituted a 'red line' for NATO that should not be crossed.[25]

The Balts strove to surmount doubts by proving that small countries could contribute to the Atlantic Alliance, particularly through the efforts of their peace-keeping troops, beginning with their service in the former Yugoslavia in the late 1990s. The Balts have sent personnel to almost every NATO mission. A key component in demonstrating their preparedness for membership of the alliance was Estonian, Latvian and Lithuanian cooperation in forming a joint infantry battalion (BALTBAT), naval squadron (BALTRON), air surveillance system (BALTNET) and staff college (BALTDEFCOL) in the latter half of the 1990s. Furthermore, Baltic governments pledged steadily to increase their defence expenditure to reach 2 per cent of GDP to conform with NATO's standard (a goal which has not yet been met).

The terrorist attacks against the USA on 11 September 2001 changed global security perceptions radically and helped to remove the remaining obstacles to Baltic membership of NATO. Baltic efforts were rewarded in 2002, when they were formally invited to join the alliance. As the USA prepared to invade Iraq in 2003, the US defence secretary, Donald Rumsfeld, rhetorically divided Europe into 'old' and 'new' – 'new' being understood as the ex-communist countries of Central and Eastern Europe, who supported the US position, as opposed to those Western European countries who did not. The Baltic states became full members of NATO on 29 March 2004. The most visible sign of NATO's presence are four fighter planes, which are based in Šiauliai, Lithuania and patrol Baltic airspace. They are contributed by NATO nations on a rotating schedule. Like most other new members from Central and Eastern Europe, the Balts have sought to preserve a strong transatlantic link. This perceived need for strong ties to the USA resulted in their sending soldiers to participate in the post-war security operation in Iraq. The Baltic states have also enthusiastically dispatched troops and civilian experts for the NATO operation in Afghanistan, even though they have suffered losses.[26] The number of military personnel participating in these missions may have been small, but in proportional terms the Baltic contribution has been among the largest of any country. In line with NATO's prioritisation of 'out-of-area' operations and rapid deployment, Latvia and Lithuania transformed their militaries into fully professional forces. Estonia, however, cautiously retained conscription and an emphasis on its own territorial defence.

## RELATIONS WITH RUSSIA

Upon achieving independence, the most pressing concern for the Baltic states was the removal of Russian troops from bases on their territory.

US pressure was instrumental in securing the withdrawal of these troops from Lithuania in 1993 and Latvia and Estonia in 1994 after social guarantees were extended to retired Soviet military personnel remaining in the Baltic states.[27] Despite the withdrawal of Russian troops, the relationship between the Baltic states and Russia remained cool. Russia has been harshly critical of the status of ethnic Russians in Estonia and Latvia and the Balts' pursuit of membership of NATO. The Balts, in turn, were alarmed by Russia's assertion of its privileged sphere of influence in its 'near abroad'.

A key obstacle to improved relations between the Baltic states and Russia was the difficulty in ratifying border treaties. Agreements were reached with all the countries by the end of the 1990s, but Russia delayed signing the treaties in the hope of hindering the Balts' progress towards NATO and EU membership by keeping the 'conflict' unresolved. Although the Lithuanians ratified their border agreement with Russia in 1997, Russia ratified the treaty only as part of a package deal with the EU to resolve the issues of Kaliningrad transit in 2002.

Lithuania is the only one of the Baltic states to have the Russian Federation as its western neighbour, in the Kaliningrad oblast, the most highly militarised area of Europe. The regulation of the transit of Russian military personnel and equipment from Kaliningrad across Lithuania to Russia proper was a source of disagreement in the first half of the 1990s. Before Lithuania and Poland were scheduled to join the EU, Kaliningrad became the main bone of contention between Russia and the EU. Russia demanded visa-free transit rights for its citizens, while the EU opposed the creation of a 'corridor' in its future Schengen space. A compromise was reached in 2002 whereby Kaliningraders would be issued 'facilitated transit documents' rather than visas.[28] After the collapse of the USSR, Kaliningrad oscillated between an optimistic vision of being a 'Hong Kong of the Baltic', with ideas of a free-trade zone or even a 'fourth Baltic republic' and the pessimistic perception of being a 'black hole' of organised crime, trafficking and infectious diseases. However, in the twenty-first century, the prerogatives of the regions of the Russian Federation have been severely restricted by the central government under President Vladimir Putin.

The situation with Latvia and Estonia was more protracted because the Russian Federation had annexed parts of the Latvian and Estonian territory at the end of World War II. The Latvian and Estonian governments renounced their territorial claims in the hope that Russia would reciprocate by recognising the validity of the 1920 peace treaties and thus acknowledging the legal continuity of their statehood. Although this did not happen, agreement was reached in 1999 and the text of a border treaty was initialled by the countries' respective foreign ministers. Further steps awaited Russia's renewed interest after the Balts achieved NATO and EU membership. The Estonian treaty was signed in Moscow in 2005 but Russia subsequently withdrew its signature. Russia objected to the references by the parliaments of Estonia and Latvia to the validity of the 1920 treaty, implicitly reaffirming legal continuity. Latvia eventually demurred and the Latvian–Russian border treaty was finally signed and ratified in 2007.

Despite expectations to the contrary, the relations between Russia and the Baltic states failed to improve after the latter became members of NATO and the EU.[29] Russia sought to portray the Baltic states as troublesome newcomers who should not be allowed to influence the policy of the two organisations towards it. This coincided with President Putin moving Russia away from democracy towards an authoritarian mode of government based on a revival of national pride. After the so-called democratic Orange Revolution in Ukraine in 2004, the Russian government began pursuing its interests in the post-Soviet space more aggressively. The Baltic states angered Russia by assisting the development of democratic reforms and moves toward the integration into the EU and NATO of former Soviet republics. For the Baltic states, this was both a moral and geopolitical imperative. After the Russian invasion of Georgia in August 2008, the Estonian president, Ilves, the Lithuanian president, Adamkus, and the Latvian prime minister, Godmanis, together with their Polish and Ukrainian colleagues, were the first heads of state to go to Tbilisi to demonstrate their solidarity with Georgia and to call for a tough EU response to Russian aggression. A delicate case of balancing between national interest and promoting democratic values has been the difficult relationship of Lithuania and Latvia with their neighbour Belarus, ruled since 1994 by 'Europe's last dictator', Alexander Lukashenko.

The Baltic states have become increasingly alarmed at Russia's use of its vast energy resources as a tool to reassert its status as a great power and to divide the EU, particularly since the Baltic states are completely dependent on Russian gas. The issue rose to the top of the political agenda after Germany and Russia struck a deal in 2005 to construct a natural gas pipeline (Nord Stream) underneath the Baltic Sea, purposely bypassing the new EU member states. The Baltic states responded by vigorously pressing for an EU common energy policy. In the 1990s the Baltic states enjoyed a lucrative oil transit trade with Russia, but this sector has been subject to political risks. Russia stopped the flow of oil to Ventspils in 2003; in 2006 the pipeline to Lithuania was closed indefinitely when the Mažeikiai oil refinery was sold to a Polish company, not a rival Russian bidder. The oil transit trade through Estonia dried up after the relocation of the Tallinn Red Army monument in 2007. Russia intends to redirect further the export of its strategic resources to its own newly constructed harbours on the Gulf of Finland.

Questions of energy supply loom large on the Baltic horizon.[30] The EU's drive to reduce carbon emissions in order to tackle global warming threatens to increase further the Baltic dependence on Russian energy supplies. Estonia's only significant natural energy resource, oil shale, is heavily polluting and will eventually have to be phased out. In accordance with Lithuania's EU Accession Treaty, the Ignalina nuclear power plant was decommissioned at the end of 2009, even though it generated the majority of the country's electricity. The Lithuanian government has been slow to make adequate preparations for the future, and a plan for Lithuania, Latvia, Estonia and Poland jointly to build a new, safer nuclear power plant near Ignalina – potentially the largest Baltic cooperation project ever – has run into difficulties.

The central battleground between the Baltic states and Russia has become the interpretation of history, particularly the events of World War II. The Balts have sought Russian acknowledgement of the crimes of communism and the fact that Soviet rule amounted to 'illegal occupation', whereas Russia rejects 'the revision of history' and absurdly warns of the 'revival of fascism' in the Baltic states. Several commemorative events which have turned into flashpoints of bilateral relations are illustrative of the emotive power of the symbols of collective memory.[31]

The annual commemorative procession of elderly Latvian veterans who fought in German uniform has been loudly condemned by Russia, which even imposed sanctions against Latvia in 1998. Russia's ire was stirred by the International Public Tribunal on the crimes of communism conducted in Vilnius in 2000. The celebration of the 60th anniversary of Victory Day in Moscow on 9 May 2005 was another occasion where contested pasts clashed. The Estonian and Lithuanian presidents declined to attend the ceremonies since most Balts considered Soviet Victory Day to be the beginning of the long years of foreign occupation, rather than liberation. In 2007, Russia reacted with fury to the Estonian government's relocation of a Red Army memorial: the Estonian embassy in Moscow was blockaded by a Kremlin-sponsored youth group, Estonian websites were hit by massive cyberattacks, and Estonian goods were boycotted.[32]

Russia displayed great annoyance at the decision of the Lithuanian parliament in 2008 to ban the public display of both Nazi and Soviet symbols. Neither the Balts nor the Russians are likely be able to convince the other to accept their narrative, but the real objective is to sway international opinion.

Apart from symbols, 'coming to terms with the past' has a legal dimension which has proved no less contentious. Baltic efforts to prosecute Soviet operatives for crimes against humanity have been vociferously opposed by Russia.[33] Claims for compensation occasionally voiced by Baltic politicians have been derided by Russia. Baltic and Eastern European governments and parliamentarians have persistently clamoured for resolutions condemning the crimes of totalitarian communism in international bodies such as the European Parliament, the Council of Europe and the OSCE, while Russia has taken active measures to defend the Soviet version of history and has repeatedly warned against 'rewriting history'. Balts who challenge the Soviet narrative of their 'liberation' in 1944–5 are routinely branded 'fascists'. The battle reached a new level in 2009 when the Russian president, Dmitry Medvedev, established a commission given the explicit task of combating the 'falsification' of history.[34]

The above illustrates that history is not merely something which is restricted to the past and solely the concern of historians; rather, its legacy is almost omnipresent in the Baltic states today, especially in the relationship with Russia. History is not confined to textbooks: in the form of collective memory, it affirms identities, inflames passions and directly or indirectly influences policy-making. It is thus prone to use and abuse as an instrument of political manipulation, which denies its multilayered nature.

This book, however, has sought to contribute to understanding, in the hope that the Baltic region will never again experience a situation like that in the Soviet-era anecdote about two intellectuals discussing the country's future: one wonders what the future will hold in a decade, and the other resignedly replies that it is useless to speculate about the future when we do not even know what our past will be by then.

# Notes

PREFACE

1. Endre Bojtár, *Forward to the Past: A Cultural History of the Baltic People* (Budapest: Central European University Press, 1999), p. 7.
2. Bojtár, *Forward to the Past: A Cultural History of the Baltic People*, p. 9.
3. Birutė Masionienė, *Baltijos Tautos* (Vilnius: Aidai, 1996), p. 14.
4. Zigmas Zinkevičius, Aleksiejus Luchtanas and Gintautas Česnys, *Where We Come From: The Origin of the Lithuanian People*, 2nd rev. edn (Vilnius: Science & Encyclopaedia Publishing Institute, 2006), p. 27.
5. Georg von Rauch, *The Baltic States: The Years of Independence, 1917–1940* (London: C. Hurst, 1974), p. ix.
6. There are more general overviews of Baltic history in German than in any other language. Two of the most recent are Ralph Tuchtenhagen, *Geschichte der baltischen Länder* (München: C. H. Beck, 2005) and Michael Garleff, *Die baltischen Länder: Estland, Lettland und Litauen vom Mittelalter bis zur Gegenwart* (Regensburg: Friedrich Pustet, 2001).
7. *The History of the Baltic Countries*, compiled by Zigmantas Kiaupa, Ain Mäesalu, Ago Pajur and Gvido Straube, 3rd edn (Tallinn: BIT, 2002).
8. Kevin O'Connor, *The History of the Baltic States* (Westport, CT: Greenwood, 2003).
9. Romuald J. Misiunas and Rein Taagepera, *The Baltic States: Years of Dependence, 1940–1990*, 2nd updated edn (Berkeley, CA: University of California Press, 1993).
10. David Kirby, *Northern Europe in the Early Modern Period: The Baltic World, 1492–1772* (London: Longman, 1990) and *The Baltic World 1772–1993: Europe's Northern Periphery in an Age of Change* (London: Longman, 1995).
11. Jörg Hackmann and Robert Schweitzer (eds), *Nordosteuropa als Geschichtsregion* (Helsinki: Aue Stiftung, 2006); Jörg Hackmann and Robert Schweitzer (eds), 'Mapping Baltic History: The Concept of North Eastern Europe', *Journal of Baltic Studies*, Special Issue, 33(4) (2002).

1 EUROPE'S LAST PAGANS

1. Valter Lang, *Baltimaade pronksi- ja rauaaeg* (Tartu: University of Tartu Press, 2007), p. 13.

2. *Prehistoric Lithuania: Archaeology Exposition Guide* (Vilnius: National Museum of Lithuania, 2000), p. 22.
3. Aivar Kriiska and Andres Tvauri, *Eesti muinasaeg* (Tallinn: Avita, 2002), pp. 25–32.
4. *Prehistoric Lithuania*, p. 26.
5. Aivar Kriiska, *Aegade alguses. 15 kirjutist kaugemast minevikust* (Tallinn: A Kriiska, 2004), pp. 51–2.
6. Lang, *Baltimaade pronksi- ja rauaaeg*, p. 16.
7. Kalevi Wiik, *Eurooplaste juured* (Tartu: Ilmamaa, 2005); Enn Haabsaar, *Soome-ugri saamine* (Tallinn: Argo, 2009).
8. Richard Villems, 'Marginalia on the Topic of Identity', in Jean-Jacques Subrenat (ed.), *Estonia: Identity and Independence* (Amsterdam: Rodopi, 2004), p. 21.
9. Valter Lang, *The Bronze and Early Iron Ages in Estonia* (Tartu: University of Tartu Press, 2007), p. 146.
10. Lang, *The Bronze and Early Iron Ages in Estonia*, p. 267.
11. The most common periodisation for the Iron Age in the Baltic states is the following: the Early Iron Age = 500 BC–AD 450, the Middle Iron Age = AD 450–800 and the Late Iron Age = AD 800–1200.
12. Lang, *The Bronze and Early Iron Ages in Estonia*, p. 265.
13. A rectangular stone cell, filled with smaller stones.
14. Lang, *Baltimaade pronksi- ja rauaaeg*, pp. 127, 209.
15. *Prehistoric Lithuania*, p. 90; Lang, *Baltimaade pronksi- ja rauaaeg*, pp. 251, 256.
16. Bojtár, *Forward to the Past*, p. 104.
17. *Prehistoric Lithuania*, p. 79; Lang, *The Bronze and Early Iron Ages in Estonia*, p. 268.
18. Andris Šnē, 'Stammesfürstentum und Egalität: Die sozialen Beziehungen auf dem Territorium Lettlands am Ende der prähistorischen Zeit (10.-12. Jh.), *Forschungen zur baltischen Geschichte*, Bd. 3 (2008): 33–56. See also Heiki Valk, 'Estland im 11.-13. Jahrhundert. Neuere Aspekte aus Sicht der Archäologie', *Forschungen zur baltischen Geschichte*, Bd. 3 (2008): 57–86.
19. Lang, *Baltimaade pronksi- ja rauaaeg*, pp. 179, 233.
20. Lang, *Baltimaade pronksi- ja rauaaeg*, pp. 234, 281.
21. Andris Šnē, 'The Emergence of Livonia: The Transformations of Social and Political Structures in the Territory of Latvia during the Twelfth and Thirteenth Centuries', in Alan V. Murray (ed.), *The Clash of Cultures on the Medieval Baltic Frontier* (Aldershot: Ashgate, 2009), p. 64.
22. Lang, *Baltimaade pronksi- ja rauaaeg*, p. 284.
23. Lang, *Baltimaade pronksi- ja rauaaeg*, p. 265.
24. Marija Gimbutas, *The Balts* (New York: Praeger, 1963), pp. 153–4.
25. Lang, *Baltimaade pronksi- ja rauaaeg*, p. 205.
26. According to the Norse *Heimskringla* saga, six years later on a journey to Estonia his uncle recognised Olaf and bought his freedom. After many adventures, Olaf ruled as King of Norway from 995 until his death in 1000.

27. Zigmantas Kiaupa, *The History of Lithuania* (Vilnius: baltos lankos, 2002), p. 24.
28. Anti Selart, *Livland und die Rus' im 13. Jahrhundert*, Quellen und Studien zur baltischen Geschichte, Bd. 21 (Köln: Böhlau, 2007), pp. 58–67.
29. Tomas Baranauskas, 'Saxo Grammaticus on the Balts', in Tore Nyberg (ed.), *Saxo and the Baltic Region: A Symposium* (Odense: University of Southern Denmark, 2004), p. 79.
30. Gimbutas, *The Balts*, p. 155.
31. Enn Tarvel, 'Sigtuna hävitamine 1187. aastal', in *Tuna. Ajalookultuuri ajakiri* 2(35), 2007, pp. 24–7.
32. Peep Peter Rebane, 'From Fulco to Theoderic: The Changing Face of the Livonian Mission', in Andres Andresen (ed.), *Muinasaja loojangust omariikluse läveni* (Tartu: Kleio, 2001), pp. 37–67.
33. *The Chronicle of Henry of Livonia* translated by James A. Brundage (New York: Columbia University Press, 2003).
34. The land of the Mother of God as opposed to the land of the Son in Palestine: Anu Mänd, 'Saints' Cults in Medieval Livonia', in Murray (ed.), *The Clash of Cultures*, pp. 194–5.
35. Iben Fonnesberg-Schmidt, *The Popes and the Baltic Crusades 1147–1254* (Leiden: Brill, 2007), pp. 139–42.
36. Although associated with the conquest of Tallinn, the legend apparently has its origins in an earlier Danish expedition against Viljandi (Fellin) in southern Estonia in 1208: John H. Lind, Carsten Selch Jensen, Kurt Villads Jensen and Ane L. Bysted, *Taani Ristisõjad – sõda ja misjon Läänemere ääres* (Tallinn: Argo, 2007), pp. 218–22.
37. The name Tallinn is commonly thought to have been derived from the Estonian words for 'Danish castle' (*Taani linna*). However, a linguistically more plausible explanation of the origin of the name is 'winter fort' (*tali linna*).
38. Selart, *Livland and die Rus' im 13. Jahrhundert*, pp. 86–121.
39. Andres Kasekamp, 'Characteristics of Warfare in the Times of Henry of Livonia and Balthasar Russow', *Lituanus* 36(1) (1990): 27–38.
40. William Urban, *The Teutonic Knights: A Military History* (London: Greenhill, 2003), p. 29.
41. William Urban, *The Baltic Crusade*, 2nd edn (Chicago: Lithuanian Research and Studies Center, 1994), pp. 190, 196.
42. Evgeniya Nazarova, 'The Crusades against Votians and Izhorians in the Thirteenth Century', in Alan V. Murray (ed.), *Crusade and Conversion on the Baltic Frontier, 1150–1500* (Aldershot: Ashgate, 2001), p. 183. Anti Selart, *Livland and die Rus' in 13. Jahrhundert*, pp. 165–6, notes that the battle was not viewed as particularly significant by contemporaries.
43. Urban, *Baltic Crusade*, p. 198. The battle was immortalised in the 1938 film *Alexander Nevsky* by Sergei Eisenstein.
44. Zinkevičius, Luchtanas and Česnys, *Where We Come From*, pp. 114, 120, 126, 129–30.

45. Zigmantas Kiaupa, Jūratė Kiaupienė and Albinas Kuncevičius, *The History of Lithuania before 1795* (Vilnius: Lithuanian Institute of History, 2000), pp. 56–8.
46. Urban, *Baltic Crusade*, p. 301.

## 2   LITHUANIA'S EXPANSION AND MEDIEVAL LIVONIA (1290–1560)

1. Kiaupa, Kiaupienė and Kuncevičius, *The History of Lithuania before 1795*, p. 78.
2. Kiaupa, Kiaupienė and Kuncevičius, *The History of Lithuania before 1795*, p. 82.
3. Stephen C. Rowell, *Lithuania Ascending: A Pagan Empire within East-Central Europe, 1295–1345* (Cambridge: Cambridge University Press, 1994), p. 132.
4. Rowell, *Lithuania Ascending*, pp. 57–8.
5. Rowell, *Lithuania Ascending*, pp. 239, 254.
6. Kiaupa, Kiaupienė and Kuncevičius, *The History of Lithuania before 1795*, p. 124.
7. Kiaupa, Kiaupienė and Kuncevičius, *The History of Lithuania before 1795*, p. 128.
8. Dov Levin, *Litvaks: A Short History of the Jews of Lithuania* (Jerusalem: Yad Vashem, 2000), p. 44.
9. William Urban, *Tannenberg and After: Poland, Lithuania and the Teutonic Order in Search of Immortality* (Chicago: Lithuanian Research and Studies Center 2002) examines how the battle has later been used by nationalist historians.
10. Kiaupa, *The History of Lithuania*, p. 76; Stasys Samalavičius, *An Outline of Lithuanian History* (Vilnius: Diemedis, 1995), pp. 40–2.
11. Samalavičius, *An Outline of Lithuanian History*, p. 47.
12. Kiaupa, Kiaupienė and Kuncevičius, *The History of Lithuania before 1795*, pp. 165–6.
13. Kiaupa, Kiaupienė and Kuncevičius, *The History of Lithuania before 1795*, pp. 219–20.
14. Kiaupa, *The History of Lithuania*, p. 86.
15. The Uniate Church would become an important vehicle for this in the seventeenth century.
16. Daniel Stone, *A History of East Central Europe*, vol. 4: *The Polish–Lithuanian State, 1386–1795* (Seattle: University of Washington Press, 2001), p. 34.
17. Juhan Kahk and Enn Tarvel, *An Economic History of the Baltic Countries*, Studia Baltica Stockholmiensia, 20 (Stockholm: Acta Universitatis Stockholmiensis, 1997), p. 55.
18. Kiaupa, Kiaupienė and Kuncevičius, *The History of Lithuania before 1795*, p. 175.

19. From 1493, Ivan III began to style himself 'the ruler of all Rus".
20. Lithuania was at war with Muscovy in 1492–4 and 1500–3.
21. Garleff, *Die baltischen Länder*, p. 62.
22. Garleff, *Die baltischen Länder*, p. 64. Although only 60 of these castles belonged to the Teutonic Order.
23. Kahk and Tarvel, *An Economic History of the Baltic Countries*, p. 32.
24. Tiina Kala, 'Põhja-Eesti kirikuelu 13.-14. sajandil: millisesse vaimulikku keskkonda tekkis Pirita klooster?', *Kunstiteaduslikke Uurimusi = Studies on Art and Architecture = Studien für Kunstwissenschaft*, 4 (2007): 57.
25. The interdict was the strongest weapon that the papal curia could use against the Teutonic Order, i.e. forbidding church services and administration of the sacraments on the order's territory: Kala, 'Põhja-Eesti kirikuelu 13.-14. sajandil': p. 58.
26. Priit Raudkivi, *Vana-Liivimaa maapäev. Ühe keskaegse struktuuri kujunemislugu* (Tallinn: Argo, 2007), pp. 117–18. Pärtel Piirimäe, 'Liivimaa maapäev Wolter von Plettenbergi ajal (1494–1535)', *Ajalooline Ajakiri* 1/2(123/124) (2008): 85–8.
27. Andris Šnē, 'The Emergence of Livonia', p. 68.
28. Garleff, *Die baltischen Länder*, p. 36; Kahk and Tarvel, *An Economic History of the Baltic Countries*, p. 66.
29. Kirby, *Northern Europe in the Early Modern Period*, p. 29.
30. Aivar Kriiska, Andres Tvauri, Anti Selart, Birgit Kibal, Andres Andresen and Ago Pajur, *Eesti Ajaloo Atlas* (Tallinn: Avita, 2006), p. 41; Ilmar Talve, *Eesti kultuurilugu. Keskaja algusest Eesti iseseisvuseni* (Tartu: Ilmamaa, 2004), p. 57.
31. Kirby, *Northern Europe in the Early Modern Period*, p. 23.
32. Talve, *Eesti kultuurilugu*, p. 56.
33. Urban, *Teutonic Knights*, p. 260.
34. Kaspars Kļaviņš, 'The Significance of the Local Baltic Peoples in the Defence of Livonia (Late Thirteenth–Sixteenth Centuries)', in Murray (ed.), *The Clash of Cultures*, pp. 337–8.
35. Among the Lithuanian graduates of the University of Königsberg was Martinus Mosvidius (Martynas Mažvydas), who produced the first Lithuanian book *Catechismus* (1547).
36. Talve, *Eesti kultuurilugu*, p. 104.
37. An Estonian-, Latvian- and Liv-language Lutheran Catechism is known to have been published in Lübeck in 1525: Pēteris Vanags, 'Die Literatur der Letten im Zeichen von Reformation und Konfessionalisierung', in Matthias Asche, Werner Buchholz and Anton Schindling (eds), *Die baltischen Lande im Zeitalter der Reformation und Konfessionalisierung: Estland, Livland, Ösel, Ingermanland, Kurland und Lettgallen. Stadt, Land und Konfession 1500–1721*, Part 1 (Münster: Aschendorff, 2009), p. 264.
38. Rimvydas Šilbajoris, 'Notes on Mažvydas' *Little Book of Good News*', *Lituanus*, 44(1) (Spring 1998): 57–8.
39. Kirby, *Northern Europe in the Early Modern Period*, p. 68.
40. Selart, *Livland and die Rus' im 13. Jahrhundert*.

3 THE POLISH–LITHUANIAN COMMONWEALTH
AND THE RISE OF SWEDEN AND RUSSIA (1561–1795)

1. Robert Frost, *The Northern Wars: War, State, and Society in Northeastern Europe, 1558–1721* (Harlow: Longman, 2000), p. 26.
2. Stone, *The Polish–Lithuanian State*, p. 62.
3. Artūras Tereškinas, *Imperfect Communities: Identity, Discourse and Nation in the Seventeenth-Century Grand Duchy of Lithuania* (Vilnius: Lietuvių literatūros ir tautosakos institutas, 2005), pp. 17–19.
4. Tereškinas, *Imperfect Communities*, p. 257.
5. Stone, *The Polish–Lithuanian State*, pp. 119–20.
6. Frost, *The Northern Wars*, pp. 64–5.
7. Kiaupa, *The History of Lithuania*, p. 136.
8. Andrejs Plakans, *The Latvians: A Short History* (Stanford, CA: Hoover Institution, 1995), p. 49.
9. Plakans, *The Latvians: A Short History*, pp. 51, 54.
10. Courland was only able to hold on to these two colonies for a few years before they were taken over by the British and Dutch respectively.
11. Bogusław Dybaś, 'Polen-Litauen und Livland im 17. und 18. Jahrhundert – drei Formen ihrer Verbindung', in Jörg Hackmann and Robert Schweitzer (eds), *Nordosteuropa als Geschichtsregion* (Helsinki: Aue Stiftung, 2006), pp. 348–51.
12. Stone, *The Polish–Lithuanian State*, p. 167.
13. Andrej Kotljarchuk, *In the Shadows of Poland and Russia: The Grand Duchy of Lithuania and Sweden in the European Crisis of the Mid-Seventeenth Century*. Södertörn Doctoral Dissertations, 4 (Huddinge: Södertörns högskola, 2006), p. 67.
14. Kiaupa, Kiaupienė and Kuncevičius, *The History of Lithuania before 1795*, p. 286.
15. Kiaupa, *The History of Lithuania*, pp. 124–5.
16. Enn Küng, *Rootsi majanduspoliitika Narva kaubanduse küsimuses 17. sajandi teisel poolel* (Tartu: Eesti Ajalooarhiiv, 2001).
17. Witch trials began before the Reformation and continued until the 1730s. Unlike elsewhere in Europe, the majority of those accused of casting magic spells were men: Aleksander Loit, 'Reformation und Konfessionalisierung in den ländlichen Gebieten der baltischen Lande von ca. 1500 bis zum Ende der schwedischen Herrschaft', in Matthias Asche, Werner Buchholz and Anton Schindling (eds), *Die baltischen Lande im Zeitalter der Reformation und Konfessionalisierung: Estland, Livland, Ösel, Ingermanland, Kurland und Lettgallen. Stadt, Land und Konfession 1500–1721* (Münster: Aschendorff, 2009), pp. 189–90.
18. Mati Laur (ed.), *Eesti ajalugu IV. Põhjasõjast pärisorjuse kaotamiseni* (Tartu: Ilmamaa, 2003), p. 15.
19. Kahk and Tarvel, *An Economic History of the Baltic Countries*, pp. 60–3.
20. Laur (ed.), *Eesti ajalugu IV*, p. 190.
21. Frost, *The Northern Wars*, pp. 265–7.

22. Laur (ed.), *Eesti ajalugu IV*, p. 35.
23. Margus Laidre, *Dorpat 1558–1708. Linn väe ja vaevu vahel* (Tallinn: Argo, 2008), pp. 655–7.
24. Frost, *The Northern Wars*, p. 13.
25. Kahk and Tarvel, *An Economic History of the Baltic Countries*, p. 73.
26. Laur (ed.), *Eesti ajalugu IV*, p. 161; Plakans, *The Latvians: A Short History*, p. 63; Kiaupa, Kiaupienė and Kuncevičius, *The History of Lithuania before 1795*, pp. 254–5.
27. Arvo Tering, 'Baltische Studenten an europäischen Universitäten im 18. Jahrhundert', in Otto-Heinrich von Elias (ed.), *Aufklärung in den baltischen Provinzen Russlands: Ideologie und soziale Wirklichkeit* (Köln: Böhlau Verlag, 1996), p. 126.
28. Michael H. Hatzel, 'The Baltic Germans', in Edward C. Thaden, Michael H. Haltzel, C. Leonard Lundin, Andrejs Plakans and Toivo U. Raun, *Russification in the Baltic Provinces and Finland, 1855–1914* (Princeton, NJ: Princeton University Press, 1981), p. 151.
29. Heide W. Whelan, *Adapting to Modernity: Family, Caste, and Capitalism among the Baltic German Nobility* (Köln: Böhlau Verlag, 1999), p. 9.
30. Whelan, *Adapting to Modernity*, p. 19.
31. Laur (ed.), *Eesti ajalugu IV*, p. 74.
32. Whelan, *Adapting to Modernity*, p. 26.
33. Or in the case of Courland's *Landesbevollmächtiger* until 1795 at the Polish court in Warsaw.
34. Reinhard Wittram, *Liberalismus baltischer Literaten. Zur Entstehung der baltischen politischen Presse* (Riga: Löffler, 1931), p. 85, cited in Ea Jansen, *Eestlane muutuvas ajas. Seisusühiskonnast kodanikuühiskonda* (Tartu: Eesti Ajalooarhiiv, 2007), p. 42.
35. Christian Kelch (1657–1710), cited in Hatzel, 'The Baltic Germans', p. 114.
36. Kahk and Tarvel, *An Economic History of the Baltic Countries*, pp. 84–5.
37. August Wilhelm Hupel (1737–1819), cited in Arnolds Spekke, *History of Latvia: An Outline* (Riga: Jumava, 2006), p. 255.
38. Laur (ed.), *Eesti ajalugu IV*, p. 193.
39. Kahk and Tarvel, *An Economic History of the Baltic Countries*, p. 83.
40. Many of the national activists of the mid-nineteenth century came from peasant households with a Herrnhuter background: Andrejs Plakans, 'The Latvians', in Thaden, *Russification in the Baltic Provinces and Finland, 1855–1914*, p. 220.
41. Ralph Tuchtenhagen, *Zentralstaat und Provinz im frühneuzeitlichen Nordosteuropa*, Veröffentlichungen des Nordost-Instituts, Bd. 5 (Wiesbaden: Harrassowitz, 2008), pp. 80–5, 176.
42. Grigorijus Potašenko, 'The Old Believers and Society in the Grand Duchy of Lithuania in the Eighteenth Century: Religious Tolerance and its Causes', *Lithuanian Historical Studies*, 6 (2001): 64.

43. Including Kant's most famous book, *The Critique of Pure Reason*, published in 1781.
44. Indrek Jürjo, *Aufklärung im Baltikum. Leben und Werk des livländischen Gelehrten August Wilhelm Hupel (1737–1819)* (Köln: Böhlau Verlag, 2006).
45. Roger Bartlett, 'Nation, Revolution und Religion in der Gesellschaftskonzeption von Garlieb Merkel', in Norbert Angermann, Michael Garleff and Wilhelm Lenz (eds), *Ostseeprovinzen, Baltische Staaten und das Nationale*, Schriften der Baltischen Historischen Kommission, vol. 14 (Münster: LIT, 2005), pp. 147–9.
46. Kiaupa, *The History of Lithuania*, p. 125.
47. After 1673 every third session met in Grodno, Lithuania: Stone, *The Polish–Lithuanian State*, p. 179.
48. Stone, *The Polish–Lithuanian State*, p. 183.
49. Anita J. Prażmowska, *A History of Poland* (Basingstoke: Palgrave Macmillan, 2004), p. 122.
50. Kiaupa, *The History of Lithuania*, p. 351; Stone, *The Polish–Lithuanian State*, p. 283.
51. Memel (Klaipėda) remained outside the Empire as part of Prussia.
52. Levin, *Litvaks*, p. 62; Kiaupa, Kiaupienė and Kuncevičius, *The History of Lithuania before 1795*, p. 256.
53. Levin, *Litvaks*, p. 54.
54. See Immanuel Etkes, *The Gaon of Vilna: The Man and His Image* (Berkeley, CA: University of California Press, 2002).

## 4   THE LONG NINETEENTH CENTURY UNDER TSARIST RULE (1795–1917)

1. Laur (ed.), *Eesti ajalugu IV*, pp. 206–7.
2. Of the 400,000 Napoleonic troops who passed through Vilnius on the way to Moscow in June 1812, only 8000 survived after retreating through the city in December: Laimonas Briedis, *Vilnius: City of Strangers* (Budapest: Central European University Press, 2009), p. 105.
3. Burghers were excluded for owning landed estates, although this had been allowed earlier under Peter the Great: Whelan, *Adapting to Modernity*, p. 77.
4. Garleff, *Die baltischen Länder*, p. 74.
5. Plakans, *The Latvians: A Short History*, p. 86.
6. Kahk and Tarvel, *An Economic History of the Baltic Countries*, pp. 91–2.
7. It had initially been merged with Pskov *guberniya* (province or governorate) in 1772 and was transferred to Vitebsk *guberniya* in 1802.
8. Initially in 1795 there were two Lithuanian provinces, Vilnius and Slonim, which were merged into one Lithuanian province in 1796. In 1801 it was split again into two provinces: Vilnius and Grodno.
9. Timothy Snyder, *The Reconstruction of Nations: Poland, Ukraine, Lithuania, Belarus, 1569–1999* (New Haven, CT: Yale University Press, 2003), pp. 27–9. Tomas Venclova, 'Native Realm Revisited: Mickiewicz's Lithuania and Mickiewicz in Lithuania', *Lituanus*, 53(3) (Fall 2007).

10. Darius Staliūnas, *Making Russians: Meaning and Practice of Russification in Lithuania and Belarus after 1863* (Amsterdam: Rodopi, 2007), p. 30.
11. Levin, *Litvaks*, pp. 64–7.
12. However, the atmosphere became more restrictive again under Alexander III (ruled 1881–94): Levin, *Litvaks*, pp. 72–4.
13. Miroslav Hroch, *Social Preconditions of National Revival in Europe: A Comparative Analysis of the Social Composition of Patriotic Groups among the Smaller European Nations* (Cambridge: Cambridge University Press, 1985).
14. Men such as Herder, Hupel, Brotze, Merkel. See Chapter 3.
15. Svennik Hoyer, Epp Lauk, and Peeter Vihalemm (eds), *Towards a Civic Society: The Baltic Media's Long Road to Freedom. Perspectives on History, Ethnicity and Journalism* (Tartu: Nota Baltika, 1993), p. 53.
16. Ulrike von Hirschhausen, *Die Grenzen der Gemeinsamkeit: Deutsche, Letten, Russen und Juden in Riga 1860–1914*, Kritische Studien zur Geschichtswissenschaft 172 (Göttingen: Vandenhoeck & Ruprecht, 2006), p. 352.
17. Vaira Vīķe-Freiberga, 'Andrejs Pumpurs's Lāčplēsis ('Bearslayer'): Latvian National Epic or Romantic Literary Creation?', in Aleksander Loit (ed.), *National Movements in the Baltic Countries during the Nineteenth Century*, Studia Baltica Stockholmiensia 2 (Stockholm: Acta Universitatis Stockholmiensis, 1985), p. 526.
18. Mart Laar, *Äratajad. Rahvuslik liikumine Eestis 19. sajandil ja selle kandjad* (Tartu: Eesti Ajalooarhiiv, 2005), pp. 366–7.
19. Uldis Ģērmanis, *Lāti rahva elurada* (Tartu: Ilmamaa, 1995), p. 145.
20. See Kristine Wohlfart, *Der Rigaer Letten Verein und die lettische National-bewegung von 1868 bis 1905*, Materialien und Studien zur Ostmitteleuropa-Forschung, vol. 14 (Marburg: Herder Institut, 2006).
21. Hans Kruus, *Eesti Aleksandrikool* (Tartu: Noor-Eesti, 1939).
22. Toivo U. Raun, 'Nineteenth- and Early Twentieth-Century Estonian Nationalism Revisited', *Nations and Nationalism*, 9(1) (2003): 141.
23. Kiaupa, *The History of Lithuania*, p. 199.
24. Theodore R. Weeks, 'Russification and the Lithuanians, 1863–1905', *Slavic Review*, 60(1) (Spring 2001): 96–114.
25. Staliūnas argues that the print ban aimed to acculturate Lithuanians to the Russian language, a precondition for the more difficult step of conversion to Orthodoxy and the long-term goal of assimilation: Staliūnas, *Making Russians*, p. 303.
26. A. S. Stražas, 'From Auszra to the Great War: The Emergence of the Lithuanian Nation', in *Lituanus*, 42(4) (Winter 1996), pp. 69–70.
27. A. S. Stražas, 'Lithuania 1863–1893: Tsarist Russification and the Beginnings of the Modern Lithuanian National Movement', in *Lituanus*, 42(3) (Fall 1996), pp. 46–8.
28. Kiaupa, *The History of Lithuania*, p. 196.
29. A. S. Stražas, 'From Auszra to the Great War', pp. 39–41.
30. Hatzel, 'The Baltic Germans', pp. 127–32.
31. Toivo U. Raun, *Estonia and the Estonians*, updated 2nd edn (Stanford, CA: Hoover Institution, 2002), p. 65.

32. Edward C. Thaden, 'The Russian Government', in Thaden, *Russification in the Baltic Provinces and Finland, 1855–1914*, pp. 33–75.
33. Toomas Karjahärm, *Ida ja lääne vahel. Eesti-Vene suhted 1850–1917* (Tallinn: Eesti Entsüklopeediakirjastus, 1998), p. 303.
34. Ea Jansen, *Eestlane muutuvas ajas. Seisusühiskonnast kodanikuühiskonda* (Tartu: Eesti Ajalooarhiiv, 2007), pp. 453–5.
35. Plakans, 'The Latvians', p. 252; Raun, *Estonia and the Estonians*, p. 78.
36. Andreas Kappeler, *The Russian Empire: A Multiethnic History* (Harlow: Pearson Education, 2001), pp. 310–11, 407.
37. Percentages for Jews in the Empire as a whole.
38. Thaden, 'The Russian Government', p. 61; Toivo U. Raun, 'The Estonians', in Thaden, *Russification in the Baltic Provinces and Finland, 1855–1914*, p. 308.
39. Hatzel, 'The Baltic Germans', p. 158.
40. Does not include the city of Narva, which was detached from Estland in 1722 and was administratively under the province of St Petersburg until 1917. Narva, nevertheless, enjoyed the same autonomous rights as the Baltic provinces.
41. Raun, *Estonia and the Estonians*, p. 72; *Latvijas vēstures atlants* (Riga: Jāņa Sēta, 1998), p. 28; Kiaupa, *The History of Lithuania*, p. 196.
42. Plakans, 'The Latvians', p. 242; Raun 'The Estonians', p. 290.
43. Of these, 81 per cent were ethnic Lithuanians and 13 per cent were Jewish: Alfonsas Eidintas, *Lithuanian Emigration to the United States: 1868–1950* (Vilnius: Mokslo ir enciklopedijų leidybos institutes, 2003), p. 56.
44. From Dvinsk (Daugavpils).
45. Hirschhausen, *Die Grenzen der Gemeinsamkeit*, p. 58.
46. Daina Bleiere, Ilgvars Butulis, Inesis Felmanis, Aivars Stranga and Antonijs Zunda, *History of Latvia: The Twentieth Century* (Riga: Jumava, 2006), pp. 41–5.
47. Maie Pihlamägi, *Eesti industrialiseerimine 1870–1940* (Tallinn: Ajaloo Instituut, 1999), pp. 23–73.
48. It joined the Russian Social Democratic Workers' Party in 1906.
49. For a recent discussion of the 1905 Revolution, see Toivo U. Raun, 'The All-Estonian Congress in Tartu, November 1905: A Reassessment'; Andrejs Plakans, 'Two 1905 Congresses in Latvia: A Reconsideration'; Saulius Sužiedėlis, 'A Century After: The "Great Diet of Vilnius" Revisited', *Journal of Baltic Studies*, 38(4) (December 2007): 383–432.
50. The figures for the victims of repression in the Baltic provinces during 1905–8 differ considerably. Karjahärm, *Ida ja lääne vahel*, p. 117, reports that 625 were killed by the punitive expeditions and 690 executed by military tribunals, while Jānis Bērziņš, 'Piektajam gadam – 100', *1905. gads Latvijā: 100* (Riga: Latvijas vēstures institūts, 2006), p. 39, claims that the total number of deaths was 2496. The same applies to the number expelled from the Baltic provinces: Karjahärm offers a figure of 2652; the figure provided by Bērziņš is double that.
51. Toivo U. Raun, 'The Nationalities Question in the Baltic Provinces, 1905–17', in John Morrison (ed.), *Ethnic and National Issues in Russian and East European History* (Basingstoke: Macmillan, 2000), pp. 121–30.

NOTES

52. Karjahärm, *Ida ja lääne vahel*, p. 156; Stražas, 'From Auszra to the Great War', pp. 54–60.
53. Kiaupa, *The History of Lithuania*, p. 220.
54. Bleiere *et al.*, *History of Latvia: The Twentieth Century*, p. 53.
55. M. Bobe, S. Levenberg, I. Maor and Z. Michaeli (eds), *The Jews in Latvia* (Tel Aviv: Association of Latvian and Estonian Jews in Israel, 1971), p. 280.

5  THE SHORT ERA OF INDEPENDENCE (1917–1939)

1. Dates prior to February 1918 – when the Gregorian (Western) calendar was introduced in the Russian Empire – are given according to the Julian calendar. The Gregorian calendar was introduced earlier in those territories which fell under German occupation.
2. See Andrew Ezergailis, *The Latvian Impact on the Bolshevik Revolution: The First Phase: September 1917 to April 1918* (Boulder, CO: East European Monographs, 1983).
3. Georg von Rauch, *The Baltic States: The Years of Independence, 1917–1940* (London: C. Hurst, 1974), p. 43.
4. The Courland *Landesrat* had done so already in March. On 8 November, Courland joined Estland, Livland and Ösel in forming a regency council for a *Landesstaat*.
5. Eduard Laaman, *Eesti iseseisvuse sünd* (Stockholm: Vaba Eesti, 1964), pp. 403, 630; Karl Siilivask (ed.), *Revolutsioon, kodusõda ja välisriikide interventsioon Eestis, 1917–1920*, vol. 2 (Tallinn: Eesti Raamat, 1982), p. 204.
6. Reigo Rosenthal, *Laidoner – väejuht. Johan Laidoner kõrgema operatiivjuhi ja strateegia kujundajana Eesti Vabadussõjas* (Tallinn: Argo, 2008), p. 522.
7. Vejas Gabriel Liulevičius, *War Land on the Eastern Front: Culture, National Identity and German Occupation in World War I* (Cambridge: Cambridge University Press, 2000), p. 243.
8. Karsten Brüggemann, 'Defending National Sovereignty Against Two Russias: Estonia in the Russian Civil War, 1918–1920', *Journal of Baltic Studies*, 34(1) (2003): 22–51; For a comprehensive recent study of the North-western Army, see Reigo Rosenthal, *Loodearmee* (Tallinn: Argo, 2006).
9. In 1935 Piłsudski was buried in Cracow alongside Polish kings, but he had his heart buried in Vilnius: Snyder, *Reconstruction of Nations*, p. 70.
10. Snyder, *Reconstruction of Nations*, pp. 58–9.
11. France, Britain, Japan, Belgium and Italy, but not the US, which delayed recognition until 1922.
12. For the political party systems, see Royal Institute of International Affairs, *The Baltic States: A Survey of the Political and Economic Structure and the Foreign Relations of Estonia, Latvia, and Lithuania* (London: Oxford University Press, 1938; repub. Westport, CT: Greenwood, 1970), pp. 41–58; V. Stanley Vardys, 'Democracy in the Baltic States, 1918–1934: The Stage and the Actors', *Journal of Baltic Studies*, 10(4) (Winter 1979): 321–35; von Rauch, *The Baltic States*, pp. 91–8.

13. Alfonsas Eidintas and Vytautas Žalys, *Lithuania in European Politics: The Years of the First Republic, 1918–1940* (New York: St Martin's Press, 1997), p. 113.
14. See Andres Kasekamp, *The Radical Right in Interwar Estonia* (Basingstoke: Macmillan, 2000).
15. The one group specifically cited by Ulmanis – the Legionnaires, a small association of decorated veterans of the war of independence – were a marginal force and did not present a genuine danger.
16. Eidintas and Žalys, *Lithuania in European Politics*, p. 115.
17. Kasekamp, *The Radical Right in Interwar Estonia*, pp. 120–31, 151–2; Eidintas and Žalys, *Lithuania in European Politics*, pp. 116–16, 121–5; Leonas Sabaliūnas, *Lithuania in Crisis: Nationalism to Communism, 1939–40* (Bloomington: Indiana University Press, 1972), pp. 25–40; Inesis Feldmanis, 'Umgestaltungsprozesse im Rahmen des Ulmanis-Regimes in Lettland 1934–1940' and Ilgvars Butulis, 'Autoritäre Ideologie und Praxis des Ulmanis-Regimes in Lettland 1934–1940', in Erwin Oberländer (ed.), *Autoritäre Regime in Ostmittel- und Südosteuropa 1919–1944* (Paderborn: Ferdinand Schöning, 2001), pp. 215–98.
18. Eidintas and Žalys, *Lithuania in European Politics*, p. 122; Sabaliūnas, *Lithuania in Crisis*, pp. 41–2.
19. The German ultimatum over Memel in 1939 and the Soviet ultimatum to Estonia in September 1939.
20. Gediminas Vaskela, 'The Land Reform of 1919–1940: Lithuania and the Countries of Eastern and Central Europe', *Lithuanian Historical Studies*, 1 (1996): 116–32.
21. Vaskela, 'The Land Reform of 1919–1940', pp. 128–9.
22. Bleiere *et al.*, *History of Latvia: The Twentieth Century*, p. 198.
23. Kahk and Tarvel, *An Economic History of the Baltic Countries*, p. 109.
24. Baltic Germans land-owners petitioned the League of Nations, claiming that the land reform acts constituted discrimination against an ethnic minority, but the League held that the issue was instead one of social justice: Royal Institute of International Affairs, *The Baltic States*, p. 30.
25. Bleiere *et al.*, *History of Latvia: The Twentieth Century*, p. 55. See also Artis Pabriks and Aldis Purs, *Latvia: The Challenges of Change* (London: Routledge, 2002), pp. 16–17.
26. Royal Institute of International Affairs, *The Baltic States*, p. 103.
27. Bleiere *et al.*, *History of Latvia: The Twentieth Century*, p. 194.
28. Toomas Karjahärm and Väino Sirk, *Vaim ja võim. Eesti haritlaskond 1917–1940* (Tallinn: Argo, 2001), pp. 21, 48, 50; Bleiere *et al.*, *History of Latvia: The Twentieth Century*, p. 223.
29. Without Memel/Klaipėda region.
30. von Rauch, *The Baltic States*, pp. 81–5.
31. Table compiled from data in Royal Institute of International Affairs, *The Baltic States*, pp. 30, 33, 36; *Latvijas vēstures atlants*, p. 43; Jüri Viikberg (ed.), *Eesti rahvaste raamat. Rahvusvähemused, -rühmad ja –killud* (Tallinn: Eesti Entsüklopeediakirjastus, 1999), p. 373; von Rauch, *The Baltic States*, pp. 81–5.

32. John Hiden, *Defender of Minorities: Paul Schiemann, 1876–1944* (London: C. Hurst, 2004), pp. 116–17.
33. Bleiere *et al.*, *History of Latvia: The Twentieth Century*, p. 237.
34. See Šarūnas Liekis, *A State within a State?: Jewish Autonomy in Lithuania 1918–1925* (Vilnius: Versus Aureus, 2003).
35. This idea was first proposed by Austrian socialists Karl Renner and Otto Bauer for the Habsburg Empire: John Hiden and David J. Smith, 'Looking beyond the Nation State: A Baltic Vision for National Minorities between the Wars', *Journal of Contemporary History*, 41(3) (2006): 387.
36. Kari Alenius, 'The Birth of Cultural Autonomy in Estonia: How, Why, and for Whom?', *Journal of Baltic Studies*, 38(4) (December 2007): 445–62.
37. At least 17,000 Latvians and 15,000 Estonians are known to have been executed, but the actual number of victims is undoubtedly larger: Professor Aadu Must (personal communication) and Björn Michael Felder, *Lettland im Zweiten Weltkrieg: Zwischen sowjetischen und deutschen Besatzern 1940–1946* (Paderborn: Ferdinand Schöningh, 2009), p. 72. See also Terry Martin, *The Affirmative Action Empire: Nations and Nationalism in the Soviet Union, 1923–1939* (Ithaca, NY: Cornell University Press, 2001), pp. 335–9.
38. Nevertheless, secret military cooperation existed between Estonia and Finland whose coastal batteries could seal off the Gulf of Finland to hostile warships: Jari Leskinen, *Vendade riigisaladus: Soome ja Eesti salajane sõjaline koostöö Nõukogude Liidu võimaliku rünnaku vastu aastatel 1918–1940* (Tallinn: Sinisukk, 2000).
39. Eidintas and Žalys, *Lithuania in European Politics*, p. 143.
40. A few rare individuals living in Vilnius at the time, such as Czesław Miłosz, the Polish-American poet who won the Nobel Prize in 1980, could appreciate both sides of the story.
41. Magnus Ilmjärv, *Hääletu alistumine. Eesti, Läti, Leedu välispoliitilise orientatsiooni kujunemine ja iseseisvuse kaotus 1920. aastate keskpaigast anneksioonini* (Tallinn: Argo, 2004), p. 245.
42. Zenonas Butkus, 'The Impact of the USSR on Lithuania's Domestic Policy and its International Orientation in the Third Decade of the Twentieth Century', *Journal of Baltic Studies*, 38(2) (June 2007): 195–214.
43. Eidintas and Žalys, *Lithuania in European Politics*, p. 164.

6   BETWEEN ANVIL AND HAMMER (1939–1953)

1. Bogdan Musial, *Sihikul oli Saksamaa. Stalini sõjaplaanid lääne vastu* (Tallinn: Tänapäeva, 2009), p. 267. Original: *Kampfplatz Deutschland. Stalins Kriegspläne gegen den Westen* (Berlin: Propyläen, 2008).
2. Although a portion of Lithuania adjacent to East Prussia was still allocated to Germany under this agreement, the USSR occupied the entire country in June 1940. Nevertheless, the USSR paid 7,500,000 gold dollars in compensation to the Reich in January 1941 for this slice of Lithuanian territory: Alfred Erich Senn, *Lithuania 1940: Revolution from Above* (Amsterdam: Rodopi, 2008), p. 146.

3. Albert N. Tarulis, *Soviet Policy toward the Baltic States 1918–1940* (Notre Dame: University of Notre Dame, 1959), p. 155.
4. Although the USSR kept most of the territory south and east of Vilnius that it had recognised as belonging to Lithuania in the 1920 peace treaty.
5. August Rei, *The Drama of the Baltic Peoples* (Stockholm: Vaba Eesti, 1970), p. 263.
6. Gert von Pistohlkors (ed.), *Baltische Länder*, Deutsche Geschichte im Osten Europas (Berlin: Siedler, 1994), p. 540.
7. In this second wave of resettlement, *Nachumsiedlung*, during the Soviet occupation 17,000 left, but many of these were Estonians and Latvians who had German spouses or could claim German descent: von Pistohlkors, *Baltische Länder*, p. 541.
8. Ago Pajur and Tõnu Tannberg (eds), *Eesti Ajalugu VI. Vabadussõjast taasiseseisvumiseni* (Tartu: Ilmamaa, 2005), p. 155.
9. Molotov's prime evidence for this absurd claim was the publication of the first issue of *Revue baltique*.
10. Magnus Ilmjärv, *Silent Submission: Formation of Foreign Policy of Estonia, Latvia and Lithuania: Period from Mid-1920s to Annexation in 1940*, Studia Baltica Stockholmiensia 24 (Stockholm: Acta Universitatis Stockholmiensis, 2004).
11. Rei, *The Drama of the Baltic Peoples*, p. 263.
12. Liudas Truska and Vygantas Vareikis, *The Preconditions for the Holocaust: Anti-Semitism in Lithuania*. The Crimes of the Totalitarian Regimes in Lithuania, vol. 1 (Vilnius: Margi raštai, 2004), p. 330.
13. Felder, *Lettland im Zweiten Weltkrieg*, pp. 90–3.
14. Toomas Hiio, Meelis Maripuu and Indrek Paavle (eds), *Estonia 1940–1945: Reports of the Estonian International Commission for the Investigation of Crimes Against Humanity* (Tallinn: Estonian International Commission for the Investigation of Crimes against Humanity, 2006), p. 217.
15. Hiio *et al.* (eds), *Estonia 1940–1945*, p. 377; Irēne Šneidere, 'The First Soviet Occupation Period in Latvia 1940–1941', in *The Hidden and Forbidden History of Latvia under Soviet and Nazi Occupations, 1940–1991*, Symposium of the Commission of the Historians of Latvia, vol. 14 (Riga: Institute of the History of Latvia, 2005), p. 41; Arvydas Anusauskas (ed.), *The First Soviet Occupation. Terror and Crimes against Humanity*. The Crimes of the Totalitarian Regimes in Lithuania. The Soviet Occupation, vol. 2 (Vilnius: Margi Raštai, 2006).
16. Ruth Bettina Birn, *Die Sicherheitspolizei in Estland 1941–1944: Eine Studie zur Kollaboration im Osten* (Paderborn: Ferdinand Schöningh, 2006), p. 258.
17. Andrew Ezergailis (ed.), *Stockholm Documents: The German Occupation of Latvia, 1941–1945. What Did America Know?*, Symposium of the Commission of the Historians of Latvia, vol. 5 (Riga: Historical Institute of Latvia, 2002), pp. 423–4.
18. Arūnas Bubnys, *The Holocaust in Lithuania between 1941 and 1944* (Vilnius: Genocide and Resistance Research Centre of Lithuania, 2005), p. 3; Yitzhak Arad, 'The Murder of the Jews in German-Occupied

Lithuania (1941–1944)', in Alvydas Nikžentaitis, Stefan Schreiner and Darius Staliūnas (eds), *The Vanished World of Lithuanian Jews* (Amsterdam: Rodopi, 2004), p. 177.

19. The most detailed analysis of the pogroms is to be found in Christoph Dieckmann and Saulius Sužiedėlis (eds), *The Persecution and Mass Murder of Lithuanian Jews during Summer and Fall of 1941*, Crimes of the Totalitarian Regimes in Lithuania, The Nazi Occupation, vol. 3 (Vilnius: Margi Raštai, 2006).

20. Andrew Ezergailis, *The Holocaust in Latvia 1941–1944: The Missing Center* (Riga: Historical Institute of Latvia, 1996), pp. 239–70.

21. Arūnas Bubnys, 'The Holocaust in Lithuania: An Outline of the Major Stages and their Results', in Nikžentaitis, Schreiner and Staliūnas (eds), *The Vanished World of Lithuanian Jews*, p. 218.

22. Aivars Stranga, 'The Holocaust in Occupied Latvia: 1941–1945', in *The Hidden and Forbidden History of Latvia under Soviet and Nazi Occupations, 1940–1991*, Symposium of the Commission of the Historians of Latvia, vol. 14 (Riga: Institute of the History of Latvia, 2005), pp. 172–3.

23. Stranga, 'The Holocaust in Occupied Latvia', p. 167.

24. Christoph Dieckmann, Vytautas Toleikis and Rimantis Zizas, *Murder of Prisoners of War and of Civilian Population in Lithuania*, The Crimes of Totalitarian Regimes in Lithuania, vol. 2 (Vilnius: Margi raštai, 2005), p. 377.

25. Alfred Erich Senn, 'Baltic Battleground', in *The Hidden and Forbidden History of Latvia under Soviet and Nazi Occupations, 1940–1991*, Symposium of the Commission of the Historians of Latvia, vol. 14 (Riga: Institute of the History of Latvia, 2005), pp. 24–6.

26. Dieckmann, Toleikis, and Zizas, *Murder of Prisoners of War and of Civilian Population in Lithuania*, p. 265.

27. Tiit Noormets, Toe Nõmm, Hanno Ojalo, Olev Raidla, Reigo Rosenthal, Tõnis Taavet and Mati Õun, *Korpusepoisid. Eesti sõjamehed 22. eesti territoriaalkorpuses ja 8. eesti laskurkorpuses Teises maailmasõjas aastatel 1940–45* (Tallinn: Sentinel, 2007), pp. 237, 239.

28. Seppo Myllyniemi, *Die Neuordnung der Baltischen Länder 1941–1944: Zum nationalsozialistischen Inhalt der deutschen Besatzungspolitik* (Helsinki: Suomen Historiallinen Seura, 1973), pp. 210–13.

29. Valdis O. Lumans, *Latvia in World War II* (New York: Fordham University Press, 2006), p. 296.

30. Laar has calculated 30,000 Soviet troops killed and over 130,000 wounded, but this is probably exaggerated. The German side lost over 2000 plus 8000 wounded: Mart Laar, *Sinimäed 1944* (Tallinn: Varrak, 2006), p. 325.

31. Lumans, *Latvia in World War II*, pp. 367–70; Geoffrey Swain, 'Latvia's Democratic Resistance: A Forgotten Episode from the Second World War', *European History Quarterly*, 39(2) (April 2009): 241–63.

32. Romuald J. Misiunas and Rein Taagepera, *The Baltic States: Years of Dependence, 1940–1990*, 2nd updated edn (Berkeley, CA: University of California Press, 1993), p. 67.

33. Kaja Kumer-Haukanõmm, 'Eestlaste Teistest maailmasõjast tingitud põgenemine läände', in Kaja Kumer-Haukanõmm, Tiit Rosenberg and Tiit

Tammaru (eds), *Suur põgenemine 1944. Eestlaste lahkumine läände ning selle mõjud* (Tartu: Tartu University Press, 2006), p. 36; Kārlis Kangeris, 'German Plans for Retreat from the Baltics: The Latvian Case', in Kumer-Haukanõmm, Rosenberg and Tammaru (eds), *Suur põgenemine 1944*, p. 47; Kiaupa, *The History of Lithuania*, p. 334.

34. Of the 2,000,000 inhabitants of Latvia in 1939, only 1,400,000 remained in Latvia in 1945: Valters Nollendorfs (ed.), *Latvia under the Rule of the Soviet Union and National Socialist Germany 1940–1991* (Riga: Museum of the Occupation of Latvia, 2002), p. 89. However, this figure includes all those who were conscripted, deported or fled as refugees. Many of these later returned to Latvia. A more precise figure is 17 per cent or 325,000 citizens: Bleiere *et al.*, *History of Latvia: The Twentieth Century*, p. 418.

35. Almost the entire Swedish minority in north-western Estonia and on the Estonian islands, 7000 people, were evacuated by the Swedish government to Sweden in 1943–4.

36. Olaf Mertelsmann, *Der stalinistische Umbau in Estland: Von der Markt- zur Kommandowirtschaft* (Hamburg: Verlag Dr. Kovač, 2006), p. 131.

37. Theodore R. Weeks, 'Population Politics in Vilnius 1944–1947: A Case Study of Socialist-Sponsored Ethnic Cleansing', *Post-Soviet Affairs*, 23(1) (March 2007): 76–95.

38. Pranas Morkus, 'The Call to Arms (1944–1953)', in Birutė Burauskaitė and Pranas Morkus, *Resistance to the Occupation of Lithuania: 1944–1990* (Vilnius: The Genocide and Resistance Research Centre of Lithuania, 2002), p. 20.

39. Tiit Noormägi and Valdur Ohmann (eds), *Hävitajad. Nõukogude hävituspataljonid Eestis 1944–1954* (Tallinn: Riigiarhiiv, 2006); Virginija Rudiene (ed.), *War after War: Armed Anti-Soviet Resistance in Lithuania in 1944–1953* (Vilnius: The Museum of Genocide Victims of the Genocide and Resistance Research Center of Lithuania, 2007).

40. A popularising account is Tom Bower, *The Red Web: MI6 and the KGB Master Coup* (London: Aurum, 1989). See also Märt Männik, *A Tangled Web: A British Spy in Estonia. The memoirs of an Estonian who fell into the clutches of MI6 and the KGB*, translated and introduced by the Earl of Carlisle (Tallinn: Grenadier, 2008).

41. Arvydas Anušauskas (ed.), *The Anti-Soviet Resistance in the Baltic States* (Vilnius: Du Ka, 1999), p. 44.

42. Jelena Zubkova, *Baltimaad ja Kreml 1940–1953* (Tallinn: Varrak, 2009), pp. 98–9.

43. Bleiere *et al.*, *History of Latvia: The Twentieth Century*, p. 351.

44. Heinrihs Strods, 'Sovietization of Latvia 1944–1991', *The Hidden and Forbidden History of Latvia under Soviet and Nazi Occupations 1940–1991*, Symposium of the Commission of the Historians of Latvia, vol. 14 (Riga: Institute of the History of Latvia, 2005), p. 223.

45. V. Stanley Vardys, *The Catholic Church, Dissent and Nationality in Soviet Lithuania* (Boulder, CO: East European Monographs, 1978), pp. 75–6.

46. Zubkova, *Baltimaad ja Kreml 1940–1953*, pp. 110–11.

47. Most of these individuals were able to resume their professions after the death of Stalin: Toomas Karjahärm and Väino Sirk, *Kohanemine*

*ja vastupanu. Eesti haritlaskond 1940–1987* (Tallinn: Argo, 2007), p. 224–7.

48. In a further ironic twist of fate, Allik managed to recover his position in 1965 after he was amnestied in 1956: Misiunas and Taagepera, *The Baltic States: Years of Dependence*, pp. 82, 149.
49. For the most detailed analysis of Stalinist economic policy in a Baltic republic, see Mertelsmann, *Der stalinistische Umbau in Estland.*
50. For the most comprehensive study of collectivisation in a Baltic republic, see David Feest, *Zwangskollektivierung im Baltikum. Die Sowjetisierung des Estnischen Dorfes 1944–1953*, Beiträge zur Geschichte Osteuropas 40 (Köln: Böhlau, 2007).
51. Heinrihs Strods and Matthew Kott, 'The File on Operation "Priboi": A Re-Assessment of the Mass Deportations of 1949', *Journal of Baltic Studies*, 33(1) (Spring 2002): 20.
52. Strods and Kott, 'The File on Operation "Priboi" ', p. 18.
53. Kiaupa, *The History of Lithuania*, p. 308.

## 7   SOVIET RULE (1953–1991)

1. Pabriks and Purs, *Latvia: The Challenges of Change*, pp. 36, 40.
2. Senn, 'Baltic Battleground', p. 19.
3. Birutė Burauskaitė, 'The Unarmed Resistance (1954–1990)', in Birutė Burauskaitė and Pranas Morkus, *Resistance to the Occupation of Lithuania: 1944–1990* (Vilnius: Genocide and Resistance Research Centre of Lithuania, 2002), p. 24.
4. William Prigge, 'The Latvian Purges of 1959: A Revision Study', *Journal of Baltic Studies*, 35(3) (Fall 2004): 211–30.
5. Pajur and Tannberg (eds), *Eesti Ajalugu VI*, p. 300.
6. Diana Mincyte, 'Everyday Environmentalism: The Practice, Politics, and Nature of Subsidiary Farming in Stalin's Lithuania', *Slavic Review*, 68(1) (Spring 2009): 31–49.
7. Misiunas and Taagepera, *The Baltic States: Years of Dependence*, p. 159.
8. Mati Graf and Heikki Roiko-Jokela, *Vaarallinen Suomi. Suomi Eestin kommunistisen puolueen ja Neuvosto-Viron KGB:n silmin* (Jyväskylä: Minerva, 2004), pp. 169–89.
9. Andrew Ezergailis, *Nazi/Soviet Disinformation about the Holocaust in Latvia: Daugavas Vanagi: Who are they? Revisited* (Riga: Occupation Museum of Latvia, 2005).
10. Those appointed to the final CPSU Politburo in 1990 were Mykolas Burokevičius, Alfrēds Rubiks and Enn-Arno Sillari, the first secretaries of the Lithuanian, Latvian and Estonian Communist Parties, respectively, after their split into pro-independence and pro-Moscow organisations.
11. Pajur and Tannberg (eds), *Eesti Ajalugu VI*, p. 311.
12. Mikk Titma, Liina Mai Tooding and Nancy Brandon Tuma, 'Communist Party Members: Incentives and Gains', *International Journal of Sociology*, 34(2) (Summer 2004): 72–99.

13. Misiunas and Taagepera, *The Baltic States: Years of Dependence*, pp. 359–60.
14. Hoyer, Lauk, and Vihalemm (eds), *Towards a Civic Society: The Baltic Media's Long Road to Freedom*, p. 217.
15. V. Stanley Vardys and Judith B. Sedaitis, *Lithuania: The Rebel Nation* (Boulder, CO: Westview, 1997), p. 86.
16. Rein Ruutsoo, *Civil Society and Nation Building in Estonia and the Baltic States: Impact of Traditions on Mobilization and Transition 1986–2000 – Historical and Sociological Study* (Rovaniemi: University of Lapland, 2002), p. 126.
17. The letter was unsigned, but it was later revealed that Berklāvs had been the main author.
18. Vardys and Sedaitis, *Lithuania: The Rebel Nation*, p. 88.
19. Table compiled from data in Misiunas and Taagepera, *The Baltic States: Years of Dependence*, p. 353; Plakans, *The Latvians: A Short History*, p. 153, 158; Raun, *Estonia and the Estonians*, p. 247. The figures for 1945 are estimates.
20. Misiunas and Taagepera, *The Baltic States: Years of Dependence*, p. 215.
21. Misiunas and Taagepera, *The Baltic States: Years of Dependence*, p. 238.
22. Robert W. Smurr, 'Lahemaa: The paradox of the USSR's first national park', *Nationalities Papers*, 36(3) (2008): 399–423.
23. Pajur and Tannberg (eds), *Eesti Ajalugu VI*, p. 316.
24. Misiunas and Taagepera, *The Baltic States: Years of Dependence*, p. 231.
25. For a systematic catalogue of absurd contradictions in Soviet life, see Lauri Vahtre, *Absurdi impeerium* (Tallinn: Tammerraamat, 2007); Enno Tammer (ed.), *Nõukogude aeg ja inimene. Meie mälestused* (Tallinn: Tänapäev, 2004).
26. Kiaupa, *The History of Lithuania*, p. 312.
27. Michael Bruchis, 'The nationality policy of the CPSU and its reflection in Soviet socio-political terminology', in Peter J. Potichnyj (ed.), *The Soviet Union: Party and Society* (Cambridge: Cambridge University Press, 1985), p. 125.
28. Pabriks and Purs, *Latvia: The Challenges of Change*, pp. 32–6.
29. Bleiere *et al.*, *History of Latvia: The Twentieth Century*, p. 526.
30. Rolf Ekmanis, 'Harmonizer of Disharmony: Latvian Poet and Editor Māris Čaklais, *Journal of Baltic Studies*, 40(2) (June 2009): 216.
31. Misiunas and Taagepera, *The Baltic States: Years of Dependence*, p. 161.
32. Vardys and Sedaitis, *Lithuania: The Rebel Nation*, p. 94.
33. Thomas Lane, *Lithuania: Stepping Westwards* (London: Routledge, 2002), p. 102.
34. *Isemajandav Eesti* (IME) – the acronym means 'miracle' or 'wonder' in Estonian – was proposed by four members of the Communist Party, Edgar Savisaar, Siim Kallas, Tiit Made and Mikk Titma: Rein Taagepera, *Estonia: Return to Independence* (Boulder, CO: Westview, 1993), pp. 128–30.
35. The term 'Singing Revolution' was invented in June 1988 to denote the peaceful nature of the dramatic political change by artist Heinz Valk, an inspiring orator for the Estonian Popular Front: Henri Vogt, *Between Utopia*

and Disillusionment: A Narrative of the Political Transformation in Eastern Europe (Oxford: Berghahn Books, 2005), p. 26. The remarkable role of choral singing in Estonia's peaceful transformation is vividly shown in *The Singing Revolution*, a documentary film by James and Maureen Tusty (Mountain View Productions, 2007).

36. Anatol Lieven, *The Baltic Revolution: Estonia, Latvia, Lithuania, and the Path to Independence* (New Haven, CT: Yale University Press, 1993), p. 113.

37. Nils Muiznieks, 'The Influence of the Baltic Popular Movements on the Process of Soviet Disintegration', *Europe–Asia Studies*, 47(1) (1995): 3–25; Mark R. Beissinger, *Nationalist Mobilization and the Collapse of the Soviet State* (Cambridge: Cambridge University Press, 2002), p. 161. Baltic events also influenced the later developments in Chechnya. The first two presidents who fought against Russia for their nation's independence, Dzhokhar Dudayev and Aslan Maskhadov, witnessed the Singing Revolution while serving as senior Soviet military officers in Estonia and Lithuania, respectively.

38. For an inside account of the work of the Baltic members of the USSR Congress of Peoples' Deputies, see Heiki Lindpere, *Molotov–Ribbentrop Pact: Challenging Soviet History* (Tallinn: Estonian Foreign Policy Institute, 2009).

39. Taagepera, *Estonia: Return to Independence*, pp. 174–5.

40. Andres Kasekamp, 'Paths to Baltic Independence', *Slovo: A Journal of Contemporary Russian and East European Affairs*, 5(1) (December 1992): 26–7.

41. Rein Taagepera, 'The Baltic Perspectives of Estonian Turning Points', *Acta Historica Tallinnensia*, 4 (2000): 13.

42. Lieven, *The Baltic Revolution*, p. 245.

43. Ainius Lasas, 'Bloody Sunday: What Did Gorbachev Know about January 1991 Events in Vilnius and Riga?', *Journal of Baltic Studies*, 38(2) (June 2007): 179–194.

44. Kristina Spohr Readman, 'Between Rhetoric and *Realpolitik*: Western Diplomacy and the Baltic Independence Struggle in the Cold War Endgame', *Cold War History*, 6(1) (February 2006): 1–42.

## 8   RETURN TO THE WEST (1991–2009)

1. Unlike the Estonian and Lithuanian constitutions, the Latvian one had not been altered in the 1930s during the era of authoritarian rule. Substantial additions – the establishment of a constitutional court and 27 paragraphs on civil and human rights – were made to it in 1998: Hermann Smith-Sivertsen, 'Latvia', in Sten Berglund, Joakim Ekman and Frank H. Aarebrot (eds), *Handbook of Political Change in Eastern Europe*, 2nd edn (Cheltenham: Elgar, 2004), p. 131.

2. The first presidential election in Estonia was only for a four-year term and the first two elections in Latvia were only for three-year terms.

3. Initially three years in Latvia. The Lithuanian Supreme Council was renamed *Seimas* in 1996.

4. Latvia and Lithuania initially had a threshold of 4 per cent.
5. A two-round run-off electoral system as in France was employed in Lithuania until 2000.
6. The best analyses of the evolution of the current political party systems are provided by the respective country chapters – Estonia by Mikko Lagerspetz and Henri Vogt, Latvia by Hermann Smith-Sivertsen, and Lithuania by Kjetil Duvold and Mindaugas Jurkynas – in Berglund, Ekman and Aarebrot (eds), *Handbook of Political Change in Eastern Europe*, and the respective country chapters – Estonia by Evald Mikkel, Latvia by Artis Pabriks and Aiga Štokenberga, and Lithuania by Ainė Ramonaitė – in Susanne Jungerstam-Mulders (ed.), *Post-Communist EU Member States: Parties and Party Systems* (Aldershot: Ashgate, 2006).
7. The social democrats were officially named the 'Moderates'.
8. Allan Sikk, *Highways to Power: New Party Success in Three Young Democracies*, Dissertationes rerum politicarum Universitatis Tartuensis 1 (Tartu: Tartu University Press, 2006).
9. Emsis's actual green credentials were questionable: David J. Galbreath and Daunis Auers, 'Green, Black and Brown: Uncovering Latvia's Environmental Politics', *Journal of Baltic Studies*, 40(3) (September 2009): 342–5.
10. All three currencies were later pegged to the euro.
11. Zenonas Norkus, 'Why did Estonia Perform Best? The North–South Gap in the Post-Socialist Economic Transition of the Baltic States', *Journal of Baltic Studies*, 38(1) (2007): 21–42.
12. European Commission, *Regular Report from the Commission on Estonia's Progress towards Accession* (Brussels, European Commission, 1998), p. 51; European Commission, *Regular Report from the Commission on Latvia's Progress towards Accession* (Brussels, European Commission, 1998), p. 56; European Commission, *Regular Report from the Commission on Lithuania's Progress towards Accession* (Brussels, European Commission, 1998), p. 50.
13. On the liquidation of collective farms and its consequences for rural communities, see Ilkka Alanen, Jouko Nikula, Helvi Põder and Rein Ruutsoo, *Decollectivisation, Destruction and Disillusionment: A Community Study in Southern Estonia* (Aldershot: Ashgate, 2001) and Sigrid Rausing, *History, Memory, and Identity in Post-Soviet Estonia: The End of a Collective Farm* (Oxford: Oxford University Press, 2004).
14. Magnus Feldmann, 'The Fast Track from the Soviet Union to the World Economy: External Liberalization in Estonia and Latvia', *Government and Opposition*, 36(4) (2001): 537–58.
15. The International Monetary Fund approved a €1.7 billion rescue loan as part of a €7.5 billion bailout which included the European Union (€3.1 billion) and Nordic countries (€1.8 billion).
16. Nationalists opposed to the liberalisation of the citizenship law initiated a national referendum, but 53 per cent of voters approved the legislation in the referendum held on 3 October 1998.
17. Vello Pettai and Kristina Kallas, 'Estonia: Conditionality amidst a Legal Straitjacket'; David J. Galbreath and Nils Muižnieks, 'Latvia: Managing

Post-Imperial Minorities'; Dovile Budryte and Vilana Pilinaite-Sotirovic, 'Lithuania: Progressive Legislation without Popular Support', in Bernd Rechel (ed.), *Minority Rights in Central and Eastern Europe* (London: Routledge, 2009), pp. 104–18, 135–65.

18. Anton Steen, *Between Past and Future: Elites, Democracy and the State in Post-Communist Countries: A Comparison of Estonia, Latvia and Lithuania* (Aldershot: Ashgate, 1997), pp. 93–8.

19. Lane, *Lithuania: Stepping Westwards*, p. 187.

20. Peter van Elsuwege, *From Soviet Republics to EU Member States: A Legal and Political Assessment of the Baltic States' Accession to the EU* (Leiden: Brill, 2008), pp. 118, 141.

21. Mikko Lagerspetz, 'How Many Nordic Countries? The Possibilities and Limits of Geopolitical Identity Construction', *Cooperation and Conflict*, 38(1) (2003): 48–60. For a discussion of spatial narratives in identity discourse in the Baltic Sea region, see Marko Lehti, 'Possessing a Baltic Europe: Retold National Narratives in the European North', in Marko Lehti and David J. Smith (eds), *Post-Cold War Identity Politics: Northern and Baltic Experiences* (London: Frank Cass, 2003), pp. 11–49.

22. Until 1995, the OSCE was known as the Conference on Security and Cooperation in Europe (CSCE).

23. Van Elsuwege, *From Soviet Republics to EU Member States*, pp. 286–7.

24. David Galbreath and Jeremy W. Lamoreaux, 'Bastion, Beacon or Bridge? Conceptualising the Baltic logic of the EU's Neighbourhood', *Geopolitics*, 12(1) (2007): 109–32.

25. See an insider's account of NATO enlargement by a key US State Department official during the Clinton administration: Ronald D. Asmus, *Opening NATO's Door: How the Alliance Remade Itself for a New Era* (New York: Columbia University Press, 2002).

26. Partly in recognition of these contributions, the 2006 NATO Summit was held in Riga and an indication of the strength of the relationship with the USA was the fact that US President George W. Bush visited the Baltic states on three separate occasions.

27. The last Russian military installation, the radar station at Skrunda in Latvia, was demolished only in 1999. The best account of the international diplomacy to remove the Russian troops is Lars Fredén, *Återkomster: Svensk säkerhetspolitik och de baltiska ländernas första år I självständighet 1991–1994* (Stockholm: Atlantis, 2006).

28. Klaudijus Maniokas, Ramūnas Vilipišauskas and Darius Žeruolis (eds), *Lithuania's Road to the European Union: Unification of Europe and Lithuania's EU Accession Negotiation* (Vilnius: Eugrimas, 2005), pp. 297–348.

29. Within the EU, Lithuania has taken a more uncompromising stance than the other Baltic states with regard to Russia. In the spring of 2008 Lithuania temporarily blocked the opening of negotiations for a new Partnership and Cooperation Agreement between the EU and Russia.

30. See Andris Sprūds and Toms Rostoks (eds), *Energy: Pulling the Baltic Sea Region Together or Apart?* (Riga: Latvian Institute of International Affairs, 2009).

31. Eiki Berg and Piret Ehin (eds), *Identity and Foreign Policy: Baltic–Russian Relations* (Aldershot: Ashgate, 2009); Jörg Hackmann and Marko Lehti (eds), *Contested and Shared Places of Memory: History and Politics in North Eastern Europe* (London: Routledge, 2009).
32. Karsten Brüggemann and Andres Kasekamp, 'The Politics of History and the "War of Monuments" in Estonia', *Nationalities Papers*, 36(3) (July 2008): 425–48.
33. At the same time, the Simon Wiesenthal Center has accused the Baltic authorities of dragging their feet in bringing suspected Nazi war criminals to trial: Efraim Zuroff, *Operation Last Chance: One Man's Quest to Bring Nazi Criminals to Justice* (New York: Palgrave, 2009), Chs 10–12.
34. 'Russia sets up commission to prevent falsification of history', *RIA Novosti*, 19 May 2009, http://en.rian.ru/russia/20090519/155041940.html (accessed 30 August 2009).

# Chronology

| | |
|---|---|
| 11,000 BC | First nomads enter the Baltic region |
| 9000 BC | Emergence of Kunda Culture |
| 9000–5000 BC | Mesolithic period in the Baltic region |
| 5000–1800 BC | Neolithic period |
| 4000 BC | Emergence of Comb Ware Culture |
| 3000 BC | Emergence of Corded Ware Culture |
| 1800–500 BC | Bronze Age |
| 500 BC–AD 450 | Early Iron Age |
| 450–800 | Middle Iron Age |
| 800–1200 | Late Iron Age |
| 1009 | First recorded mention of Lithuania |
| 1186 | Pope appoints Meinhard first Bishop of Üxküll |
| 1198 | First crusade against the Livs |
| 1199 | Albert ordained Bishop of Üxküll |
| 1201 | Founding of Riga |
| 1202 | Establishment of the Swordbrothers |
| 1206 | Crusaders subjugate the Livs |
| 1219 | Danes conquer northern Estonia |
| 1227 | Subjugation of the Estonians by the Swordbrothers |
| 1236 | Swordbrothers annihilated at Saulé |
| 1237 | Swordbrothers merged with Teutonic Knights |
| 1242 | Novgorodians defeat Livonian knights on ice of Lake Peipus |
| 1253 | Mindaugas crowned King of Lithuania after adopting Christianity |
| 1255 | Riga elevated to archbishopric |
| 1263 | Mindaugas assassinated |
| 1282 | Riga becomes first Hanseatic town in Livonia |

| | |
|---|---|
| 1290 | Semigallians conquered, present-day Latvia fully subjugated by the Teutonic Order |
| 1316 | Gediminas becomes Lithuanian grand duke |
| 1323 | Vilnius established as Lithuanian capital |
| 1343 | St George's night uprising of Estonians |
| 1346 | Danes sell Estonia to the Teutonic Order |
| 1386 | Lithuanian Grand Duke Jogaila crowned King of Poland |
| 1387 | Adoption of Christianity by Lithuanians |
| 1388 | Lithuanian Grand Duke Vytautas grants privileges for Jews |
| 1410 | Defeat of the Teutonic Knights by Poles and Lithuanians at Tannenberg |
| 1422 | Peace of Melno; end of wars between Lithuanians and Teutonic Order |
| 1435 | Establishment of the Livonian Confederation |
| 1481 | First Muscovite invasion of Livonia |
| 1524 | Protestant reformation triumphs in Livonian cities |
| 1525 | First Estonian and Latvian book printed |
| 1529 | First Lithuanian Statute (law code) |
| 1547 | First Lithuanian book printed |
| 1558 | Tsar Ivan the Terrible launches the Livonian War |
| 1561 | Dissolution of the Livonian Confederation; northern Estonia under Swedish protection and the rest of Livonia under Polish rule |
| 1562 | Last Master of Livonian Order becomes Duke of Courland |
| 1569 | Polish–Lithuanian Commonwealth formed |
| 1579 | Founding of University of Vilnius |
| 1583 | End of Livonian War |
| 1585 | Denmark sells the Bishopric of Courland to Poland–Lithuania |
| 1588 | Third Lithuanian Statute (law code) |
| 1595 | Establishment of Uniate Church in Grand Duchy of Lithuania |
| 1629 | Peace of Altmark grants Livonia to Sweden |
| 1632 | Founding of University of Dorpat (Tartu) |
| 1642 | Beginning of Duke Jacob's illustrious reign in Courland |
| 1645 | Sweden gains Ösel (Saaremaa) from Denmark |
| 1655 | Muscovite invasion of Lithuania; Act of Kėdainiai creating abortive Lithuanian–Swedish union |
| 1689 | Publication of Latvian-language Bible |
| 1697 | Great famine |
| 1700 | Start of Great Northern War |

| | |
|---|---|
| 1703 | Founding of St Petersburg |
| 1709 | Sweden defeated by Russia at Poltava |
| 1710 | Estland and Livland capitulate to Russia |
| 1710–11 | Devastating plague |
| 1721 | Peace of Nystad ends Great Northern War |
| 1739 | Publication of Estonian-language Bible |
| 1772 | First partition of Poland–Lithuania |
| 1783 | Empress Catherine integrates Baltic provinces into Russia |
| 1791 | Constitution for Poland–Lithuania |
| 1793 | Second partition of Poland–Lithuania |
| 1794 | Polish–Lithuanian uprising against Russia |
| 1795 | Final partition of Poland–Lithuania |
| 1802 | Re-establishment of the University of Dorpat (Tartu) |
| 1802–4 | Beginning of agrarian reforms in Baltic provinces |
| 1812 | Napoleon's invasion of Russia |
| 1816–19 | Emancipation of serfs in Courland, Estland and Livland |
| 1824 | Latvian Literary Society founded |
| 1830–31 | Polish–Lithuanian uprising against Russia |
| 1832 | Wilno (Vilnius) University closed |
| 1838 | Establishment of Estonian Learned Society |
| 1840 | Abolition of the Lithuanian Statute |
| 1845 | Orthodox conversion movement in Baltic provinces |
| 1849 | Peasants allowed to purchase land in Livland |
| 1856 | First regular Latvian newspaper – *Mājas Viesis* |
| 1857 | First regular Estonian newspaper – *Perno Postimees*; Estonian national epic – *Kalevipoeg* |
| 1861 | Emancipation of serfs in the Russian Empire, including Lithuania and Latgale |
| 1863–4 | Polish and Lithuanian uprising against Russia |
| 1864 | Ban on use of Latin alphabet in Lithuanian |
| 1868 | Founding of Riga Latvian Association |
| 1869 | First Estonian song festival |
| 1873 | First Latvian song festival |
| 1883 | First Lithuanian newspaper – *Aušra* |
| 1885 | Start of Russification in Baltic provinces |
| 1888 | Publication of Latvian national epic – *Lāčplēsis* |
| 1897 | Latvians achieve control over first municipal government Wolmar (Valmiera) |

| | |
|---|---|
| 1904 | End of ban on Lithuanian and Latgalian publications using Latin alphabet |
| 1905 | Failed Russian Revolution; political mobilisation in Baltic region |
| 1906 | Retribution by tsarist punishment units; elections to Russian Duma |
| 1914 | Beginning of World War I |
| 1915 | Lithuania occupied by Germany; Latvian territory becomes frontline |
| 1917 | Collapse of tsarist regime; Bolshevik seizure of power |
| 1918 | Lithuanian, Estonian and Latvian independence declared |
| 1919 | Estonians, Latvians and Lithuanians fight Russian Bolsheviks and German volunteers |
| 1920 | Peace treaties with Soviet Russia |
| 1921 | International recognition: Estonia, Latvia and Lithuania join League of Nations |
| 1923 | Military alliance concluded between Estonia and Latvia; Lithuanian seizure of Memel |
| 1924 | Failed communist putsch in Tallinn |
| 1925 | Estonian Cultural Autonomy Law |
| 1926 | Smetona comes to power in Lithuania after military coup |
| 1934 | Coups d'état in Estonia and Latvia; Baltic Entente |
| 1938 | Polish ultimatum to Lithuania |
| 1939 | Nazi–Soviet Pact; Red Army bases in the Baltic states; resettlement of Baltic Germans |
| 1940 | Incorporation of Baltic states into USSR |
| 1941 | Mass deportations; German invasion; murder of the Jews |
| 1944–45 | Red Army reconquers the Baltic states |
| 1945 | End of World War II; resistance continues |
| 1949 | Collectivisation and mass deportations |
| 1950 | Purge of Estonian Communist Party leadership |
| 1953 | Death of Stalin |
| 1956 | Thaw under Khrushchev |
| 1959 | Purge of Latvian Communist Party leadership |
| 1968 | Soviet invasion of Czechoslovakia ends Thaw |
| 1972 | Self-immolation of Romas Kalanta in Kaunas |
| 1974 | Death of Lithuanian Communist leader Antanas Sniečkus |
| 1979 | Baltic dissidents' appeal to the UN |
| 1980 | Youth riot in Tallinn |

| | |
|---|---|
| 1985 | Gorbachev becomes leader of the USSR |
| 1987 | First demonstrations against Soviet rule |
| 1988 | The Singing Revolution; Estonian declaration of sovereignty; establishment of Baltic Popular Fronts |
| 1989 | Baltic Way – human chain from Tallinn to Vilnius to demand freedom |
| 1990 | Election of pro-independence governments |
| 1991 | Independence of Estonia, Latvia and Lithuania recognised |
| 1992–93 | Constitutions adopted and founding elections; currency reforms; liberalisation of economies |
| 1993–94 | Russian troop withdrawal |
| 1995 | Baltic states apply for EU membership |
| 1997 | Estonia invited to begin EU accession negotiations |
| 1999 | Latvia and Lithuania invited to begin EU accession negotiations |
| 2002 | EU membership negotiations completed; invitation to join NATO |
| 2004 | Baltic membership of the EU and NATO |
| 2006 | NATO summit held in Rīga |
| 2007 | Riot over relocation of Red Army monument in Tallinn |
| 2008 | Drastic budget cuts in response to world financial crisis |
| 2009 | EU adopts Baltic Sea Strategy |

# Place Names

| Current Estonian, Latvian or Lithuanian | German | Russian (pre-1917)* | Other |
|---|---|---|---|
| Cēsis | Wenden | Kes' | Võnnu (Est.) |
| Daugava (river) | Düna | Dvina | Dźwina (Pol.) |
| Daugavpils | Dünaburg | Dvinsk | Dwińsk |
| | | | Dyneburg (Pol.) |
| Eestimaa | Estland | Estliandiia | Estonia |
| Gardinas | Garten | Grodno | Hrodna (Bel.) |
| | | | Grodno (Pol.) |
| Jelgava | Mitau | Mitava | Mitawa (Pol.) |
| Karaliaučius | Königsberg | Kaliningrad (from 1946) | |
| Kaunas | Kowno Kauen | Kovno | Kowno (Pol.) Kovne (Yid.) |
| Klaipėda | Memel | Memel' | |
| Kurzeme | Kurland | Kurliandiia | Curonia (Latin) Courland |
| Latgale | Lettgallen | | Lettigallia (Latin) Inflanty (Pol.) |
| Liepāja | Libau | Libava | Libawa (Pol.) |
| Lietuva | Litauen | Litva | Litwa (Pol.) Lithuania |
| Liivimaa (Est) Vidzeme (Lv.) | Livland | Lifliandiia | Livonia (Latin) Inflanty (Pol.) |
| Narva | Narwa | Narva | Narva |
| Nemunas (river) | Memel | Neman | Nieman (Pol.) |
| Pärnu | Pernau | Pernov | Parnawa (Pol.) |
| Peipsi (lake) | Peipus | Chudskoe | Peipus |
| Saaremaa | Ösel (Oesel) | Ezel' | Osilia (Latin) |
| Salaspils | Kirchholm | Kirhol'm | |

| Current Estonian, Latvian or Lithuanian | German | Russian (pre-1917)* | Other |
|---|---|---|---|
| Šiauliai | Schaulen | Shauliai | Szawle (Pol.) |
| Suvalkija | Sudauen | Suvalki | Suwałki (Pol.) |
| | | | Sudovia (Latin) |
| Tallinn | Reval | Revel' | |
| Tartu | Dorpat | Derpt/Yur'ev | Tērbata (Lv.) |
| Trakai | Traken | Troki | Troki (Pol.) |
| Valga (Est.) | Walk | Valk | |
| Valka (Lv.) | | | |
| Valmiera | Wolmar | Vol'mar | Volmari (Est.) |
| Ventspils | Windau | | |
| Vilnius | Wilna | Vil'na | Wilno (Pol.) |
| | | | Vilne (Yid.) |
| Žalgiris (battle) | Tannenberg | | Grunwald (Pol.) |
| Žemaitija | Schamaiten | Zhmud' | Samogitia (Latin) |
| Zemgale | Semgallen | Zemgaliia | Semigallia (Latin) |

* Russian names prior to 1917 are mainly transliterations of German and Polish place names, whereas later Russian usage is primarily a transliteration of the current Estonian, Latvian and Lithuanian forms.

# Further Reading

## GENERAL

Only two general histories of the Baltic states have been published in the English language. The first is a well-illustrated textbook, *The History of the Baltic Countries*, 3rd edn (Tallinn: BIT, 2002), written by a team of Estonian, Latvian and Lithuanian historians headed by Zigmantas Kiaupa, Ain Mäesalu, Ago Pajur and Gvido Straube, and funded by the European Commission explicitly to foster Baltic cooperation. More readable, but less reliable, is Kevin O'Connor, *The History of the Baltic States* (Westport, CT: Greenwood, 2003). These will undoubtedly soon be surpassed by Andrejs Plakans' forthcoming book in Cambridge University Press's *Concise Histories* series.

A survey of Baltic history from an economic perspective is provided by Juhan Kahk and Enn Tarvel, *An Economic History of the Baltic Countries*, Studia Baltica Stockholmiensia 20 (Stockholm: Acta Universitatis Stockholmiensis, 1997). John Hiden and Patrick Salmon, *The Baltic Nations and Europe: Estonia, Latvia & Lithuania in the Twentieth Century*, 2nd edn (London: Longman, 1994) is best on the diplomatic history of the inter-war era. David Kirby took the analysis to a new level when he first wrote about the wider 'Baltic World', including all the peoples and territories along the Baltic Sea rim in his *Northern Europe in the Early Modern Period: The Baltic World, 1492–1772* (London: Longman, 1990) and *The Baltic World 1772–1993: Europe's Northern Periphery in an Age of Change* (London: Longman, 1995). Together with Merja-Liisa Hinkkanen, Kirby also explores the maritime history of the region in *The Baltic and North Seas* (London: Routledge, 2000). Alan Palmer, *Northern Shores: A History of the Baltic Sea and its Peoples* (London: John Murray, 2005) is intended for a wider audience and is an ideal companion on a Baltic cruise.

## INDIVIDUAL NATIONS

History writing has generally followed national lines and thus more has been written about Estonia, Latvia and Lithuania separately than together. Comparative study has been impeded by the lack of knowledge of the relevant languages and the fact that the concept of the Baltic states is a relatively recent one. For Estonia, the authoritative overview is Toivo Raun, *Estonia and the Estonians*, updated 2nd edn (Stanford, CA: Hoover Institution, 2002). A reliable textbook is Ain Mäesalu, Tõnis Lukas, Mati Laur, Tõnu Tannberg and Ago Pajur, *History of Estonia* (Tallinn: Avita, 2004); a livelier account is Mart Laar, *Estonia's Way* (Tallinn: Pegasus, 2006).

For Latvia, the standard overview is Andrejs Plakans, *The Latvians: A Short History* (Stanford, CA: Hoover Institution, 1995). A more detailed account of the modern era is Daina Bleiere, Ilgvars Butulis, Inesis Felmanis, Aivars Stranga and Antonijs Zunda, *History of Latvia: The Twentieth Century* (Riga: Jumava, 2006). The only general survey of Lithuania in English is Zigmantas Kiaupa, *The History of Lithuania* (Vilnius: baltos lankos, 2002). The same author, together with Jūratė Kiaupienė and Albinas Kuncevičius, has written the definite account of pre-modern Lithuania: *The History of Lithuania before 1795* (Vilnius: Lithuanian Institute of History, 2000). A quick read is Stasys Samalavičius, *An Outline of Lithuanian History* (Vilnius: Diemedis, 1995).

Three highly useful reference books, containing entries on the most significant individuals, events and institutions, have been published by Scarecrow Press of Lanham, MD: Andrejs Plakans, *Historical Dictionary of Latvia* (1997), Saulius Sužiedėlis, *Historical Dictionary of Lithuania* (1997) and Toivo Miljan, *Historical Dictionary of Estonia* (2004).

## NATIONAL MINORITIES

There is a rapidly expanding literature examining the various ethnic groups who have lived in the Baltic countries, with attention primarily devoted to the Jews of Lithuania and the Baltic Germans. Dov Levin, *Litvaks: A Short History of the Jews of Lithuania* (Jerusalem: Yad Vashem, 2000) and Masha Greenbaum, *The Jews of Lithuania: A History of a Remarkable Community 1316–1945* (Jerusalem: Gefen, 1995) provide good overviews, while *The Vanished World of Lithuanian Jews* (Amsterdam: Rodopi, 2004), edited by Alvydas Nikžentaitis, Stefan Schreiner and Darius Staliūnas, concentrates on the nineteenth and twentieth centuries. Šarūnas Liekis provides a detailed analysis of *'A State within a State?' Jewish autonomy in Lithuania 1918–1925* (Vilnius: Versus Aureus, 2003), and the most revered figure among Lithuanian Jews is the subject of Immanuel Etkes, *The Gaon of Vilna: The Man and His Image* (Berkeley, CA: University of California Press, 2002). Latvia's Jewish community is covered by Josifs Steimanis, *History of Latvian Jews* (New York: Columbia University Press, 2002).

Much has been written about the Baltic Germans by themselves, but these books have naturally been in German, the authoritative volume being Gert von Pistohlkors (ed.), *Baltische Länder* (Berlin: Siedler, 1994), in the series *Deutsche Geschichte im Osten Europas*. In English, John Hiden and Martyn Housden, *Neighbours or Enemies? Germans, the Baltic and Beyond* (Amsterdam: Rodopi, 2008) discusses the relationship between the Germans and the indigenous peoples of the region in the twentieth century. Hiden portrays a rare apostle of tolerance in *Defender of Minorities: Paul Schiemann, 1876–1944* (London: C. Hurst, 2004). Heide W. Whelan, *Adapting to Modernity: Family, Caste, and Capitalism among the Baltic German Nobility* (Köln: Böhlau Verlag, 1999) dissects the life of the landed gentry in the nineteenth century, while Anders Henrikssen, *The Tsar's*

*Loyal Germans: The Riga German Community: Social Change and the Nationality Question, 1855–1905* (Boulder, CO: East European Monographs, 1983) focuses on their urban compatriots.

## EARLY HISTORY

On the prehistory of the Indo-European Baltic peoples, Marija Gimbutas, *The Balts* (New York: Praeger, 1963) has been highly influential but is now quite outdated. Endre Bojtár, *Forward to the Past: A Cultural History of the Baltic People* (Budapest: Central European University Press, 1999) discusses theories of the origins and development of the Baltic peoples from a linguistic perspective. Two highly accessible publications on the prehistory of Lithuania are Zigmas Zinkevičius, Aleksiejus Luchtanas and Gintautas Česnys, *Where We Come From: The Origin of the Lithuanian People*, 2nd rev. edn (Vilnius: Science & Encyclopaedia Publishing Institute, 2006) and *Prehistoric Lithuania: Archaeology exposition guide* (Vilnius: National Museum of Lithuania, 2000). The most detailed up-to-date archaeological research in English on any part of the region is Valter Lang, *The Bronze and Early Iron Ages in Estonia* (Tartu: University of Tartu Press, 2007).

For the Christianisation of the Baltic region, the classic single-volume overview is Eric Christiansen, *The Northern Crusades,* 2nd edn (London: Penguin, 1997). The most prolific scholar is William L. Urban. His books, *The Baltic Crusade*, 2nd edn (1994), *The Livonian Crusade*, 2nd edn (2004), *The Samogitian Crusade* (1989) and *Tannenberg and After: Poland, Lithuania and the Teutonic Order in Search of Immortality* (2002) have all been published in Chicago by the Lithuanian Research and Studies Center. Urban has also written *The Teutonic Knights: A Military History* (London: Greenhill, 2003). A major contribution to the field, which looks at developments from the perspective of the natives rather than that of the crusaders, is Stephen C. Rowell, *Lithuania Ascending: A Pagan Empire within East-Central Europe, 1295–1345* (Cambridge: Cambridge University Press, 1994). Recent studies on specific aspects of the crusades can be found in Iben Fonnesberg-Schmidt, *The Popes and the Baltic Crusades 1147–1254* (Leiden: Brill, 2007), Nils Blomkvist, *The Discovery of the Baltic: The Reception of a Catholic World-System in the European North (AD 1075–1225)* (Leiden: Brill, 2005) and in two collections of articles edited by Alan V. Murray, *Crusade and Conversion on the Baltic Frontier 1150–1500* (Aldershot, 2001) and *The Clash of Cultures on the Medieval Baltic Frontier* (Aldershot: Ashgate, 2009). The most important primary source is *The Chronicle of Henry of Livonia* translated by James A. Brundage (New York: Columbia University Press, 2003), a participant's account of the early years of the Livonian crusade.

## EARLY MODERN ERA

For the early modern period, most attention has been devoted to the contest between Sweden, Russia and Poland–Lithuania for dominance of the Baltic Sea region. Stewart P. Oakley, *War and Peace in the Baltic, 1560–1790* (London: Routledge, 1992) chronicles the struggle for hegemony, and Robert Frost, *The Northern Wars: War, State, and Society in Northeastern Europe, 1558–1721* (Harlow: Longman, 2000) brilliantly analyses the military developments. The history of the Polish–Lithuanian Commonwealth is the subject of Daniel Stone, *The Polish–Lithuanian State, 1386–1795*, A History of East Central Europe, vol. 4 (Seattle: University of Washington Press, 2001). Andrej Kotljarchuk, *Making the Baltic Union: The 1655 Federation of Kedainiai between Sweden and the Grand Duchy of Lithuania* (Saarbrücken: VDM, 2008) examines an episode when the Commonwealth almost broke apart. Artūras Tereškinas, *Imperfect Communities: Identity, Discourse and Nation in the Seventeenth-Century Grand Duchy of Lithuania* (Vilnius: Lietuvių literatūros ir tautosakos institutas, 2005) provides insights into the mentality of the Lithuanian nobility.

## THE TSARIST ERA

The integration of the Baltic Provinces and Lithuania into the Russian Empire are the subject of Edward C. Thaden, *Russia's Western Borderlands, 1710–1870* (Princeton, NJ: Princeton University Press, 1984), his *Russification in the Baltic Provinces and Finland, 1855–1914* (Princeton, NJ: Princeton University Press, 1981) co-authored with Michael H. Haltzel, C. Leonard Lundin, Andrejs Plakans and Toivo Raun; Theodore R. Weeks, *Nation and State in Imperial Russia: Nationalism and Russification on the Western Frontier, 1863–1914* (DeKalb: Northern Illinois University Press, 1996) and Darius Staliūnas, *Making Russians: Meaning and Practice of Russification in Lithuania and Belarus after 1863* (Amsterdam: Rodopi, 2007).

The rise of nationalism is addressed in *National Movements in the Baltic Countries during the Nineteenth Century*, Studia Baltica Stockholmiensia, vol. 2 (Stockholm: Acta Universitatis Stockholmiensis, 1985), edited by Aleksander Loit. Virgil Krapauskas, *Nationalism and Historiography: The Case of Nineteenth-Century Lithuanian Historicism* (Boulder, CO: East European Monographs, 2000) and Tomas Balkelis, *The Making of Modern Lithuania* (London: Routledge, 2009) trace the construction of a modern Lithuanian national identity. Timothy Snyder, *The Reconstruction of Nations: Poland, Ukraine, Lithuania, Belarus, 1569–1999* (New Haven, CT: Yale University Press, 2003) contrasts the pre-modern and modern concepts of nation in the lands of the former Polish–Lithuanian Commonwealth.

Social and economic change at the turn of the twentieth century and its political ramifications are discussed in *The Baltic Countries 1900–1914*. Studia Baltica Stockholmiensia, vol. 5 (Stockholm: Acta Universitatis Stockholmiensis, 1990) edited by Aleksander Loit. Specific related topics are covered in Leonas Sabaliūnas, *Lithuanian Social Democracy in Perspective 1893–1914* (Durham, NC: Duke University Press, 1990) and Alfonsas Eidintas, *Lithuanian Emigration to the United States: 1868–1950* (Vilnius: Mokslo ir enciklopedijų leidybos institutes, 2003). Reginald E. Zelnik's *Law and Disorder on the Narova River: The Kreenholm Strike of 1872* (Berkeley, CA: University of California Press, 1995) uses a strike at a factory in Narva to examine larger issues of relations between the state, labour, industry and nationalities in the Russian Empire.

The experience of German soldiers in the 'Wild East' during World War I, primarily Lithuania and Latvia, is the subject of Vejas Gabriel Liulevičius's masterfully written *War Land on the Eastern Front: Culture, National Identity and German Occupation in World War I* (Cambridge: Cambridge University Press, 2000). *The 1917 Revolution in Latvia* (Boulder, CO: East European Monographs, 1974) and *The Latvian Impact on the Bolshevik Revolution: The First Phase: September 1917 to April 1918* (Boulder, CO: East European Monographs, 1983) by Andrew Ezergailis examine the role of Latvia and the Latvians in the Russian Revolution. Surprisingly, there have been no recent English-language studies on the establishment of independent statehood to supplant Stanley W. Page, *The Formation of the Baltic States: A Study of the Effects of Great Power Politics upon the Emergence of Lithuania, Latvia, and Estonia* (New York: Howard Fertig, 1970) which focuses on external factors. Estonian social democratic leader August Rei, a key participant in the events, chronicles the achievement and loss of independence in *The Drama of the Baltic Peoples* (Stockholm: Vaba Eesti, 1970). Alfred Erich Senn, *The Emergence of Modern Lithuania* (New York: Columbia University Press, 1959) is still valuable.


## INDEPENDENCE

The classic account of the independence era between the two world wars, and a pioneering work of comparative Baltic studies, is Georg von Rauch, *The Baltic States: The Years of Independence, 1917–1940* (London: C. Hurst, 1974). A wealth of information can be found in *The Baltic States: A Survey of the Political and Economic Structure and the Foreign Relations of Estonia, Latvia, and Lithuania* first published by the Royal Institute of International Affairs (London, 1938) and republished by Greenwood Press (Westport, CT, 1970). *The Baltic States in War and Peace, 1917–1945* (University Park, PA: Pennsylvania State University Press, 1978), edited by V. Stanley Vardys and Romuald Misiunas, contains several important essays. Alfonsas Eidintas and Vytautas Žalys provide a comprehensive account of both foreign and domestic affairs in *Lithuania in European Politics: The Years of the First Republic, 1918–1940* (New York: St Martin's Press, 1997). There is as yet no equivalent survey of inter-war Estonia or Latvia.

The foreign policies of the Baltic states are examined in *The Baltic in International Relations Between the Two World Wars*, Studia Baltica Stockholmiensia 3 (Stockholm: Acta Universitatis Stockholmiensis, 1988), edited by John Hiden and Aleksander Loit. Alfred Erich Senn, *The Great Powers, Lithuania and the Vilna Question, 1920–1928* (Leiden: Brill, 1966) analyses Lithuania's major foreign policy dilemma, and John Hiden, *The Baltic States and Weimar Ostpolitik* (Cambridge: Cambridge University Press, 1987) concentrates on the perspective of Berlin. Baltic cooperation has been a popular subject, covered by Hugh I. Rodgers, *Search for Security: A Study in Baltic Diplomacy, 1920–1934* (Hamden: Archon Books, 1975), Bronis J. Kaslas, *The Baltic Nations – The Quest for Regional Integration and Political Liberty: Estonia, Latvia, Lithuania, Finland,*

*Poland* (Pittston, PA: Euramerica Press, 1976) and, more recently, Marko Lehti, *A Baltic League as a Construct of the New Europe: Envisioning a Baltic Region and Small State Sovereignty in the Aftermath of the First World War* (Frankfurt: Peter Lang, 1999).

In contrast to external relations, domestic politics has received scant attention: the major works are Leonas Sabaliūnas, *Lithuania in Crisis: Nationalism to Communism, 1939–1940* (Bloomington: Indiana University Press, 1972) and Andres Kasekamp, *The Radical Right in Interwar Estonia* (Basingstoke: Macmillan, 2000), both of which are wider in scope than their titles suggest.

Several volumes on inter-war economic developments have been published in Stockholm University's Studia Baltica Stockholmiensia series: a collection of conference papers, *Emancipation and Interdependence: The Baltic States as New Entities in the International Economy, 1918–1940* (1994), edited by Anders Johansson *et al.*; Anu-Mai Kõll, *Peasants on the World Market: Agricultural Experience of Independent Estonia 1919–1939* (1994); Anu-Mai Kõll and Jaak Valge, *Economic Nationalism and Industrial Growth: State and Industry in Estonia 1934–39* (1998), and Jaak Valge, *Breaking away from Russia: Economic Stabilization in Estonia 1918–1924* (2006). International trade is analysed in Merja-Liisa Hinkkanen-Lievonen, *British Trade and Enterprise in the Baltic States, 1919–1925* (Helsinki: SHS, 1984).

The diplomatic prelude to the loss of independence is covered in David M. Crowe, *The Baltic States & the Great Powers: Foreign Relations, 1938–1940* (Boulder, CO: Westview, 1993) and in *The Baltic and the Outbreak of the Second World War* (Cambridge: Cambridge University Press, 1992), edited by John Hiden and Thomas Lane. Although polemical and outdated, Albert Tarulis, *Soviet Policy toward the Baltic States, 1918–1940* (Notre Dame: University of Notre Dame Press, 1959) still provides a good overview of the subject. Magnus Ilmjärv has used Soviet archives to argue that the Baltic authoritarian governments were largely responsible for their own demise in *Silent Submission: Formation of Foreign Policy of Estonia, Latvia and Lithuania: Period from Mid-1920s to Annexation in 1940*, Studia Baltica Stockholmiensia 24 (Stockholm: Acta Universitatis Stockholmiensis, 2004). The Soviet takeover is analysed in detail in Alfred Erich Senn, *Lithuania 1940: Revolution from Above* (Amsterdam: Rodopi, 2008).

## WORLD WAR II

Valdis O. Lumans provides a useful overview of *Latvia in World War II* (New York: Fordham University Press, 2006), while Geoffrey Swain examines events at the micro-level, focusing on the ethnically diverse eastern Latvian city of Daugavpils in *Between Stalin and Hitler: Class War and Race War on the Dvina, 1940–46* (London: RoutledgeCurzon, 2004). A riveting and unconventional account of Latvia during the Second World War, interwoven with the experiences of his own family, is Canadian historian Modris Eksteins's *Walking since Daybreak: A Story of Eastern Europe, World War II, and the Heart of our Century* (Boston: Houghton Mifflin, 1999). Roger D. Petersen uses Lithuania in the 1940s as his central case study to test the role of emotions in determining individual motivation in *Resistance and Rebellion: Lessons from Eastern Europe* (Cambridge: Cambridge University Press, 2001) and *Understanding Ethnic Violence: Fear, Hatred, and Resentment in Twentieth-Century Eastern Europe* (Cambridge: Cambridge University Press, 2002).

On the Holocaust, and the role of Lithuanians, Latvians and Estonians in it, the major works are Alfonsas Eidintas, *Jews, Lithuanians and the Holocaust* (Vilnius: Versus Aureus, 2003), Joseph Levinson (ed.), *The Shoah (Holocaust) in Lithuania* (Vilnius: Vilna Gaon Jewish State Museum, 2006), Andrew Ezergailis, *The Holocaust in Latvia 1941–1944: The Missing Center* (Riga: Historical Institute of Latvia, 1996) and Anton Weiss-Wendt, *Murder without Hatred: Estonians and the Holocaust* (Syracuse, NY: Syracuse University Press, 2009). A useful collection of articles is *Collaboration and Resistance during the Holocaust: Belarus, Estonia, Latvia, Lithuania* (Bern: Peter Lang, 2004) edited by David Gaunt, Paul A. Levine and Laura Palosuo.

In all three countries, international commissions have been convened by the president of the republic to examine crimes against humanity committed during both the Nazi and Soviet eras. The findings of the Estonian commission have been published in two volumes edited by Toomas Hiio, Meelis Maripuu and Indrek Paavle, *Estonia 1940–1945: Reports of the Estonian International Commission for the Investigation of Crimes Against Humanity* (Tallinn: Estonian International Commission for the Investigation of Crimes against Humanity, 2006) and *Estonia since 1944* (Tallinn: Eesti Mälu Instituut, 2009). The Commission of the Historians of Latvia has produced over twenty volumes of articles on various aspects of Nazi and Soviet rule, one of which has been published in English as *The Hidden and Forbidden History of Latvia under Soviet and Nazi Occupations, 1940–1991*, Symposium of the Commission of the Historians of Latvia, vol. 14 (Riga: Institute of the History of Latvia, 2005). The International Commission for the Evaluation of the Crimes of the Nazi and Soviet Occupation Regimes in Lithuania has published a series of volumes reproducing archive documents and analyses, in the Lithuanian and English languages in parallel, on specific facets of Nazi and Soviet rule, notably vol. III, *The Persecution and Mass Murder of Lithuanian Jews during Summer and Fall of 1941* (Vilnius: Margi Raštai, 2006), compiled by Christoph Dieckmann and Saulius Sužiedėlis, and vol. IV: *The Second Soviet Occupation. Political Bodies of the Soviet Union in Lithuania and their Criminal Activities* (Vilnius: Margi Raštai, 2008), compiled by Vytautas Tininis.

## THE SOVIET ERA

The neglected issue of the international status of the Baltic states during and after World War II is the subject of a volume edited by John Hiden, Vahur Made and David J. Smith, *The Baltic Question during the Cold War* (London: Routledge, 2008). James T. McHugh and James S. Pacy trace the activities of Baltic ambassadors in exile in *Diplomats without a Country: Baltic Diplomacy, International Law, and the Cold War* (Westport, CT: Greenwood, 2001). A legal perspective is provided by Lauri Mälksoo, *Illegal Annexation and State Continuity: The Case of the Incorporation of the Baltic States by the USSR: A Study of the Tension between Normativity and Power in International Law* (Leiden: Nijhoff, 2003). The pioneering overview of the Soviet period, the foundation for almost all subsequent works, is Romuald J. Misiunas and Rein Taagepera, *The Baltic States: Years of Dependence, 1940–1990*, 2nd updated edn (Berkeley, CA: University of California Press, 1993). Two rather uneven volumes of conference proceedings, *The Baltic Countries under Occupation: Soviet and Nazi rule 1939–1991*, Studia Baltica Stockholmiensia 23 (Stockholm: Acta Universitatis Stockholmiensis, 2003), edited by Anu-Mai Kõll, and *Regional Identity under Soviet Rule: The Case of the Baltic States* (Hackettstown, NJ: Association for the Advancement of Baltic Studies, 1990) edited by Dietrich André Loeber, V. Stanley Vardys, and Laurence P. Kitching, cover a diverse variety of topics. A more focused collection of essays, *The Sovietization of the Baltic States, 1940–1956* (Tartu: Tartu University Press, 2003), has been compiled by Olaf Mertelsmann. A highly useful study aid is a collection of documents edited by Andrejs Plakans: *Experiencing Totalitarianism: The Invasion and Occupation of Latvia by the USSR and Nazi Germany 1939–1991: A Documentary History* (AuthorHouse, 2007).

For the post-war Soviet period, there are plenty of publications dealing with repression and resistance, but very little has been written about other facets of life during the post-Stalin era. The most reliable and comprehensive book on the resistance in all three countries is *The Anti-Soviet Resistance in the Baltic States* (Vilnius: Du Ka, 1999) edited by Arvydas Anušauskas. Dissent and resistance to Soviet rule is documented in Thomas Remeikis, *Opposition to Soviet Rule in Lithuania, 1945–1980* (Chicago: Institute of Lithuanian Studies Press, 1980), V. Stanley Vardys, *The Catholic Church, Dissent and Nationality in Soviet Lithuania* (Boulder, CO: East European Monographs, 1978) and Rein Taagepera, *Softening without Liberalization in the Soviet Union: The Case of Jüri Kukk* (Lanham, MD: University of America Press, 1984) which masterfully places the life and death of one dissident in a wider perspective. An oral history of the forest brethren is Mart Laar, *War in the Woods: Estonia's Struggle for Survival, 1944–1956* (Washington DC: Compass, 1992).

## THE SINGING REVOLUTION

The most widely read account of the 'Singing Revolution' and the recovery of independence is Anatol Lieven's incisive but at times patronising eye-witness account, *The Baltic Revolution: Estonia, Latvia, Lithuania, and the Path to Independence* (New Haven, CT: Yale University Press, 1993). *The Baltic Way to Freedom: Non-violent Struggle of the Baltic States in a Global Context* (Riga: Zelta grauds, 2003), edited by Jānis Škapars, is a comprehensive collection of short texts by many of the leading figures in the Baltic popular fronts, with the main emphasis on Latvia.

Studies of an individual country's experiences have been most abundant in the case of Lithuania: Alfred Erich Senn, *Lithuania Awakening* (Berkeley, CA: University of California Press, 1990) and *Gorbachev's Failure in Lithuania* (New York: St Martin's Press, 1995); V. Stanley Vardys and Judith B. Sedaitis,

*Lithuania: The Rebel Nation* (Boulder, CO: Westview, 1997), and Richard J. Krickus, *Showdown: The Lithuanian Rebellion and the Breakup of the Soviet Empire* (Washington DC: Brassey's, 1997). Latvia is treated in Rasma Karklins, *Ethnopolitics and Transition to Democracy: The Collapse of the USSR and Latvia* (Baltimore, MD: Johns Hopkins University Press, 1994) and Estonia is the subject of Rein Taagepera, *Estonia: Return to Independence* (Boulder, CO: Westview, 1993) and Rein Ruutsoo, *Civil Society and Nation Building in Estonia and the Baltic States: Impact of Traditions on Mobilization and Transition 1986–2000 – Historical and Sociological Study* (Rovaniemi: University of Lapland, 2002).

The 'Singing Revolution' is placed in the wider context of developments in the USSR by Kristian Gerner and Stefan Hedlund, *The Baltic States and the End of the Soviet Empire* (London: Routledge, 1993) and Mark R. Beissinger, *Nationalist Mobilization and the Collapse of the Soviet State* (Cambridge: Cambridge University Press, 2002). The role of Western diplomacy in the achievement of Baltic independence is one of the main subjects of Kristina Spohr Readman's *Germany and the Baltic Problem after the Cold War: The Development of a New Ostpolitik, 1989–2000* (London: Routledge, 2004).

## THE TRANSITION PERIOD

The transition period of the 1990s and recent history is treated most accessibly and comprehensively in *The Baltic States: Estonia, Latvia and Lithuania* (London: Routledge 2002), which consists of three separate books put within a single cover: David J. Smith, *Estonia: Independence and European Integration*, Artis Pabriks and Aldis Purs, *Latvia: The Challenges of Change*, and Thomas Lane, *Lithuania: Stepping Westwards*. Their work supersedes earlier volumes by Ole Nørgaard and Lars Johannsen, *The Baltic States after Independence*, 2nd edn (Cheltenham: Edward Elgar, 1999) and Graham Smith (ed.), *The Baltic States: The National Self-determination of Estonia, Latvia and Lithuania* (Basingstoke: Macmillan, 1994), which cover similar ground. A sympathetic but idiosyncratic approach is taken by Walter C. Clemens, *The Baltic Transformed: Complexity Theory and European Security* (Lanham, MD: Rowman & Littlefield, 2001) which explains why the Baltics were more successful than the Balkans in the 1990s. *Baltic Democracy at the Crossroads: An Elite Perspective* (Kristiansand: Norwegian Academic Press, 2003), edited by Sten Berglund and Kjetil Duvold, looks at post-communist elite networks and the functioning of the new democracies.

The Latvian case is analysed in Juris Dreifelds, *Latvia in Transition* (Cambridge: Cambridge University Press, 1997) and Marja Nissinen, *Latvia's Transition to a Market Economy: Political Determinants of Economic Reform Policy* (New York: St Martin's Press, 1999). Daina Stukuls Eglitis, *Imagining the Nation: History, Modernity and Revolution in Latvia* (University Park, PA: Pennsylvania State University Press, 2002) discusses the yearning of Latvians for a return to 'normality' and Katrina Z. S. Schwartz, *Nature and National Identity after Communism: Globalizing the Ethnoscape* (Pittsburgh: University of Pittsburgh Press, 2006) looks at the relationship between Latvian identity and the environment. The Estonian case is examined in *Return to the Western World: Cultural and Political Perspectives on the Estonian Post-Communist Transition* (Tartu: Tartu University Press, 1999) and *Estonia's Transition to the EU: Twenty Years On* (London: Routledge, 2009), both edited by Marju Lauristin and Peter Vihalemm.

The Russian minority in the Baltic states has been the most popular research topic in recent years. A pathbreaker was David Laitin's *Identity in Formation: The Russian-speaking Populations in the Near Abroad* (Ithaca, NY: Cornell University Press, 1998). Mark A. Jubulis covers Latvia in *Nationalism and Democratic Transition: The Politics of Citizenship and Language in Post-Soviet Latvia* (Lanham, MD: University Press of America, 2001), and Marju Lauristin and Mati Heidmets (eds), *The Challenge of the Russian Minority: Emerging Multicultural Democracy in Estonia* (Tartu: Tartu University Press, 2002) examines the Estonian case. David J. Galbreath, *Nation-Building and Minority Politics in Post-Socialist States: Interests, Influence and Identities in Estonia and Latvia* (Stuttgart: ibidem-Verlag, 2005) covers both cases. Lithuania receives attention in Vesna Popovski, *National Minorities and Citizenship Rights in Lithuania, 1988–93* (Basingstoke: Macmillan, 1993).

Dovile Budryte's *Taming Nationalism? Political Community Building in the Post-Soviet Baltic States* (Aldershot: Ashgate, 2005) analyses the role of historical memory in the relationship between the titular and minority groups in all three states. Indeed, memory politics have become a hot topic in the wake of the relocation of the Soviet war memorial in Tallinn in 2007, which was the main catalyst for *Contested and Shared Places of Memory: History and Politics in North Eastern Europe* (London: Routledge, 2009), edited by Jörg Hackmann and Marko Lehti.

The influence of international organisations on the evolution of minority policies are examined in Judith Kelley's *Ethnic Politics in Europe: The Power of Norms and Incentives* (Princeton, NJ: Princeton University Press, 2004) and Elena Jurado, *Complying with European Standards of Minority Protection: The Impact of the European Union, OSCE and Council of Europe on Estonian Minority Policy, 1991–2000* (Saarbrücken: VDM, 2008). *Minority Rights in Central and Eastern Europe* (London: Routledge, 2009), edited by Bernd Rechel, contains excellent chapters on the impact of EU conditionality on Estonia, Latvia and Lithuania.

## EUROPEAN INTEGRATION AND FOREIGN RELATIONS

A comprehensive analysis of the process of joining the European Union is Peter Van Elsuwege, *From Soviet Republics to EU Member States: A Legal and Political Assessment of the Baltic States' Accession to the EU* (Leiden: Brill, 2008). An exhaustive account of the Lithuanian case is *Lithuania's Road to the European Union: Unification of Europe and Lithuania's EU Accession Negotiation* (Vilnius: Eugrimas, 2005), edited by Klaudijus Maniokas, Ramūnas Vilipišauskas and Darius Žeruolis.

The most notable recent scholarly analyses of Baltic foreign policies are dominated by a constructivist approach, highlighting the centrality of identity in international relations: Eiki Berg and Piret Ehin (eds), *Identity and Foreign Policy: Baltic–Russian Relations* (Aldershot: Ashgate, 2009); David Galbreath, Ainius Lasas and Jeremy W. Lamoreaux, *Continuity and Change in the Baltic Sea Region: Comparing Foreign Policies* (Amsterdam: Rodopi, 2008); Merje Kuus, *Geopolitics Reframed: Security and Identity in Europe's Eastern Enlargement* (New York and Basingstoke: Palgrave Macmillan, 2007), and Maria Mälksoo, *The Politics of Becoming European: A Study of Polish and Baltic Post-Cold War Security Imaginaries* (London: Routledge, 2009).

## OTHER LANGUAGES AND JOURNALS

In addition to the selection of English-language books included in the above survey (and, of course, to research published in Estonian, Latvian and Lithuanian), there is a rich literature on Baltic history (primarily that of Estonia and Latvia) in German. Recent introductory surveys similar in scope to the present work are Ralph Tuchtenhagen, *Geschichte der baltischen Länder* (München: C. H. Beck, 2005) and Michael Garleff, *Die baltischen Länder: Estland, Lettland und Litauen vom Mittelalter bis zur Gegenwart* (Regensburg: Friedrich Pustet, 2001). The most comprehensive and authoritative history of the three Baltic countries ever in any language promises to be *Das Baltikum: Geschichte einer europäischen Region*, in three volumes currently being edited by Karsten Brüggemann, Konrad Maier and Ralph Tuchtenhagen. There is also a substantial literature on Baltic history in Russian, much of which was produced during the Soviet period by Estonian, Latvian and Lithuanian scholars. However, there are some important recent works by younger Russian scholars, notably Elena Zubkova, *Pribaltika i Kreml' 1940–1953* (Moscow: ROSSPEN, 2007). Additionally, there is a significant amount of research in Finnish, mainly on Estonia, and in Polish, mainly on Lithuania. References to some of these works can be found in the endnotes.

As for academic journals, *Journal of Baltic Studies* is the main source. *Lituanus* is the best for Lithuanian topics. Articles on Baltic history appear regularly in *Slavic Review, Slavonic and East European Review, Europa-Asia Studies* and *Nationalities Papers. Zeitschrift für Ostmitteleuropa-Forschung* also publishes some articles in English.

# Index